"Love is the greatest power in the world, and Alan Sears and Craig Osten deal with a very delicate subject in *The Homosexual Agenda* in a spirit of tough love. The message of this book is must-reading for every concerned American."

—*Bill Bright,* Founder and Chairman
Campus Crusade for Christ

"The Alliance Defense Fund . . . is doing a wonderful work in defending religious liberty and preserving the rights of Christian people."

—*Dr. James Dobson,* Author and
Founder of Focus on the Family

"If any right-thinking American has found the gay and lesbian agenda difficult to understand or hard to believe, all of the answers—clear, irrefutable, convincing, and frightening—are here in this salient and timely volume from the highly respected Alliance Defense Fund. The six-point strategy of the homosexual community is completely dismantled, in terms of legality, morality, politics, psychology, and funding. This book could be the instrument that will reverse the tide of influence that this devastating vice is having on American society today."

—*D. James Kennedy,* Senior Minister
Coral Ridge Presbyterian Church

"The homosexual rights movement is built on a foundation of lies, deception, and factual disinformation. In spite of the flood of data on the destructive nature of homosexual practices, homosexuality is being normalized and promoted in movies, television, music, and to children and young people in our public schools and universities. Contrary to the common wisdom, we do not exhibit true compassion when we remain silent about the true nature of homosexuality. Genuine compassion requires cold honesty and brutal frankness about the popular mythologies that surround the gay and lesbian lifestyle. It is this structure of lies, deception, and factual disinformation that Americans must understand if we are to save our civilization. I commend Alan Sears and Craig Osten for having the courage to tell the truth about this highly destructive movement."

—*Marlin Maddoux,* USA Radio

"The sexual revolution of the last half-century amounts to the most sweeping and significant reordering of human relationships in all of human history. This did not come to pass by accident. Indeed, it was driven by social and sexual revolutionaries who intended to 'liberate' humanity for the polymorphous perversity described by Freud and celebrated by the cultural elite.

"The legitimation and celebration of homosexuality stands at the center of this sexual revolution. In *The Homosexual Agenda*, Alan Sears and Craig Osten reveal the strategy and the ambition that now drive the homosexual movement—a movement that will settle for nothing less than total victory for its cause. Sears and Osten prove their case and reveal the facts, and we are all in their debt. Most helpfully, they also prove the fact that the homosexual agenda cannot succeed unless religious liberty is forfeited. This may well be the most significant religious liberty issue of our times. Read this book—get angry—and get active in the cause of religious liberty."

—*R. Albert Mohler Jr.*, President
The Southern Baptist Theological Seminary

"This ground-breaking book destroys the myth that homosexual activists simply want equal rights. Of the book's many strengths is its reliance upon homosexual activists' own stated agenda. Sears and Osten copiously document this agenda in what can only be described as a manifesto for sexual terrorism against marriage, family, and the church. They show how this agenda has radically reshaped public opinion even to threatening our religious liberties in their desire to codify their immoral agenda in our nation's laws. I commend Sears and Osten for their love of the gospel and desire to help those in real bondage to sin. A must-read for every pastor."

—*Alfred Poirier*, Senior Pastor
Rocky Mountain Community Church

"This book is courageously but compassionately written. Obviously, the subject engenders confusion, confrontation, and sometimes hostility. The facts are thoughtfully and forthrightly presented and are worthy of honest consideration no matter what persuasion one may have concerning homosexuality."

—*Adrian Rogers*, Senior Pastor,
Bellevue Baptist Church

"This is riveting reading. . . . As this book shows through its review of the aggressive march of militant homosexuals through the courts, the legislatures, cultural institutions, and churches, the pretense of homosexuals' 'tolerance' of non-homosexuals is over."

—*The Wanderer*

THE HOMOSEXUAL AGENDA

Exposing the Principal Threat
to Religious Freedom Today

ALAN SEARS & CRAIG OSTEN

BROADMAN
&HOLMAN
PUBLISHERS

NASHVILLE, TENNESSEE

13-digit ISBN: 9780805426984
10-digit ISBN: 0805426981

Published by Broadman & Holman Publishers, Nashville, Tennessee

Dewey Decimal Classification: 261.7
Subject Heading: GAY LIBERATION MOVEMENT
HOMOSEXUALITY \ FREEDOM OF RELIGION

Unless otherwise stated all Scripture citation is from the Holy Bible, New International Version, © 1973, 1978, 1984 by International Bible Society.

7 8 9 10 11 12 13 14 15 09 08 07 06

Contents

117373

This book is dedicated
to the founding members of the Alliance Defense Fund including:
the late Bill Bright, the late Larry Burkett, James C. Dobson,
D. James Kennedy, Marlin Maddoux, and the late William Pew.

Each has taken a strong and uncompromising stand for the gospel and has withstood the slings and arrows of those who desire to silence its dissemination in America. It has been an honor for both of us to stand with these brave men for the sake of the gospel.

Acknowledgments

The authors wish to thank Al Janssen, Jordan Lorence, Glen Lavy, Jeff Ventrella, Marv McCarthy, Paul Weber, Ben Bull, Rich Jefferson, Elizabeth Murray, and Julie Michael for their assistance on this project. Most of all, we express appreciation to our wives and our families. Their insight and help was invaluable as we tackled this often difficult and contentious subject.

A Note
from the Authors

While this book deals with a difficult and contentious issue, we want to state up front that both authors and the ministry of the Alliance Defense Fund have nothing but respect, compassion, and sensitivity toward those ensnared in homosexual behavior. Both of us have family members, respected acquaintances, and friends who have been trapped in this behavior and know something of the incredible pain and sorrow it has brought to them and their families. With God's grace we carefully balance this love and respect for these individuals with warnings about the carrying out, promotion, and demand for legal approval for homosexual behavior that will stifle religious freedom and trap millions of more people in its deadly grip.

—*Alan Sears and Craig Osten*

Introduction

Homosexuality is a condition; gay and lesbian is a decision.
—Father Benedict Groeschel, *With Mind and Heart Renewed*

John had never known a loving, stable family. When he was just five, his biological parents divorced, beginning a revolving door of different father figures, none of whom lasted. What he learned from these men was that they were something he didn't want to be.

By the time he was eighteen, John's mother and father were each on their third spouses, and he had learned that men "were unstable, they hurt you, and they put your mother down."[1] He spent his childhood as his mother's caretaker, and as a result, he bonded and attached himself to her.

John grew up ashamed of himself and his male identity. As a young man, dressing himself up as "Candy," he would masquerade as a female impersonator. This disguise was a cover-up for the inner hatred he had for himself and the misery he felt as a result. He was crying out for love, the love that only Christ could completely provide, but he had never heard. He said, "When I would come home from a bar with a partner I didn't know, I would break down in tears . . . feel like a piece of meat. . . . I was just a hollow shell. . . . I was twenty-four but felt like eighty. I tried to take my life. . . . I was tired and worn out. . . . I didn't want to die; I wanted to escape. . . . I wanted someone to tell me that 'I love you. There is something of value to you'"[2]

This tortured young man did not know at the time that God had a different plan for his life, a plan that would slowly be revealed through the quiet, consistent witness of a Christian couple.

John thought the couple was "quaint" when they visited him at the print shop he managed. Over a period of months, the couple's Christ-like love started to break down the hardened exterior he had put up to suppress the pain he felt inside. Wherever he went, he seemed to run into this couple. He could not escape their kindness.

Through the witness of this couple, John finally came face-to-face with the unconditional love he had missed so much as a child: the love of Jesus Christ and God the Father. The young man would eventually accept Christ, but as part of the healing process and because of his fear of the organized church, the couple would provide him with a personal church service, complete with music, sermon, and morning offering. He would read the Bible and weep as the pain of twenty-four years of hurt slowly melted away and he poured himself into the words. For the first time he knew he had a Father who loved and cared for him in a way he had never experienced before.

John moved to Northern California to join a church that specifically ministered to others trying to escape the trap of homosexual behavior. It was there he met his future wife, Anne, who was seeking healing from her past of lesbian behavior. The two fell in love and in 1992 they were married. As the years went by, the Lord blessed them with three sons and a relationship that would be a witness to the world of what the love of Jesus Christ can do to heal a broken heart.

Who is this person? His name is John Paulk. We both know and love him and can attest that he is one of the warmest, gentlest, and most courageous individuals we have ever met. He has faced every sling and arrow that could be thrown at him, along with numerous temptations—and some human weakness—but has remained strong in the faith. We personally know only a few ex-homosexuals, but we know there are thousands of John and Anne Paulks throughout America who have heard and responded to the redemptive love of Jesus Christ. How many more are out there who need to learn of his saving grace?

Unfortunately, if many homosexual activists have their way, Christ's message of redemptive love will be silenced and those who share it through the preaching of the uncensored words of Scripture will be punished. Thus, those who need to respond to the gospel will never have the opportunity to hear it. The effort of homosexual activists to convince Americans to tolerate (i.e., "affirm") homosexual behavior* tramples religious freedom and leaves a trail of broken

---

*Author's note: In this book, we will only use the word gay when it is part of a direct quote from other material. It is our belief that gay is primarily a political term used by radical homosexual activists to take attention away from their sexual behavior. In a conference in the early 1970s, a decision was made

bodies in the dust. Broken bodies, broken souls who without the chance to hear and respond to the gospel will never know that there is a way out of a lifestyle, and its accompanying behaviors, that falls far short of the joy their Creator intended and leads to despair, disease, and early death.[3†] Yet despite these dangers, it is a behavior that is being promoted as nothing more than an alternative lifestyle, and any dissent is ridiculed, vilified, and censored.

John Paulk was living such a life. But through Christ's redeeming love, John's life is now one of joy and fulfillment. He now knows that he is living the life that God intended for him. For every John and Anne Paulk we know who have been able to overcome homosexual behavior and come to a personal relationship with Jesus Christ, we know several other individuals who are still trapped in homosexual behavior, whether they are former classmates or family members.

What we all must remember is that Christ died for all of our sins. It is not "hate" or "hate speech" to tell someone to turn from sin and embrace Christ's love. It is an act of love, for the greatest act of love the world has ever known is what Christ did for all of us on the cross.[‡]

We recently received another reminder of how the love and power of the gospel can bring healing to a broken life.

Melissa Fryrear is a former lesbian who, in Jesus Christ, found the love that she had been searching for all her life. Her testimony is touching and a reminder to all of us of God's amazing and transforming grace. Melissa has graciously agreed to allow us to share it.

I am the second and last child my parents adopted in the '60s. I grew up in a nice upper-middle class neighborhood

by a group of activists to purposefully label homosexuals and their behaviors as gay in order to reposition them politically. One of their goals was to get the general public to use the word *gay* instead of *homosexual* since they believed *gay* would take the onus off homosexual behavior. That stated, homosexuality is "intrinsically disordered" and contrary to Scripture and natural law. Homosexual persons, as are all unmarried and married persons, are called to chastity and sexual fidelity. We also differentiate between the word *homosexuality* and homosexual behavior, as noted hereafter. On Valentine's Day 2003, a group of academics gathered to discuss the proper usage of "lavender" language. Bill Leap, coordinator of the 10th Annual American University Conference on Lavender Languages and Linguistics said that homosexuals around the world "still struggle with the complex terminology and double-meanings of homosexual language." Leap said that TV shows such as *Will & Grace* are used by homosexuals to teach them about the basics of communication in "gayspeak." Words such as "top," "pitcher," and "catcher" have totally different meanings in homosexual culture. Lionel Tiger, Darwin professor of anthropology at Rutgers University added: "It's just a courting language . . . like any courtship language for a particular group of people interested in mating with each other." The use of the word *gay* instead of *homosexual* is just another form of so-called "lavender" language. See Michael L. Betsch, "University Conference Focuses on 'Gay Language,'" CNSNews.com, February 6, 2003.
†It was reported in late 2003 that syphilis rates are growing dramatically in America, particularly among homosexual and bisexual men, which could also lead to a large increase in future HIV/AIDS cases. The Centers for Disease Control says that 40 percent of the new cases are in homosexual/bisexual men. Source: Steve Mitchell, "Syphilis Increase Sparks AIDS Concerns," United Press International, November 20, 2003.
‡See 1 Peter 2:24.

in the east end of Louisville. Thirty-six years later, my parents continue to live in the same home.

I grew up attending church . . . . At Trinity, I was dedicated as a baby; I went to Vacation Bible School in the summer; and I played in the children's handbell choir. Although I had grown up attending church, I had not yet made a personal decision for Jesus Christ. Attending church seemed like something we did because it was the "right thing to do." In retrospect, I remember hearing stories about Jesus and about people in the Bible, but I never recall hearing a story about salvation. I did not yet know I was a sinner in need of a Savior.

I remember one Sunday morning when I was thirteen. I was sitting in the sanctuary with my parents waiting for the 11:00 a.m. service to begin. I picked up a Bible that was resting on the back of the pew in front of me and I began to flip through the pages at random. As I was flipping through the pages, the Bible fell open to the book of Leviticus, the eighteenth chapter. My eyes fell upon the 22nd verse: "A man should not lie with another man as one lies with a woman; that is detestable." My eyes hung on that semicolon and then swung to the words that followed: "that . . . is . . . detestable." Without looking around and without saying a word to anyone, I closed that Bible, placed it back on the pew in front of me, and in my heart I said "No" to God. When I read that verse, the words that I read after the semicolon were, "Melissa is detestable."

Even at thirteen, I had already known for a couple of years that something seemed different about me. Many gays and lesbians believe they are born homosexual. This is what I believed. I had made that decision because as early as the age of seven, I could remember being drawn to girls. My assumption was, "Well, if I have always felt this way, then I must have been born this way." That was a beginning seed, I believe, that began to take root in the soul of my heart.

As my adolescent years continued to unfold, my mind was filled with a barrage of screaming questions: 'What is wrong with me?!'" "Why don't I seem to be attracted to the boys like the other girls?!" "Why do I seem attracted to the girls?!" "Why do I hate being a girl?!" "What is wrong with me?!" In an attempt to answer those screaming questions,

I opened up a dictionary one day and read the definitions to words like *homosexual* and *lesbian* and *gay*. That seed sprouted.

I was sixteen when I became involved in my first lesbian relationship . . . . Unaware, unable, and unwilling to resist the temptation and draw any longer, I embraced with outstretched and welcoming arms my lesbian identity. When I left home at eighteen to attend the University of Kentucky, I immersed myself in the gay community. Everything in my world revolved around being gay. I had three goals in life: have a good time, make a lot of money, and without overusing the cliché, find the woman of my dreams . . . and the seed flourished.

In the late '80s, I began working for an advertising agency in Lexington. The agency was owned by three men, one who was a Christian. Bill was the Christian. He was always kind, considerate, and respectful toward me. He was unlike the other two men . . . .

These years of my life continued to unfold and from my perspective, I was well on my way to achieving my three goals in life. I was having some really good times; I was making a lot of money; and yet again, I was in a relationship with a woman. Yet something was stirring within me.

One Saturday night unexpectedly, I asked my partner at the time if she wanted to go to church the next morning. Because we were so emotionally enmeshed, she agreed to almost anything I ever suggested. This time was no exception. Because I had grown up in the Presbyterian church, that seemed the most familiar place to start and so we looked in the phone book. In the small community of Versailles, there was only one Presbyterian church, appropriately named Versailles Presbyterian, and as one might expect, it was located on Main Street. It was a small congregation of predominantly older couples. Needless to say, when my partner and I walked in, it was obvious. The members of that church, though, received us with warmth and without condemnation. I immediately became involved in all the activities they offered: the Wednesday night potlucks, Sunday morning Bible studies, and I even joined the adult handbell choir.

There was a couple in their seventies, L. J. and Doris Crain, who took me under their wings and into their hearts.

L. J. was an intelligent and kind man. He was the clerk of session and led our adult Sunday morning Bible study . . . . Bill from my workplace, and L. J. and Doris from my church, knew the life I was living. They were discerning people and at that time I looked like a lesbian woman . . . sporting a short, cropped hairstyle, very little makeup, and masculine attire. And although they knew about me and the life I was living, they never said a word about my homosexual lifestyle. Instead, they met me where I was, accepted me with grace, loved me unconditionally, and prayed for me fervently. It was through relationship with them that I was led to make the most important decision of my life. One afternoon, sitting alone on the edge of my bed in the stillness of my bedroom, I said quietly in my heart, "Jesus, Jesus please, please come and be the Savior of my life and the Lord of my life." He did; and a new seed was planted.

My partner at the time actually gave me my first Bible . . . It was the New International Version Study Bible in blue leather with silver edged pages and the words of Jesus in red. I began to read that Bible, and it was not long before I discovered what a concordance is. Just in case you were wondering, "homosexuality" in the NIV concordance is listed alphabetically between "hometown" and "honesty." I soon learned there were a number of Scriptures that address the issue of homosexuality. I read again the Scripture in Leviticus that I had read so many years before. I also found verses in Deuteronomy, Romans, and 1 Corinthians. And this is when the wrestling ensued.

For months I went around and around with the Lord. I did not yet understand; my faith was so new. I argued with Him; I pleaded with Him; I fled from Him; I yelled at Him; and I opposed Him. "God," I said, "I know Your Word says that it's wrong, that it's a sin, but to me it feels like I've been born this way. It's all I've ever known. To me it feels normal, but You say it's an abomination. God help me!"

The Bible says the Word of God is living and active, sharper than a double-edged sword; it penetrates even to dividing soul and spirit, joints and marrow. It judges the thoughts and attitudes of the heart. Isaiah 55:11 says that God's Word will not return empty, but it will accomplish what God desires and achieve the purposes for which He sends it. For the next four, eight, and twelve months the Holy Spirit of God continued to work those truths into my heart until I came to the point of convicting revelation where I knew what I was doing was sin. But God demonstrated in His own love for me in this, that while I was still a sinner, Christ died for me. The Bible says that repentance is a gift and that it's God's kindness that leads us to repentance. During those months, even in my confusion, even in my anger, even in my rebellion, God showered me with His love. In 1992, by His grace, I repented of my years of sexual sin and the new seed sprouted.

The separation, though, from my partner at the time was not immediate. Although at the time of repentance all sexual immorality stopped, we still shared a bed together, a home together, and a life together. That was one of the first tangible experiences I had of God's patient and tender mercy. He knew how incredibly enmeshed we were. It was as if we were two infected wounds that had been crudely bandaged together with dirty and soiled gauze. But like a sensitive and compassionate doctor, the Lord began to slowly and gently unwrap that dressing. Over the next months, He continued to move in our lives and we eventually separated completely.

Can you imagine if Melissa had never had the chance to hear and respond to the gospel? If the law had forbidden it? If it were considered hate speech to tell her? She would still be trapped in a behavior that brought her so much shame. She would have no idea that Christ loves her and can forgive her for her past. It would be an incredible tragedy but one that *can* and *will* happen if we remain silent to the threat that the homosexual agenda represents to religious freedom in America.

Melissa's story is also a reminder that Jesus himself is why we must treat individuals who practice homosexual behavior with respect, compassion, and sensitivity. To do otherwise would mean a disservice to the gospel and Christ's sacrifice.

Another example of a hurting individual who came to know the healing grace of Jesus Christ is Teresa Britton. Teresa was raised Baptist, but by her senior year, she was going to "gay" bars in search of love. She never found it, regardless of how many lesbian relationships she was involved in. One night, crying in bed, she said that she felt God touch her: "The next thing I knew I was on the floor in a fetal position. Within that instant, all the lies I believed and all the gray areas of my life became black and white. The truth had been revealed to me, and I knew the way I was living was wrong."

The lie was that she was born homosexual and couldn't change. Teresa traced her entrapment in lesbianism to her father's alcoholism and physical abuse. "I will never, ever let a man treat me like that," she would say to herself. "If that's what a man is all about, why would I want to be with one?" In September 2000, she accepted Jesus Christ as her Lord and Savior. One of the reasons? The love of Christ shown through church members. Without her church, she said, "I would probably still be bouncing from one relationship to another. I would be on the road to destruction instead of the road to life."[4] This is the love that God calls us to, and this is the love that we must defend against those who seek to silence it.

Craig is also a good friend with another woman who had escaped from lesbian behavior. His friend had served as the press secretary to Patricia Ireland, the former president of the National Organization for Women. She knew deep down about the sinfulness of her lesbian behavior and *wanted to escape,* but she felt nothing but anger and condemnation from individuals who called themselves Christians. The anger she felt repelled her from Christianity for many years. Despite this, God continued to work on her heart and eventually brought her to him. She still struggles with the anger she experienced from Christians when she was a lesbian but has remained strong in the faith.

The experiences of Craig's friend remind us that, as with all sin by persons of whatever orientation, we must differentiate between condemning the sin of homosexual behavior and condemning the individual. Ultimately only God judges the heart. We vehemently disagree and disassociate ourselves with the actions of individuals, such as Fred Phelps of Topeka, Kansas, who would picket the funerals of AIDS victims, post messages that "God Hates Fags" on the World Wide Web, condemn those who have compassion for those trapped in homosexual behavior,[5]* and state that there is no redemption for the homosexual.

However, on the other hand, we cannot stand idly by while many well-meaning individuals provide spiritual cover for and enable those who are caught in and/or promote this destructive behavior. We are called by a living God to serve him, and there are crystal-clear,

---

*Fred Phelps and his followers have picketed Focus on the Family because the ministry employs three former homosexuals on its staff: John Paulk, Amy Tracy, and Mike Haley.

non-debatable issues that cannot be dismissed if we are to live in obedience to him. One of those issues is homosexual behavior. God the
Creator has written the rule book (the Bible) for his creation, and
despite reinterpretations and explanations by activists and some
members of the clergy, his Word undeniably condemns homosexual
behavior.*

Christ's healing power has never been more powerful than today,
as proven in the cases of these former homosexuals. The hurt and
shame that homosexual behavior can bring to an individual is devastating. In a *USA Today* article, Sharon Sherrard, a San Rafael,
California, accountant, said that she found solace with regard to her
lesbian behavior by drinking alcohol to excess. "'No matter what I
did,'" she said, "'I knew in my mind that I could never, quote, get to
heaven as long as I was an active lesbian.'"[6] Ms. Sherrard desperately
needs to know Christ's love for her and that only he can heal the
wounds in her heart that have caused her to fall into lesbian behavior. However, if the gospel is silenced, she will be forced to continue
to find her solace elsewhere, such as in a liquor bottle, rather than
having it quenched by the living water that is Jesus Christ.

Alan has witnessed the pain of those who are trapped in homosexual behavior firsthand from the time he spent as a full-time and
special prosecutor—both on the local and federal levels—and as the
head of several criminal investigative task forces. In addition, he
served as the executive director of the Attorney General's
Commission on Pornography in 1985–86. In the various roles he
served across the United States, he had in-depth and personal exposure to not only the criminal enterprise surrounding hard-core
pornography's production and distribution, but to much of the
related sex trade, especially to those who practiced homosexual
behavior. In multiple prosecutions of people involved in every level
of the pornography trafficking industry, Alan learned firsthand, many
times from hours of conversations with defendants and their counsel, of these individuals' real view of the First Amendment (it was a
joke and a smoke screen). He also learned what the profiteering

---

*1 Corinthians 6:9–10 says: "Do you not know that the wicked will not inherit the kingdom of God?
Do not be deceived: Neither the sexually immoral nor idolaters nor adulterers nor male prostitutes *nor
homosexual offenders* nor thieves nor the greedy nor drunkards nor slanderers nor swindlers will inherit
the kingdom of God" (emphasis added). Romans 1:24–28 states: "Therefore God gave them over in the
sinful desires of their hearts to sexual impurity for the degrading of their bodies with one another. They
exchanged the truth of God for a lie, and worshiped and served created things rather than the Creator—
who is forever praised. Amen. Because of this, God gave them over to shameful lusts. Even their women
exchanged natural relations for unnatural ones. In the same way, the men also abandoned natural relations with women and were inflamed with lust for one another. Men committed indecent acts with
other men, and received in themselves the due penalty for their perversion." Leviticus 18:22 reads: "Do
not lie with a man as one lies with a woman; that is detestable."

pornographers thought of the homosexual persons who were plied with every manner of video, magazine, and appliance. To be blunt, the pornographers had nothing but disgust and ridicule for those who paid them hard cash.

In years of public speaking during and after this period of his life, Alan called pornography the "true hate literature" of our age, because of its hatred and exploitation of the human person, regardless of size, shape, color, and gender. It reduced human beings to valueless commodities to be ogled at and disposed of like used tissue. And sad to say, many of these individuals who were disposed of by the pornographers were practicing homosexuals.

One of the unique experiences Alan had was to meet many young homosexual men and women who were struggling with the issue of pornography and the various forms of sex trade outlets. These included the so-called gay bars, many of which he, and his other commission members, discovered to be often owned or controlled not by homosexuals, but by exploitive heterosexuals and criminal enterprises. These individuals and organizations just wanted to make a buck off the weakness of others. Alan talked with these men and women in depth about their pain, their heart needs, and the role that this material played in their formation and their sexual behavior. Alan has maintained some of these relationships for more than seventeen years by occasional correspondence, and some of the individuals he knew have since died of sexually transmitted diseases.

Based on these years and experiences with those trapped in homosexual behavior, we must express real outrage at the merciless exploitation of those with homosexual urges and temptations. Overt efforts are made by many to lead young men and women into homosexual behavior, many for simple, base reasons that have nothing to do with political agendas—instead, the new recruits are "fresh meat" and sources of new cash, new sex partners, and new profit.

It is for these tragically exploited people that Christ died. Those who are trapped in homosexual behavior have been deceived, just like anyone else who does not know the fullness of Christ. They are often told that their greatest enemies are the church (and in the case of Craig's friend many have sadly given credence to that thought) and the traditional family, the two entities that could bring the healing they so desperately need. The result is that the immense inner pain of many has been channeled into an incessant drive to silence, punish, and, ultimately, eliminate these two institutions. It is the church (a church that proclaims the gospel) that can guide them to the healing of their pain through faith in Jesus Christ, and it is the traditional family that can keep future generations of children from falling into homosexual behavior.

John Paulk's story is an example of what can happen when the traditional family breaks down and children are left hurt and confused. With only one parent—in most cases, the mother—to bond with and attach to, boys in particular are vulnerable to falling into homosexual behavior. John's experiences remind us that we *must* support and defend the traditional family, in order to prevent such pain from being spread to an entire generation of children.*

The Alliance Defense Fund® was founded to defend the right to hear and speak the Truth—that truth is the Gospel of Jesus Christ.† The Alliance Defense Fund has been involved in countless cases involving the rights of people to live and express their faith, to share Christ's love with a hurting world, to protect the sanctity of human life, and to defend marriage and the family from those who seek to redefine these terms into meaninglessness. We will discuss some of the legal cases that the Alliance Defense Fund has been part of and how what we have experienced has alarmed both of us with regard to how the homosexual agenda threatens religious freedom, and in particular, evangelism.

Almost daily, we hear from another parent whose children have been exposed to homosexual activism in the classroom, or from an employee forced to undergo so-called diversity training at work (training that ridicules the Christian position on homosexual behavior), or from a business person forced to violate his or her sincerely held religious beliefs about homosexual behavior. These cases are not going away. We are seeing them happen with increasing frequency as the homosexual activist movement strives to censor or marginalize all speech that is in accord with biblical teaching on homosexual behavior, and with it, the gospel of Jesus Christ.

In the pages following, we will outline how these attacks on religious freedom are being played out in all aspects of our culture. We

---

*We have both, one through personal experience, and the other through an immediate family member's experience, known the pain, the shame, and the sorrow when God's plan for the traditional family has been broken by divorce. Only by God's grace, his forgiveness, restoration, and healing in our lives do our own families today experience the richness of living his model lifestyle.

†The Alliance Defense Fund is a one-of-a-kind legal service organization founded in 1994 by the late Dr. Bill Bright, Dr. James Dobson, Dr. D. James Kennedy, the late Larry Burkett, Marlin Maddoux, the late William Pew, and more than thirty other national ministry leaders to provide strategy and coordination, training, and funding in the legal battle for religious freedom, sanctity of human life, and the traditional family and its values. ADF has provided funding and assistance in hundreds of legal matters, including twenty-nine cases before the U.S. Supreme Court, has trained more than 715 volunteer attorneys to serve the Body of Christ across America, and partnered with more than one hundred ministries and organizations. Since its formation, ADF has been involved in nearly every legal case of national scope concerning the definition of marriage and attempts to redefine the family.

know from personal experience that many Christians we come in contact with are uncomfortable with this whole issue of homosexuality. They hear such words as "intolerance," and they want to be considered tolerant. They hear the term "hateful," and they want to appear loving. They say, "All we need to do is share the gospel," yet are unaware that their ability to do even that is quickly eroding away. Many choose to avoid the subject totally, rather than set themselves up for ridicule and vilification.

So why are we insisting that we examine this issue? Because, whether you realize it or not, this issue affects your marriage, it threatens your children, and if we don't do something soon, it will drastically limit your religious liberty.

For the sake of evangelism, for the sake of freedom and human rights, and for the sake of the very souls of those who desperately need to hear about the love of Jesus Christ, like John Paulk and the others we have mentioned who have responded to the gospel, *we cannot allow this to happen.*

And the church is confused on the issue. This is why we believe, with the strongest sense of urgency, that the faith community must be fully educated on the threat that is coming to the front door of their places of worship and their homes. We need to do this not only for those trapped in homosexual behavior, but also for the future of our children, our country, and the church.

Consider the following illustration. You are on vacation, visiting the Grand Canyon. As you are standing on an observation platform, you witness the typical scene of a person below the platform with his back to the edge of the canyon posing for a picture. Then something unusual and disturbing happens. The person keeps backing closer and closer to the edge. From your vantage point you can see that if the person backs up any farther, he is going to plunge thousands of feet to his death. From his vantage point, he cannot see what is about to happen.

You run toward him and shout a warning. Then something even more unusual happens. The people standing below the platform, taking the picture, yell back at you and tell you to stop your hate speech. They tell you that you need to respect diversity and the decision to stand as close to the ledge as they want. Before their last words are finished, the person near the edge continues backing up, loses his footing, and falls to a horrible death.

To your astonishment, the photographer runs over to you, shakes his fist in your face, and says that your bigotry caused the person's death.

Sound preposterous? Yes, it does.

But due to the incredible, amazing grace of God, believers have been granted the vantage point to see and warn the individuals of the dangers ahead if they continue to engage in sinful behavior. He has given us the ability to see from the observation tower the big picture that others cannot see.

Few, if any, would condemn people standing dangerously close to the edge. However, we would warn them and others of the physical dangers ahead if they keep moving in the direction they are going. Compassion does not mean that you provide the person with a pat on the back as he heads over the cliff. It means loving our neighbors as ourselves and warning them of the dangers ahead if they continue down the same path. As Christians, we cannot sit idly by as individuals engage in behavior that will result in their eternal demise. Yet, the concern we have for our brothers and sisters—for their physical, psychological, and eternal welfare—has now often been classified as hate speech, and in the near future we face the real likelihood of punishment if we issue even the slightest of warnings about what may await them. As Christians, we cannot remain silent, nor can we allow others to silence us when it comes to the eternal soul of an individual. However, if the homosexual agenda continues to go unchecked that is *exactly what is going to happen.*

The other question we have to ask ourselves is this: are we willing to take a stand for our children and our grandchildren? What type of world will they inherit if we do not take a stand? Will they inherit a world of broken families and broken lives, a world in which any mention of the sinfulness of homosexual behavior and the need for the redemptive love of the gospel is a criminal offense? Or will they inherit a world in which the gospel can be freely lived out and proclaimed, in which traditional families are encouraged by society, and in which the religious beliefs of parents are supported, and not undermined, by the state?

In the pages to follow, we will strive to make the point that the future of our children and grandchildren is in our hands. We will outline how the homosexual agenda touches every area of our lives, from the media to education to families to corporate America and to government. We will document how the religious freedoms of all Americans are under attack from radical homosexual activists.

Will we avert our glance while Rome burns and our children are lost because we were afraid . . . afraid to offend, afraid to be labeled intolerant, afraid to take action in fear of repercussions? Or will we take a stand for Christ and for our children and grandchildren?

How far down the road have homosexual activists taken us toward their goal of unbridled sexual behavior and silencing of the church? Let us look at four stages that lead to the moral demise of a culture. Prepare yourselves to be alarmed.

1. *The Community Establishment Stage.* In this stage, a group of like-minded individuals (homosexual activists) who practice a lifestyle or sinful behavior discover each other and start to play a larger role in society. They start to feel empowered.
2. *The Organization Stage.* In this stage, the group now feels empowered and starts to get organized and develop a game plan for legitimizing their behavior in society.
3. *The Mobilization Stage.* The group starts to pool together all of its resources. They develop a common language and strategy for presenting their case to the public. They reframe the issue, taking it out of the moral realm, and present it as a "human rights" issue. Those who oppose their argument are deemed "hateful" or "intolerant" toward those that are "different" even though the group's only identification is that of a chosen sexual behavior.
4. *The Legitimization Stage.* Once an issue has been redefined from a moral absolute to an individual choice, society starts to be reprogrammed that the arguments of the group are valid and therefore special privileges for previous "injustices" and for the affirmation of the behavior occur.*

We are at stage 4 and are at the eleventh hour with regard to homosexual activism and religious freedom. The homosexual activists have the ball on our ten-yard line, and it is first and goal. We can either put up a brave defensive stand, or we can let them cross the goal line unhindered. If believers choose to do nothing, there may be a day that people of faith will have to tell their children and grandchildren, "I'm sorry. I did nothing to protect your religious freedom and now it's gone." They will have to say to those caught in homosexual behavior and wish to escape, like John Paulk, "I'm sorry, I cannot help you." Let us pray that we never have to face that scenario and that God's eternal truth, as expressed through the death and resurrection of his Son, Jesus Christ, will continue to be proclaimed boldly and without apology in our land . . . that together on our knees the door will remain open for the gospel.

---

*These stages were developed by S. Michael Craven.

CHAPTER ONE

How Did We Get Here?

*If we reflect on the dreadful consequences of sodomy to a state,
and on the extent to which this abominable vice may be secretly carried
on and spread; we cannot, on the principles of sound policy, consider
the punishment as too severe. For if it once begins to prevail, not only
will boys be easily corrupted by adults, but also by other boys; nor will
it ever cease; more especially as it must thus soon lose all its
shamefulness and infamy and become fashionable and the national
taste; and then . . . national weakness, for which all remedies
are ineffectual, most inevitably follow; not perhaps in the first
generation, but certainly in the course of the third or fourth. . . . To
these evils may be added yet another, viz. that the constitutions
of those men who submit to this degradation are, if not always,
yet very often, totally destroyed, though in a different way
from what is the result of the whoredom.
Whoever, therefore, wishes to ruin a nation, has only to get this
vice introduced; for it is extremely difficult to extirpate it where
it has once taken root because it can be propagated with much
secrecy . . . and when we perceive that it has once got a footing
in any country, however, powerful and flourishing, we may venture
as politicians to predict that the foundation of its future decline
is laid and that after some hundred years it will no longer
be the same . . . powerful country it is at the present.*
—Sir John David Michaelis, *Commentaries on the Laws of Moses,* 1814

In the June 2004 issue of the homosexual magazine *The Advocate,* the editors took a wishful look at their vision for America in the year 2054:

> Evan Wolfson, director of Freedom to Marry, a national group that advocates for marriage rights for same-sex couples, predicts a scenario in which a student in a rural classroom announces during recess that he's going to marry the boy who sits next to him. There will be no punishment from the teacher or taunts from classmates. After all, the boy might have two moms who are frequently seen at parent-teacher conferences . . . . After winning the Super Bowl, a gay quarterback could scream at TV crews, "I'm going to Disney World with my boyfriend!" The first lady could be the "first womyn." . . . Gay-themed TV shows, movies, and music now reserved for cable and other specialized outlets will likely be a staple of broadcast networks, multiplexes, and major labels, and no one will bat an eye at fictional portrayals of same-sex relationships.

The article quotes University of Southern California Anthropology and Gender Studies Professor Walter L. Williams: "I think we'll see more progress in the gay movement in the next 10 years than we saw in the past 50."[1]

That is an alarming thought considering what has happened over the past twenty years. In 1983, 30 percent of Americans said that they knew someone who was homosexual. By 2000, that figure had skyrocketed to 73 percent. In 1985, only 40 percent of those polled said they were comfortable around individuals who practice homosexual behavior. By 2000, that number had risen to 60 percent. Also in 1985, 90 percent of Americans said they would be upset if their son or daughter announced they were homosexual. By 2000, that figure stood at just 37 percent.[2]

Those of us who have dealt with the issue of the homosexual agenda issue over the years often stop and ask ourselves in disbelief: How has 1 to 2 percent of the population* achieved so much success in transforming American culture and restricting religious freedom?

The road leading to the grave threat that the homosexual agenda poses to evangelism, faith, and religious freedom did not happen

---

*Homosexual activists often proclaim that 10 percent of the population is homosexual. The 10 percent figure is based on studies and publications by Dr. Alfred C. Kinsey. However, Dr. Kinsey's methodology was defective. He used data gathered from interviews with felons, including sex offenders; volunteers who were coached to give answers that skewed the results; and the sexual stimulation of boys ages two months to fifteen years old. (See Judith Reisman, *Kinsey: Crimes & Consequences* [Arlington, Va.: The overnight. It has been part of a long-term strategy implemented by radical homosexual activists to dramatically transform America's perception of homosexuality and of those who oppose homosexual behavior.

As Gene Edward Veith wrote about the tremendous gains made by the homosexual activist movement: "Homo-sexuality used to be considered a vice; now even those it makes uncomfortable now must avow—as in a *Seinfeld* episode—'not that there's anything wrong with it,' while those who think there is something wrong with it are considered to have the vice of intolerance."[3]

> *That's how lasting social change happens—the barriers suddenly come down when nobody's looking.*
>
> —Walter Shapiro, *USA Today* columnist, on the success of the homosexual rights movement

What has caused such a radical shift in public attitudes toward homosexual behavior? And how did this shift happen in less than a generation?

The reason is a well-thought-out strategy that was devised in part by homosexual activists Marshall Kirk and Hunter Madsen and publicized in two publications: a 1987 article titled "The Overhauling of Straight America" and a 1989 book titled *After the Ball.*† When one reads both of these works, one sees how radical homosexual activists have implemented the strategy laid out in these publications almost to the letter.

The homosexual activists laid out a six-point strategy to radically change America's perception of homosexual behavior. Their six points were:

1. Talk about gays and gayness as loudly and often as possible.
2. Portray gays as victims, not aggressive challengers.
3. Give homosexual protectors a "just" cause.
4. Make gays look good.

Institute for Media Education, 1998]; Wardell Pomeroy, *Dr. Kinsey and the Institute for Sex Research* [New York: Harper & Row, 1972], 97–137.) In contrast, a 1993 report from the Alan Guttmacher Institute (part of Planned Parenthood and thus not a conservative organization) found that only 1.1 percent of 3,321 men surveyed considered themselves to be exclusively homosexual, and only 2.3 percent had engaged in sex with another man in the prior ten years (John O. G. Billy, et al., *Family Planning Perspectives* [Alan Guttmacher Institute, March/April 1993]). *Sex in America: A Definitive Survey* reported that of 3,432 respondents, "about 1.4 percent of women said they thought themselves as homosexual or bisexual and about 2.8 percent of men identified themselves in this way" (Robert T. Michael, et al. [New York: Warner Books, 1995], 176). An article published in *Pediatrics* likewise reported that of 34,706 adolescents surveyed (grades 7-12), 1.1 percent said they were bisexual or predominantly homosexual (Gary Remafedi, et. al., abstract, "Demography of Sexual Orientation in Adolescents," *Pediatrics*, Vol. 89, 1992, pp. 714–21). No survey using random sampling techniques has duplicated Kinsey's results.

†The following information is included in both places. The article "The Overhauling of Straight America" is found in chapter 3, "Strategy: Persuasion, Not Invasion." In addition, Madsen used the pseudonym Erastes Pill in the article but used his real name in the book.

5. Make the victimizers look bad.
6. Solicit funds: the buck stops here (i.e., get corporate America and major foundations to financially support the homosexual cause).

We are going to examine all six of these points and show how each is being played out in present-day American culture.

"Talk about Gays and Gayness as Loudly and Often as Possible"

In "The Overhauling of Straight America," Kirk and Madsen write, "The principle behind this advice is simple: almost all behavior begins to look normal if you are exposed to enough of it at close quarters and among your acquaintances."

This principle has proven itself time and time again throughout history as inhumane and outrageous behavior have become commonplace and ordinary. Every modern dictator has understood this principle as well.

In the past decade it has often seemed that every time you blink there is another newspaper article and another television show talking about otherwise "ordinary" individuals who practice homosexual behavior. The onslaught is relentless. This continual promotion of homosexual behavior eventually has one of two effects: (1) it convinces people that homosexual behavior is just another lifestyle, or (2) causes them to get so sick of the issue that they throw their hands up in disgust or become exhausted and then withdraw. Either way, the radical homosexual activists win, as they have either convinced people that they are "just like my fishing buddy" or make them so fed up with the issue that they can no longer stand it and just say to themselves, "I'm tired. I give up. Give them what they want so they will be quiet."

Kirk and Madsen wrote, "The main thing is talk about gayness until the issue becomes thoroughly tiresome." This ties into the concept of perseverance, the gradual wearing-down of people until they get to the point of total fatigue and give in on an issue. As we will see throughout this book, homosexual activists continue to hammer away time and time again until people just say, "Forget it" and then homosexuals get their way.

The activists were also very much aware that the unseemly sides of homosexual behavior—the types of sexual activity and its consequences—would have to be suppressed in order to gain acceptance. They wrote: "In the early stages of the campaign to reach straight America, the masses should not be shocked and repelled by premature exposure to homosexual behavior itself. Instead, the imagery of sex should be downplayed and gay rights should be reduced to an abstract social question as much as possible."[4] Therefore, the link between the practices of homosexual behavior and pedophilia, as well as the other dark sides of homosexual behavior, are intentionally suppressed or denied. Kirk and Madsen added: "First let the camel get his nose inside the tent—and only later his unsightly derriere!"[5]

An example of this was found in article that appeared in the February 8, 2004, *San Francisco Chronicle*. Reporting on the growing acceptance of homosexual behavior, Rona Marech wrote,

> First, there was the term "homosexual," then "gay" and "lesbian," then the once-taboo "dyke" and "queer." Now all bets are off. With the universe of gender and sexual identities expanding, a gay youth culture is emerging, acceptance of gays rising and label loyalty falling, the gay lexicon has exploded with scores of new words and blended phrases that delineate every conceivable stop on the identity spectrum—at least for this week. . . . Someone who is "genderqueer," for example, views the gender options as more than just male and female or doesn't fit into the binary male-female system. A "trannydyke" is a transgender person attracted to people with a more feminine gender, while a "pansexual" is attracted to people of multiple genders. A "boi" describes a boyish gay guy or a biological female with a male presentation; and "heteroflexible" refers to a straight person with a queer mindset. . . . The list of terms—which have hotly contested definitions—goes on: "FTM" for female to make, "MTF" for male to female, "boy dyke," "trannyboy," "trannyfag," "multigendered," "polygendered," "queerboi," "transboi," "transguy," "transman," "half-dyke," "bi-dyke," "stud," "stem," "trisexual," "omnisexual," and "multisexual."[6]

Carolyn Laub, of the Gay-Straight Alliance Network, added, "We in society and our generation are developing new understandings of sexual orientation and gender identities and what that means to us. We don't really have enough language to describe that; therefore, we have to create new words."[7]

Sam Davis, founder of a group called "United Genders of the Universe," continued: "If you're not a man or a woman, words like 'gay' or 'lesbian' don't fit you anymore. The words from just a few years ago aren't adequate to talk about who we are, where we're coming from and who we like."[8]

Kirk and Madsen also knew full well that the media would play an important role in their crusade. They stated, "The average American watches over seven hours of TV daily. Those hours open up a gateway into the private world of straights, through which a Trojan Horse might be passed."[9] Homosexual behavior has not only become commonplace on network television and in movies, but homosexual characters are often portrayed as the most compassionate, funny, "normal," and "human" individuals in the show. Shows such as *Queer Eye for the Straight Guy* on the Bravo network now portray homosexual behavior as superior to heterosexual behavior.

The next target for Kirk and Madsen was organized religion. They wrote, "While public opinion is one primary source of mainstream values, religious authority is the other. When conservative churches condemn gays, there are only two things we can do to confound the homophobia of the true believers. First, we can use talk to muddy the moral waters. This means publicizing support for gays by more moderate churches, raising theological objections of our own about conservative interpretations of Biblical teachings, and exposing hatred and inconsistency."[10] The homosexual activists have found a more than willing ally in liberal churches, many which threw out the gospel years ago anyway. Many of these churches now seemingly exist for few purposes besides the promotion of homosexual behavior.

With regard to churches that hold fast to the biblical teaching on homosexual behavior, Kirk and Madsen said, "We can undermine the moral authority of homophobic churches by portraying them as antiquated backwaters, badly out of step with the times and with the latest findings of psychology. Against the mighty pull of institutional religion, one must set the mightier draw of science and public opinion. . . . Such an unholy alliance has worked well against churches before, on such topics as divorce and abortion."[11] Therefore, conservative Christians have been referred to in the media as "largely poor, uneducated, and easy to command."[12]

In addition, even in traditional churches, dissenting advocates of homosexual politics are portrayed as enlightened, cutting-edge thinkers.

"Portray Gays as Victims, Not Aggressive Challengers"

Kirk and Madsen's next point, "Portray gays as victims, not as aggressive challengers," is a direct play to most Americans' basic sense of fairness and liberal guilt about anyone who claims to have been oppressed. Therefore, despite demographic statistics to the contrary,* homosexual activists have skillfully played the media like a drum to portray themselves as a victimized class in need of special protections.

In addition, they have been extremely skillful at turning tragedies into opportunities to move the homosexual agenda forward and portray anyone who opposes them as "murderers" or at least sympathetic to murder. This was evident in the assassination of Harvey Milk (the first open homosexual on the San Francisco Board of Supervisors); the AIDS epidemic of the early 1980s, when homosexual activists turned a deadly disease spread primarily by homosexual behavior into a civil rights issue; and the Matthew Shepard murder, when two non-religious thugs shamefully and brutally killed a young homosexual man by hanging him on a fence to die. In this last instance, homosexual activists went on the *Today* show and immediately blamed the murder on conservative Christian organizations such as Focus on the Family.[13] Dr. Dobson, the president of Focus on the Family, holds sincere religious objections to homosexual behavior but denounces violence of any kind. Instead, it was two thugs with no consciences at all who murdered Shepard. It is likely that if these two individuals had a strong relationship with Jesus Christ, Shepard would still be alive today.

Perhaps the most vicious diatribe came from Deborah Mathis who wrote in the *Orlando Sentinel:*

> The opponents [of homosexual behavior] prefer not to acknowledge their own bigotry. Hence, the disguise—or self-delusion—of noble purpose. They insist that they mean no harm. 'Hate the sin, love the sinner' is their mantra. How tiresome. How empty. But a handy little motto it is, for sure. Thanks to it, homophobes the world over don't have to reconcile their hate that writhes in their hearts with the Christianity that rests on their sleeves. Chant it enough times, and you can feel almost sanctified. . . . Did the anti-homosexual crowd help kill Matthew Shepherd? Nor per

---

*Later in the book we will present statistics to demonstrate that many individuals who practice homosexual behavior have higher incomes, more disposable income, and are more likely to travel overseas, among other things.

se. But it poisoned the air, which poisoned the minds which connived to attract, deceive, and destroy a young man who deserved, in the least, to be left alone. They share in the complicity.[14]*

Mathis also adds that conservative Christians are like Adolf Hitler, who exterminated 6 million Jews. Perhaps she has forgotten the brave actions of Christians such as Dietrich Bonhoeffer, Titus Brandsma, and Corrie ten Boom, who stood up to Hitler and his tragic slaughter of millions. However, her column is a vivid example of how far the homosexual activists and their allies are willing to go to demonize people of faith.

Randy Thomas, a former homosexual, succinctly summed up what has happened: "As a former homosexual, when I was involved in the 1980s promoting the gay agenda, our only focus was to seek tolerance, whereas today's political activism has moved from true tolerance into political domination and power. It's an amazing thing to watch a group that said they were oppressed become oppressors."[15]

"Give Homosexual Protectors a 'Just' Cause"

This strategy ties naturally into the almost natural inclination of people on the left side of the political spectrum to embrace any group that they become convinced has been "wronged" in the past. While there have been groups with legitimate grievances (e.g., African-Americans), radical homosexual activists have tried to piggyback on these legitimate efforts to right past wrongs to move the ball forward for their agenda. They have accomplished this through the manipulation of statistics on teen suicide, the creation of a Christian boogeyman in the Matthew Shepard tragedy, and so forth. The result is that individuals motivated by social justice issues, including some evangelicals, have felt that they need to protect practicing homosexuals from a so-called hostile society.

Another natural market for radical homosexual activists to tap in this area is Hollywood (see chap. 2 and the previous discussion in this chapter) with its liberal sensitivities and large homosexual com-

---

*In Chicago, a homosexual teenager killed a Catholic woman who was trying to persuade him to change his sexual orientation. The woman, Mary Stachowicz, was found strangled and then was placed in a crawl space under the floor. Yet there was no "hue and cry" over this "hate crime" and it was barely reported in the national press. Peter LaBarbera said: "If a gay man had been murdered for trying to convince someone to be gay, it would be a national news story and be deemed a hate crime. But when a gay man murders a woman who tried to convince him to change, the media spike the story." See Ellen Sorokin, "Some Say Gay Teen Should Face Hate Crime in Slaying," *Washington Times*, November 26, 2002.

munity. Kirk and Madsen wrote, "A media campaign that casts gays as society's victims and encourages straights to be their protectors must make it easier for those who respond to assert and explain their new perspectives."[16]

Just as Hollywood did much in the late 1930s to early 1940s (back when it was in more conservative hands) to convince Americans of the need to become involved in World War II, and then later in the 1960s to help support the civil rights and anti-war movements, it has adopted homosexual behavior as one of its latest causes. Therefore, as we will see later, homosexuals are almost always innocent—the hero who needs protection in films, television, etc.—while those who oppose them are either boorish or religious fanatics.

But homosexual activists are finding resistance from groups, such as African Americans who had legitimate civil rights grievances, to their efforts to piggyback homosexual behavior on the decades-long struggle by blacks for equal rights. Star Parker, a conservative black activist, writes,

> The gay front would like to be viewed as the latest chapter of the civil rights movement. According to their reasoning, gays are America's newest oppressed minority, seeking fairness, justice, and the right to pursue happiness in the same manner as other social groups in this country. Homosexuals today feel they are fighting the same battle that blacks fought 40 years ago. But, in fact, the gay movement is the civil rights movement turned on its head . . . . The civil rights movement of the 1960s was about living up and applying our principles, not re-writing or reinventing them. There was no tradition on which this country was founded that Dr. King challenged. It was upon those very traditions that he made his challenge and claim . . . . In a fashion quite the opposite of Dr. King— who challenged an unjust nation to return to its principles and traditions from which it had strayed—gay political operatives work to re-write our traditions to suit their own proclivities. They say their struggle is about equality, but it's really about the exercise of political power and claims for entitlement.[17]

Even liberal African-American civil rights activists like Jesse Jackson refute the claim by homosexual activists that they have legitimate civil rights concerns. When asked about the "right" of homosexuals to "marry," Jackson said that there was no comparison with the legitimate civil rights struggles of black Americans. Jackson commented: "The comparison with slavery is a stretch in that some slave masters were gay, in that gays were never called three-fifths human in the Constitution, and in that they did not require the Voting Rights Act to have the right to vote."[18]

"Make Gays Look Good" and "Make the Victimizers Look Bad"

This manifests itself in many ways: from rewriting history to convince people that many famous individuals were homosexual to the sympathetic portrayal of homosexuals in the media. The other part of this strategy, according to Kirk and Madsen, is to "make the victimizers look bad." Kirk and Madsen wrote, "We intend to make the anti-gays look so nasty that average Americans will want to disassociate themselves from such types."[19]

Unfortunately, some individuals have played right into the hands of radical homosexual activists in helping them bludgeon the Christian community on the homosexual issue. In the introduction, we mentioned Fred Phelps and his followers who go around the country with signs that read "God Hates Fags," picket funerals of AIDS victims, and host a Web site showing homosexuals being thrown into the fire of hell. Others have used less than ideal discernment in discussing the homosexual issue in the media. By not practicing Christ-like speech, sincere Christians have often been their own worst enemy in assisting radical homosexual activists move their agenda forward, especially when they are looking for the absolutely worst-case examples to prop up as representatives of orthodox and evangelical, Bible-believing Christians.

This is why the behavior of people of faith must always be above reproach. When Christians speak out against homosexual behavior with unconfessed sins in our own closets, we only validate the mindset that Christians are hypocrites who cannot remove the planks in our own eyes.* When believers use less than Christ-like speech, we give credence to arguments of homosexual activists that we are less than compassionate, to put it nicely.

None of this means that people of faith should avoid the truth, even unpleasant truth, but we must speak the truth in love.†

---

*See Matthew 7:3–5.
†See 1 Corinthians 6:9–10; Romans 1:24–28; Leviticus 18:22; Psalm 24:3–4.

Anyone who has followed the agenda of the radical homosexual activists for the past ten to fifteen years can see how they have been successful in virtually every area mentioned by Kirk and Madsen. In subsequent chapters in this book, we will describe how each area of this agenda has been implemented in the media, in public schools, the church, and every other aspect of contemporary American life.

In addition, despite the claims that "we are everywhere," a survey of the 2000 census data found that more than one-quarter of same-sex households were concentrated in five urban areas (listed with the percentage of residents who state they are homosexual): New York City: 8.9%, Los Angeles: 6.6%, San Francisco: 4.9%, Washington, D.C.: 3.3%, and Chicago: 3.1%.[20]*

"Solicit Funds: The Buck Stops Here"

The other method used by homosexual activists is to falsely accuse the other side of having billions of dollars in resources while they are struggling to put food on the table. Nothing could be further from the truth. Homosexual activist groups are backed by millions of dollars, including generous grants from numerous corporations.† This ties into their final strategy: "Solicit funds: the buck stops here."

An example of how homosexual activists use money to advance their agenda is illustrated through the work of the Gill Foundation, which has $255 million in assets, in Colorado.[21] Started by Quark software founder Tim Gill (an open homosexual) in response to the state's passage of Amendment 2, which would have barred special rights and privileges for homosexual behavior, the foundation alone has poured at least $800,000 into the Colorado Springs area, home of several conservative religious organizations, including Focus on the Family.[22]

The Gill Foundation has provided an additional $3.4 million in grants to promote the homosexual agenda through its subsidiary, the Gay and Lesbian Fund for Colorado, to groups such as the Easter Seals, the American Lung Association, the Urban League, and the Girl Scouts. The money comes with strings, however. Each organization that accepts a Gill Foundation grant must agree to add homosexual behavior to its anti-discrimination policies and publicly credit the

---

*The same Census report stated the cities with the highest concentration of same-sex households in proportion to all households in a metropolitan area were as follows: San Francisco, California; Santa Fe, New Mexico; Portland, Maine; Burlington, Vermont; Seattle, Washington; Miami, Florida; and Austin, Texas.
†The Ford Foundation, for example, has provided grants to the pro-homosexual Gill Foundation, the National Gay and Lesbian Task Force, International Gay and Lesbian Human Rights Commission, National Gay and Lesbian Task Force Policy Institute, and the Lambda Legal Defense and Education Fund, which actively lobbies for same-sex marriage.

fund in its materials. More than $9 million of the foundation's money has gone directly to groups such as the Lambda Legal Defense and Education Fund, which lobbies for same-sex marriage.[23] In 2001, the foundation gave $18.5 million in donations to homosexual organizations and causes.[24]

Will Perkins, who helped spearhead Amendment 2, says, "What the Gill Foundation is attempting to do—and they're quite successful at it—is to buy legitimacy for the homosexual lifestyle. They've put a lot of money in the Springs area, and part of the deal is to neutralize public opinion on homosexual behavior, and it's been working."[25]

The result has been that in Colorado Springs now a majority of its city council members are sympathetic to homosexual behavior, going so far as to proclaim a gay pride week in a city that is home to headquarters or regional offices for more than seventy-two Christian ministries.[26] In November 2002, the Colorado Springs City Council voted to grant same-sex partners tax-funded health-care benefits. The transformation from "ground zero" of "hate" (as radical homosexual activists called it after the passage of Amendment 2) to funding the homosexual agenda was complete. And, with the exception of Focus on the Family, the response from the other 70+ Christian ministries in town was deafeningly silent.[27]

The American Civil Liberties Union (ACLU) has wholeheartedly embraced the homosexual agenda and appointed as its new executive director in 2001 Anthony Romero, who is an openly homosexual person with a record of activism.[28] The ACLU boasts of 400,000 members and more than 1,000 volunteer and 60 staff attorneys.[29] Its various components have a $45 million budget, a $50 million endowment fund,[30] which includes a $7 million grant from the Ford Foundation,[31] and three hundred chapters nationwide.[32] The Lambda Legal Defense and Education Fund, which advocates same-sex marriage and has been the leader in the attack against the Boy Scouts (see chap. 8) for its policy regarding homosexual scoutmasters, boasts of corporate support from IBM and United Airlines.[33] The Human Rights Campaign, which actively lobbies for and provides direct financial support to political candidates sympathetic to the homosexual agenda, lists American Airlines and Subaru as corporate sponsors.[34]

The Gill Foundation has assets of more than $165 million.[35] The budget of the Human Rights Campaign has more than tripled in six short years.[36] David Bohnott, a venture capitalist who developed the GeoCities Web site, gave about $2 million to the Human Rights Campaign,[37] and Karen Levinson, founder of E-Trade, has donated $500,000 to pro-homosexual groups.[38]

Meanwhile, many Christian organizations are finding themselves in a time of financial retrenchment, and the one organization in the state of Arizona lobbying for family values finds itself always scrambling to find the cash just to keep the doors open. While homosexual activists say they are not the aggressive challengers, the fact is that they are the aggressive, well-financed challengers.

Eric Pollard, the founder of ACT-UP (a militant homosexual group) openly admitted that lying was part of the strategy of homosexual activists. He even said that Adolf Hitler's *Mein Kampf* was the model used for their strategy.[39] It is a strategy of lies and intimidation. Consider the following excerpts from Hitler's work:

> [T]he magnitude of a lie always contains a certain factor of credibility, since the great masses of the people in the very bottom of their hearts tend to be corrupted rather than consciously and purposely evil, and that, therefore, in view of the primitive simplicity of their minds, they more easily fall a victim to a big lie than to a little one, since they themselves lie in little things, but would be ashamed of lies that were too big. . . .[40]
>
> [S]omething of even the most insolent lie will always remain and stick—a fact which all the great lie-virtuosi and lying-clubs in this world know only too well and also make the most treacherous use of. . . .[41]
>
> [B]y clever and persevering use of propaganda even heaven can be represented as hell to the people, and conversely the most wretched life as paradise.[42]

When you read these quotations, coupled with the strategy outlined by Kirk, Madsen, and others to transform American culture to accept homosexual behavior and condemn those who hold sincere religious objections to such behavior, it might be said that activists have followed a strategy akin to what Hitler used back in the 1920s and 1930s to take over Germany. In fact, Kirk and Madsen, in the book *After the Ball,* which fleshed out the strategy discussed in "The Overhauling of Straight America," said regarding advertisements that would place homosexuals in a positive light: "It makes no difference that the ads [portraying homosexuals as icons of normality] are lies, not to us . . . not to bigots."[43]

Much of the homosexual agenda has been based on deception. For example, while several studies throughout the past ten years have placed the percentage of homosexuals at no higher than 1 to 2 percent, homosexual groups and their allies continue to cite the now-discredited figure of 10 percent when it comes to estimating the percentage of homosexuals in America. Yet, despite research to the contrary, homosexual activists continue to push the 10 percent figure, or even greater numbers, and government entities and the media seldom, if ever, question the inaccuracy of the puffed-up statistic.

Kirk and Madsen also added that they knew that they would have to wage a war of propaganda, just as Hitler did so masterfully in Nazi Germany, to get the American public on their side. Here is a direct quote from *After the Ball:* "We have in mind a strategy as calculated and powerful as that which gays are accused of pursuing by their enemies—or, if you prefer, a plan as manipulative as that which our enemies themselves employ. It's time to learn from Madison Avenue, to roll out the big guns. Gays must launch a large-scale campaign—we've called it the Waging Peace campaign—to reach straights through the mainstream media. WE'RE TALKING ABOUT PROPAGANDA"[44] [emphasis added].

Kirk and Madsen continue: "Even when it sticks to the facts, propaganda can be unabashedly subjective and one-sided. There is nothing necessarily wrong with this. Propaganda tells its own side of the story as moving (and credibly) as possible, since it can count on its enemies to tell the other side with a vengeance [another reminder to us about using Christ-like speech to help our credibility]. In its battle for hearts and minds, effective propaganda knows enough to put its best foot forward. This is what our media campaign must do."[45]

In the chapters following, we will see how the homosexual activists have successfully implemented Kirk and Madsen's propaganda campaign in the media, the public schools, the medical profession, corporate America, the workplace, and most of all, the church. In fact, the activists have followed this plan to the letter. They have achieved the goals they set out in the late eighties through careful coordination and relentless effort. As a result, the very future of our nation is at risk if the homosexual agenda continues to advance unchecked.

CHAPTER TWO
That's Entertainment?

*A Martian gathering evidence about American society, simply
by monitoring our television, would certainly assume that there were
more gay people in America than there are evangelical Christians.*
—Michael Medved

Will & Grace is one of the highest rated comedies on network television. It has won a slew of Emmy awards and is part of NBC's "Must See TV" promotion on Thursday nights, following in the footsteps of such classic shows as *The Cosby Show* and *Family Ties*.

It is also the most upfront show on network television in regard to the promotion of homosexual behavior. In fact, the stars of *Will & Grace* even got involved politically, cutting an advertisement in 2000 urging California voters to oppose Proposition 22, which stated that California would only recognize marriages between one man and one woman. The star, Eric McCormick, who plays the openly homosexual Will, stated the intentions of the producers early on. He said, "I would love to get to the point where grandmothers in Kansas are saying, 'I just hope that Will finds a nice man.' We're not a political show, but that would be a real coup."[1]

In one particularly egregious episode of the show, John and Anne Paulk are mercilessly mocked. When one of the lead characters attends a meeting of ex-homosexuals, he meets the leader of the group who talks about how they are all going to be restored to "righteousness." After incessant taunting by the homosexual character, all the ex-homosexuals in the room return to homosexual behavior, and the leader does as well, accepting a date with the homosexual.

After this show aired, Mike Haley, a former homosexual who works at Focus on the Family, sent the following letter to Jon Kinnally, the executive story editor of *Will & Grace:*

> Dear Mr. Kinnally:
>
> I am writing to request a meeting with you regarding a recent episode of *Will & Grace.* The show in question grossly misrepresented thousands of individuals struggling to come out of homosexuality. As a former gay man, and now a national spokesman and expert on homosexuality and youth issues for Focus on the Family—one of the country's largest organizations, who, among other things, assists gays and lesbians who desire to be heterosexual—I know first-hand how frustrating and painful it is to be mocked by those who haven't taken the time to find out what the process is all about. I'm specifically talking about references in the show to former homosexuals, and those wrestling with their sexual identity, as "freaks," "self-loathing closet cases," "morally wrong," and as members of "cults." Nowhere in this episode are we portrayed as honest men and women seeking help.
>
> You may vehemently disagree with this position, but I'd at least like the opportunity to sit down and talk to you about it. Our conversation may not change your mind about the possibility of coming out of homosexuality, but at the very least it will put a real face behind the caricature you depicted on prime-time TV. And in the end, hopefully it will encourage you to think twice before ridiculing the belief systems of those who differ from you. With that in mind, please respectfully consider my request.

The last thing Mike received was respect, based on the reply on *Will & Grace* letterhead he received:

> Dear Mr. Haley:
>
> I received your letter dated June 9, and was very interested in your point of view. The issues you raised are the very same ones that we on the *Will & Grace* writing staff debate on a daily basis. Our decision to present the story on the ex-gay ministry was solely in the interest of creating the most comedic episode possible. And it was certainly

not our intention to offend you in any way. But come on, Mike, even you've got to admit that fags trying to pretend they're straight is pretty funny.

In response to your request for a meeting, well, I think I can read between the lines on that one. I'm about 6'1", brown hair, green eyes, and I'm into rollerblading, baking cookies, and cleaning up afterwards. My dislikes include game-playing, negative attitudes, and condoms.

If any of this interests you, I can be found every Sunday at the Brunch and Beer Bust at the Motherlode in West Hollywood. I do hope you show, because like you, I am an expert on homosexuality, and in my expert opinion, this "hard-to-get thing" you're playing is Hot, Hot, Hot![2]

Mike had written a serious and thoughtful letter and was treated with a mocking sexual proposition in reply. This response shows not only the hostility of homosexual activists in the entertainment industry to traditional values and those who have overcome homosexual behavior, but also the general tone in the entertainment media to anyone who objects to homosexual behavior. What was communicated to Mike in a letter is what is communicated on the small screen every week.

Will & Grace is an example of Kirk and Madsen's stated strategy to use the media to help desensitize Americans to homosexual behavior.* Perhaps nowhere else has the homosexual activist movement had more success than in gaining control of the entertainment media to promote its agenda.

For example, alarming statistics are coming to the forefront that document the role that the media has played in the growing acceptance of homosexual behavior and its effect on American society.

Using data from the National Opinion Research Center at the University of Chicago, the study showed that in 1988, 74.9 percent of respondents said that sex between two people of the same sex is always wrong. By 1998, that number had dropped to 54.6 percent. The number of women who said they had had a sexual encounter with another woman rose from 0.2 percent to 2.8 percent, while the percentages of men having a sexual encounter with another man rose from 1.7 percent to 4.1 percent.[3†]

---

*In 2003, shows such as *Queer Eye for the Straight Guy* and *It's All Relative* made their debuts on cable and network television. Both of these shows portrayed homosexuals in a positive light while ridiculing heterosexuals or people with religious beliefs that do not affirm homosexual behavior. An episode of ESPN's *Playmakers* about a homosexual football player ended with a recitation of the Twenty-third Psalm in support of his behavior.

†A "sexual encounter" does not mean the person engaging in the act was a "homosexual," nor did many of those who had an encounter repeatedly replicate the behavior.

Amy Butler, a professor at the University of Iowa, explained some of the reasons why the increase in homosexual behavior had occurred: "Declining social, legal, and economic sanctions against same-gender sexual behavior in recent years and more positive images of gay men and women in the media may have made it easier for people to recognize their same-gender sexual interest and act upon it."[4] The Associated Press report on the study added: "Whether more positive media portrayals play a role in the increasing reports of homosexual activity is hard to determine, Butler said. For certain, the media wouldn't put shows on television or produce movies that portray gay lifestyles if the public wasn't willing to accept it, she said. Her study says the way gays and lesbians appear in the media may make some people more comfortable with their homosexual impulses."[5]

For many young people, the open promotion of homosexual behavior in the media and the classroom, along with the breakdown of the traditional family, has led to their "coming out" at younger and younger ages.*

Not a New Phenomenon

We would be incorrect if we stated that homosexual behavior was a fairly recent phenomenon in Hollywood.

Hollywood has long had a large homosexual contingent, and, as a result, many there have had a natural sympathy for the homosexual cause. That is why you see old-time Hollywood stars such as Elizabeth Taylor and Debbie Reynolds support radical homosexual organizations.[6] Taylor has said, "Without homosexuals there would be no Hollywood, no theater and no arts."[7]†

It is well known that some of the most famous writers, directors, and other creative talent from Hollywood's so-called golden era engaged in homosexual behavior. However, these facts were well concealed from the general public who would have heartily disap-

---

*A new teenage lesbian pop duo named Tatu recently reached the top of England's pop charts and have closed in on the American Top 20. They strip and kiss between songs and dress in revealing school girl outfits. Their "discoverer," a Russian psychologist named Ivan Shapovalov, says: "All our inspiration is from childhood. Why should this be hidden? . . . They are two teenagers singing about love." Shapovalov then accused those who have spoken out about the group and its lesbian pedophile image as "prudes." See Sabrina Tavernise, "A Bubblegum Duo Sets Off Squeals and Squirms," *New York Times,* March 4, 2003.

†At least one veteran Hollywood star has had the courage to stand up to Hollywood's liberal agenda. Actress Jane Russell said at a recent national conference that she was tired of Christian conservatives being labeled intolerant when they stand up for their beliefs. "The Lord put this country together or we wouldn't be like we are," Russell said. See Marc Morano, "Hollywood Actress Declares Herself 'Right-Wing Christian Bigot," *CNSNews.com,* February 3, 2003.

proved. Ramon Navarro, the star of the silent version of *Ben Hur* was a practicing homosexual.[8] William Haines, another star of the late twenties and early thirties, publicly disclosed his homosexual behavior, and it immediately ended his career[9] (back in the days when homosexual behavior was frowned upon by the general public). Greta Garbo was a notorious bisexual, equally promiscuous with both men and women.[10] Montgomery Clift[11] and Rock Hudson,[12] screen icons of the 1950s, practiced homosexual behavior.

George Cukor, director of such films as *A Star Is Born, The Women,* and *The Philadelphia Story,* was one of the first publicly acknowledged homosexuals in Hollywood. He was the so-called women's director because of his gentle, feminine ways.[13] Clark Gable asked for Cukor's removal from the set of *Gone With the Wind* because of his personal discomfort with Cukor's homosexuality and had him replaced with the vigorously heterosexual Victor Fleming.[14] Today, Gable (the biggest star of his era) would be labeled a homophobe and blacklisted from Hollywood because of his actions. In fact, in perhaps a belated attempt to extract some revenge from the "King," as he was called, radical homosexual activists now claim that Gable was bisexual,[15] despite the numerous stories told by Joan Crawford, Loretta Young, and many other of his leading ladies about his very virile heterosexuality. The King must be rolling in his grave.

Besides Gable, other Hollywood icons, such as Cary Grant, have seen their lives rewritten by radical homosexual activists, despite long histories of heterosexual behavior.[16]

Despite the prevalence of homosexual behavior (as well as promiscuous heterosexual behavior) in Hollywood's history, the golden age was a different era. Homosexual behavior was not openly promoted on screen, and when it was implied, it was done so in a humorous fashion. There were stereotypical homosexual characters in movies, most notably Edward Everett Horton's fussy characters in the Fred Astaire/Ginger Rogers musicals *The Gay Divorcee, Top Hat,* and *Shall We Dance* (Horton himself was a well-known homosexual in Hollywood).[17] Franklin Pangborn's cowardly actions in W. C. Fields' films and Gus Schilling's effeminate male secretary in the Astaire/Rita Hayworth film *You Were Never Lovelier* are more examples.

However, these characters tended to be comic relief, and their behavior was implied, not openly promoted as a viable alternative to heterosexuality or as something to be admired and followed. They were portrayed much like a dotty old aunt whose eccentric behavior is to be winked at.

While many cultural observers point to the 1990s as the time when the portrayal of active homosexuals came "out of the closet," so to speak, it was in the late 1960s that a significant shift started to happen in Hollywood's portrayal of homosexual behavior.

In 1967, the movie *Who's Afraid of Virginia Woolf?*, starring Richard Burton and Elizabeth Taylor, was released. Written by the homosexual playwright Edward Albee, it trashed traditional marriage as it portrayed a warring couple who had nothing but the most absolute contempt for each other. It went on to win Best Picture that year.*

In the same year, Norman Lear, who later created and produced *All in the Family*, released *Divorce American Style*, with Dick Van Dyke and Debbie Reynolds, which also openly mocked the institution of marriage. The door had been opened to the weakening of marriage in the mass media and the exaltation of alternative lifestyles. Once marriage was attacked, other sexual behaviors, such as premarital and homosexual sex, were not only seen and promoted as viable options but as more desirable than the institution that God had intended for mankind. The Pandora's box had been opened.

Homosexual Behavior on Network Television

In 1971, the CBS television network, in an attempt to appeal to young, urban viewers with disposable incomes, purged its schedule of such light-humored shows as *The Beverly Hillbillies, Green Acres, Hogan's Heroes, Petticoat Junction,* and *The Andy Griffith Show.* These fairly conservative and generally family-friendly shows were replaced by the loud, raucous, in-your-face liberalism of Norman Lear's *All in the Family* and *Maude* and the elite contempt for authority sensibilities of Larry Gelbart's *M*A*S*H.*

(The movie *M*A*S*H* was not the first but was definitely the most blatant film to that date to† openly ridicule Christianity in its portrayal of Frank Burns as a Bible-reading, adulterous hypocrite. In one scene he is reading the Twenty-third Psalm, and his tentmates make demeaning and obscene comments about the Bible and his faith. The television program started down this road in the first two seasons but eventually painted religious faith in a more positive

---

*Alan has debated Albee on a program that aired on PBS where Albee expanded his attack on traditional marriage to include support for pornography (even including taxpayer funded support for it).
†The attacks by Hollywood on Christians started in earnest in 1960 with the release of *Elmer Gantry* and *Inherit the Wind.* Christians were portrayed as either corrupt or ignorant buffoons.

manner in the character of Father Mulcahy, as long as his faith was liberal and did not suggest moral absolutes.)

Part of this new "hipness" was the sexualization of network comedy, until everything seemingly became a joke about sex. Much of this new emphasis came from an influx of homosexual writers and directors. However, it would be erroneous to say that it took until the 1990s for this new direction to be used to promote homosexual behavior on network television.

In an early episode of *All in the Family,* the "enlightened" liberal characters invite a seemingly stereotypical homosexual friend over to the Bunker house for dinner with the conservative and bigoted Archie. Archie immediately engages in the type of behavior that would be described today as "homophobic." The friend is straight, of course, and Archie ends up with egg on his face. Later on, Archie retreats to his neighborhood bar to be with "real men," one of whom is a tough-as-nails former football player and a "man's man" Archie admires. As the episode unfolds, Archie eventually realizes that this man's man practices homosexual behavior, and he is forced to rethink his stereotype of homosexuals.[18]

A 1977 episode dealt with the death of Edith's lesbian cousin and the issues surrounding the leaving of her estate to her lover.[19] Another episode featured the "hate crime" murder at Christmas time of a transvestite whom the Bunkers had come to know, shaking Edith's faith in God.[20]

In 1974, the TV show M*A*S*H aired an episode titled "George," which served as a precursor to the attempt to allow individuals who engage in homosexual behavior to serve openly in the armed forces. George arrives at the 4077th M*A*S*H hospital badly bruised and cut up. Both Hawkeye and Trapper John, the two liberal doctors, suspect that they are not normal war wounds and that the guys beat him up in his platoon for being "different" (i.e., homosexual). Of course, the conservative, hypocritical Frank Burns figures out George's secret and attempts to have him drummed out of the military. Hawkeye and Trapper John then dig up a secret on Frank (he cheated on his medical exams) and blackmail him to allow George to continue to serve, otherwise they will air Frank's dirty laundry and get him thrown out of the military on a dishonorable discharge. George is painted in the most sympathetic of lights, while Frank is shown to be narrow-minded, hypocritical, and bigoted.[21]

In the late '70s, in an attempt to catch up with the new direction launched by CBS, the ABC television network aired the then-controversial program *Soap,* which was filled with sexual humor. It also introduced the first openly homosexual regular character on network television, Jodie Dallas, portrayed by comedian Billy Crystal, and America met his "boyfriend."[22]

While most media observers cite *Ellen* as the first show to feature an openly homosexual leading character, they are in error. In 1981, NBC aired *Love, Sydney* starring Tony Randall as an openly homosexual commercial artist. His sexuality was played down after initial public backlash and was only brought back into story lines when the program was on its last legs.[23]

In 1983, in the first season of *Cheers* on NBC, an episode ran that featured a group of homosexuals who start frequenting the bar, much to the discomfort and alarm of the "regulars." At first, the regulars will have nothing to do with the homosexuals and force them to sit in a secluded area of the bar. However, Diane, the enlightened barmaid, takes up the cause of the homosexual characters and eventually shows the regulars how ridiculous their behavior is. The episode ends with the homosexual and heterosexual characters embracing each other and joining together for a round of drinks.[24]

There is a definite link here. All the shows mentioned above were comedies. Homosexual activists have noticed very astutely that the use of humor is a primary vehicle to help them reach their goal of cultural acceptance. Humor had been used by the entertainment industry in the past to stir up anti-war sentiment (the Marx Brothers' *Duck Soup, M*A*S*H, Dr. Strangelove*) and to promote feminism (*Nine to Five*) and cross-dressing (*Some Like It Hot* and *Tootsie*).

Homosexual producers and directors readily admit that humor is their best weapon to soften up the American public for the future promotion of their agenda. If you can get people to laugh about something, you are then on the way to convincing them to accept the behavior as normal. Thus, the portrayal of homosexual behavior gradually moved into prime-time dramas, such as ABC's *thirtysomething*, the first show to portray two men in bed together.

For many years, the number-one prime-time comedy was *Friends*, a show about oversexed heterosexuals, which was produced by an open homosexual. In one episode, the ex-wife of one of the heterosexual leads marries her lesbian lover in a ceremony officiated by Newt Gingrich's lesbian sister, Candice.* A pointed political statement is made in the midst of all the laughter.

---

*Newt Gingrich is the former Speaker of the House of Representatives and a Republican.

When homosexual activists and their allies cannot use overt means to promote homosexual behavior, they often resort to so-called "camp humor" with the underlying homosexual themes. In the early 1980s, Alan saw firsthand homosexual "camp humor" as he prosecuted hard core obscenity cases in federal court.

For instance, in one case, one of the materials purchased from the defendants (who at the time controlled the largest distribution network for hard core pornography in the world) was a graphic series of illustrations of homosexual sexual behavior of every type imaginable (and beyond Alan's imagination). These illustrations were accompanied with violent imagery of beating, stomping, and kicking of a very young-looking man or teenager by an older, more powerful man dressed in black leather. The subsequent depictions of bruising and serious injury ended with the victim being abandoned naked and unconscious in a forest.

The professional obscenity defense lawyers, who had been assembled from across the nation to, in their words, "defend the First Amendment," called an expert witness. This individual was a professor from Johns Hopkins University and was called to prove a claim by the defense that such violent material was not obscene, could not be interpreted as obscene, and, in fact, was high comedy.

Under oath, and with a straight face, the professor went through one graphic depiction of sex and violence after another, explaining that the depictions were nothing more than homosexual "camp humor." He explained in detail how everyone in the enlightened homosexual community who saw this material would laugh and wink because to them it was an "inside joke" that would leave "ignorant straights" puzzled. The "straights" would then stupidly think that it was actually a dirty depiction of men fighting and engaging in sodomy.

The grinning Ph.D. went on to explain to the jury that homosexuals throughout the entertainment industry love to have fun with "straight ignorance" by inserting homosexual "inside jokes" into scripts and visual imagery (such as having a homosexual man play the lead romantic role with a female). Thus, the homosexuals in the entertainment industry and their friends would see and understand these "jokes" and laugh while foolish "straights" who oppose homosexual behavior ignorantly watch, pay for, and share with their children the inside jokes.

What the professor could not explain, of course, was the impact of viewing such violent sex material by those who weren't in on the so-called "joke," or insiders to "campiness," such as the young boys, who are the largest consumers of hard-core pornography.*

As we stated earlier in the introduction, Alan learned later of the lack of respect and the total disgust within the pornographic production community for those who practice homosexual behavior. These peddlers of human flesh would greatly exploit their weaknesses for profit. Alan believes that those who produce and sell obscene material have their own form of "camp humor"—the taking of millions of dollars from persons caught up in homosexual behavior (who the pornographers hate) through the production of ever more effective, more arousing materials and opportunities to financially exploit homosexual sexual desires.[25]

But let's get back to the idea that making people laugh about homosexual behavior leads to desensitization toward homosexual behavior.

Given the theory that making people laugh about homosexual behavior leads to desensitization, is it any wonder that the boldest pro-homosexual move by Hollywood happened with Ellen DeGeneres, a comedian on her program *Ellen*?

Ellen had floundered for several years, never really being a hit. Ellen DeGeneres's sexuality was one of the worst-kept secrets in Hollywood.[26] To help spike the ratings of the program, ABC ran a season-long tease through promotional announcements and trial balloons in major news publications about the character of Ellen coming out. Finally, in the May sweeps, the so-called "puppy" episode was aired, which unveiled Ellen's lesbianism, with the help of several major Hollywood stars.[27] The character of Ellen's coming out was coupled with Ellen DeGeneres's own public announcement on the cover of *Time* magazine, which read simply, "Yep, I'm Gay."[28]

After high ratings, especially in urban areas with large homosexual populations, for the coming-out episode, *Ellen* quickly sank lower in the ratings than it was before, as it became a soapbox for the promotion of lesbian behavior. In one episode, Ellen expresses her love for her "girlfriend" and gets on one knee and proposes to her.[29] Even in 1998, that was a little too much for America to take. Still, Hollywood refused to acknowledge that the show's demise could have been blamed on its promotion of lesbian behavior and instead insisted that it was "too preachy."[30]

---

*The case resulted in a 11–1 hung jury. Before the retrial, the defendants pled guilty to federal felony charges, admitting that the "humorous" material was legally obscene). See the Final Report of the Attorney General's Commission on Pornography for more information.

Despite the failure of *Ellen,* along with other notable duds featuring other stars playing homosexual characters,[31] network television continues to relentlessly push the homosexual agenda. In fact, only one network show, *Will & Grace,* that promotes homosexual behavior, has been a hit. The Gay and Lesbian Alliance Against Defamation (GLAAD) now claims that there are more than thirty prime-time television characters who are openly homosexual.[32] It also claims to "control" Hollywood, having full script approval over the portrayal of homosexual behavior.[33] The result is that homosexual characters are often depicted as the most likable and emotionally healthy characters on prime-time television. This is done deliberately in order to normalize homosexual behavior to Americans. Michael Medved stated, "We're in the Sydney Poitier stage of 'gay' characters. . . . [I]n the 1950s, 60s, and early 70s, every major black character was upright and honorable and likely portrayed by Poitier. . . . [T]here's such eagerness in the gay community for a sort of compensatory treatment, that every character you meet that's gay is going to be likeable."[34] He added, "A Martian gathering evidence about American society, simply by monitoring our television, would certainly assume that there were more gay people in America than there are evangelical Christians."[35]

Graphic Portrayal

The latest salvo in the relentless promotion of homosexual behavior on network and cable television is the introduction of "transgendered" characters. The since-canceled CBS show *The Education of Max Bickford,* starring Oscar winner Richard Dreyfuss, introduced a character named Steve who undergoes a sex-change operation and becomes Erica.

GLAAD, which monitors homosexual portrayals like hawks, sent a letter to the media outlining a list of do's and don'ts for writing about the character of Erica (portrayed by actress Helen Shaver). The letter suggested:

- Do use female pronouns when referring to Erica.
- Don't use quotation marks around [the words] female, woman, Erica, or female pronouns when referring to Helen Shaver's character.

Included in the packet of material the media received was a list of "problematic terminology" such as "she-male," "he-she," "trannie," "tranny," and "gender-bender." Instead, the letter stated that "transition" should be used instead of "sex change" and "intersex person" instead of "hermaphrodite."

GLAAD spokesman Scott Seomin proudly said that the organization had done a similar mailing to the media after Hillary Swank was nominated for an Oscar for playing a girl who makes herself into a boy in *Boys Don't Cry*. (Swank won the Oscar and gave an acceptance speech promoting transgender rights).[36]

Could you imagine the uproar that might happen if the Southern Baptist Convention sent out a letter to the media stating that they should not use the words *fundamentalist, bigot, Bible thumper*, or *intolerant* to describe evangelical Christians? The howls of censorship would be heard from coast to coast, but that illustrates the control radical homosexual activists have over Hollywood.

The promotion of homosexual, bisexual, and "transgendered" characters has become so universal on network and cable television that even pro-homosexual members of the media get confused. Consider these comments from Matthew Gilbert of the *Boston Globe*:

> Claire Fisher is straight—or is she? As season four of [HBO's] *Six Feet Under* unfolds, the show's caustic art student is fanning her flames for a slamming lesbian poet named Edie. Meanwhile, Claire's terminally bummed ex-boyfriend, Russell, is chasing after her, despite his gay tryst with their bombastic professor, Olivier . . . .
>
> Talk about switch-hitting. These days, it's getting harder to hang sexual orientation labels on TV characters . . . . Writers on *Queer as Folk, The L Word*, and *Nip/Tuck* have been boldly creating men and women who fall somewhere between the extremes of the Kinsey scale—exclusively homosexual or exclusively heterosexual . . . . The blurring of the lines of sexual orientation is a step beyond "Gay TV" . . . . The sexually indefinite characters aren't closeted gays and lesbians, running from their true selves, struggling to accept the inevitable. They're more curious-seeking than that, and less tortured. They're "questioning," as a number of Lesbian, Gay, Bisexual, and Transgender organizations have put it. Yep, TV is beginning to include the LGBT *and* Q community in its electronic embrace.[37]

Another method used to promote homosexual behavior is to get two attractive heterosexual actresses to lock lips, especially in movies and TV shows geared to teenagers. We have been treated to Sarah Michelle Gellar (*Buffy the Vampire Slayer*) and an attractive female exchanging a passionate kiss in the teen sex movie *Cruel Intentions*,[38] Jennifer Aniston and Winona Ryder engaging in a prolonged kiss on *Friends*,[39] and Calista Flockhart kissing another female character on *Ally McBeal*.[40] If two seemingly "with-it," glamorous, sexy women engage in lesbian behavior, it is then demystified and not seen as odd or relegated to those who would be considered less than physically attractive.

And the trend is moving into so-called "family friendly" programming. Several years ago, the WB Network launched *The Gilmore Girls* as a so-called "wholesome" program in response to the concern of many advertisers about the ever-rising amount of sex and violence on television. The *New York Post* reported in April 2004, "It's not television's first lesbian kiss, but it ranks with the most shocking . . . . The WB cures fan's spring fever with a Sapphic smooch between . . . over-achieving star Rory and her roommate Paris." The article goes on to state that the two girls go to Florida for a spring break and a dance party, and "the butch Paris plants one on her demurring pal."[41]

Once you get past network television, all boundaries quickly disappear. On the Showtime pay network, the first episode of the show *Queer as Folk* depicted a thirty-year-old homosexual man having sex with a seventeen-year-old boy.[42] Showtime also added a series promoting lesbianism called *The L Word*. Lifetime bills itself as the "women's network" but repeatedly airs programs that promote lesbian behavior and alternative families.[43]

Noggin, a cable channel owned by media conglomerate Viacom (which also owns CBS, MTV, Nickelodeon, and other networks), beamed a Canadian drama, *Degrassi: The Next Generation* into American homes. The drama featured two male homosexual teens "falling in love" with each other. Actor John Breger, age eighteen, who plays one of the homosexual teens, said, "People grow up now with the idea of coming out and stuff like that. It's not such a surprise when they do. Our generation is growing up seeing it happen."[44]

The March 29, 2004, edition of the *Wall Street Journal* announced the intention of Viacom, Inc., chairman and chief executive Summer Redstone to launch an "all-gay" cable network. The *Journal* reported, "Viacom's renewed interest comes amid a surge in popularity of gay characters and gay-themed shows on television in the past few years . . . . The gay audience is an increasingly attractive one for advertisers [more on this later], spending nearly $500 billion a year, according to Prime Access, Inc., a gay and lesbian advertising and marketing agency in New York. Average U.S. income is 8 percent higher in gay households than straight ones, according to Forrester Research, Inc."

The article continues about the possible skepticism by homosexuals of a "watered down" network that would appeal to heterosexuals as well. Joe Flint, the author of the article, writes, "To show that it isn't a gay channel trying to build crossover appeal to a straight audience, Viacom probably will need to explore controversial issues like gay marriage and adoption."[45]

"It's about time somebody went after that audience with a network," media analyst Tom Wolzien says. "It's an important segment of the audience that has been traditionally underserved."[46]

Stephanie Gibbons, Showtime's (which is owned by Viacom) senior vice president for advertising and promotion, added, "It's just a continued evolution of something we've been doing for a long time."[47]

Brent Bozell, head of the Media Research Center, correctly pointed out that the last thing the entertainment industry has done is "underserve" homosexuals. He wrote, "Let's understand something here. This is not some kind of affirmative action proposal to bring gays into Hollywood. They're there, at every level, already. This is a move to promote the homosexual lifestyle to the public. . . . Far from being 'underserved,' gays have been pampered and catered to. Seemingly everywhere you turn you find the gay character, the gay theme, the gay argument inserted, and so often for no reason other than to placate the gay community. As the pundit Camille Paglia put it a few years ago, 'Entertainment, media, and the arts are non-stop advertisements for homosexuality these days.'"[48]

Bozell then described what we are in for, citing the example of PrideVision in Canada:

> So what might we expect from the proposed gay cable channels? In the online magazine *Slate,* Michael Joseph Gross looks at PrideVision TV, a nearly five-month-old Canadian gay cable network. . . . "PrideVision," relates Gross, "addresses the diversity issue with shows like 'You Don't Know D—k,' a documentary about female-to-male transsexuals . . . . As far as the sex goes, PrideVision is fairly soaked in it. 'Hard-core erotica,' for both gay men and lesbians is [shown] at midnight . . . and a men's soft-core porn feature at 10:30 p.m., called 'Steamy Knights' is the channel's top-rated show. PrideVision also offers porn-dressed-as-documentary; one show called 'Urinal,' explores the 'policing of washroom sex in Ontario.'" Near the close of his story, Gross gets to the heart of the matter: "News programs, talk shows, and dramas (on any U.S. gay net-

work) will have to be fearlessly candid about the *centrality of sex in much of gay life* for gay viewers to take them seriously"[49][emphasis added].

Bozell then nailed the target when he concludes: "Think of all the gay men you've heard equate their sexual orientation with 'who I am' or 'what I am.' Then try to remember if you've ever heard a straight man say the same thing. Sex is important to the typical heterosexual, but the difference between 'important' and 'central' is, undeniably, vast. So, too, is the difference between the way heterosexuality has always been discussed on television and how homosexuality is portrayed on a gay channel."[50]

Viacom went ahead with their plans and announced on May 25, 2004, that their MTV Network Division would launch LOGO, a new cable network specifically targeted to homosexual audiences. The network will start on February 17, 2005. Tom Freston, chairman and CEO of MTV Networks, said, "Creating a network specifically for the LGBT community is something we've wanted to do for a long, long time, and it's an idea we feel is overdue . . . . We have big plans and hopes for LOGO, and I'm thrilled to announce its arrival."[51]

Perhaps the silver lining in all of this is, as Bozell pointed out, that a gay channel will show the American public the real version of homosexual life, a life based on rampant sex and despair, rather than the whitewashed portrayals presently shown on network television.

Homosexual Portrayals on the Silver Screen

Up until this point we have focused on how the homosexual agenda has been pushed on television. We are now going to turn our focus to what has occurred on the silver screen.

While homosexual-themed movies were becoming staples in European cinemas in the late 1960s and early 1970s, the subject was still pretty much taboo in America.[52] Only one major film, 1962's *The Children's Hour* with Audrey Hepburn and Shirley MacLaine, went near the subject of homosexual behavior. It was considered box-office and public relations poison by Hollywood to produce a movie with blatant homosexual themes.

The first toe in the water, so to speak, was in 1978 with the movie *Making Love*. It was the first film to show two men in bed with each other and was a film that took years to make since no up-and-coming young actor, such as Harrison Ford or Michael Douglas, would go near the movie because of the effect it would have had on his career.[53] (This is quite a change from 2004 when several leading men seem to be trying to "out-gay" each other.) Eventually, two unknowns at the time, Harry Hamlin and Michael Ontkean, took the parts in the movie, which dealt with a man leaving his wife for another man. It was a financial dud at the box office.[54]

So Hollywood decided that America wasn't quite ready for the sight of two men in bed together and decided to push the agenda in a less direct way: cross-dressing comedies featuring heterosexual characters. Thus, we were given *Tootsie* with Dustin Hoffman portraying a man masquerading as a woman to get a job on a soap opera, *Mrs. Doubtfire* with Robin Williams disguising himself as a frumpy nanny so he can spend time with his children, and *Victor/Victoria* about a woman, played by Julie Andrews, who dresses up as a male impersonator.

Again, all of these films were successful comedies, designed to soften up America for the coming onslaught.

The breakthrough film for the homosexual agenda was *Philadelphia* (1993) starring Tom Hanks. The makers of the film deliberately went out of their way to find the most likable actor possible (Hanks—who has been compared to a modern-day Jimmy Stewart)[55] in order to push their agenda that AIDS was a civil rights rather than a public health issue and that homosexuals are victims of discrimination. Every major news magazine trumpeted the movie, and the entire Hollywood publicity machine and homosexual community got behind it to ensure that it was a success. Hanks was nominated and won Best Actor for the role.[56] In his rambling acceptance speech, Hanks gave tribute to his homosexual drama teacher.[57]

Philadelphia opened the floodgates and gave us subsequent movies such as *The Birdcage,* which depicted Robin Williams and Nathan Lane as two homosexual partners who faced rejection from their ultraconservative families, and *In and Out,* inspired by Hanks's speech and which dealt with a high school teacher who is "outed" during an acceptance speech. The film featured a prolonged kiss between actors Kevin Kline and Tom Selleck. Again, both of these films were comedies and pushed the envelope a little further.

In 1999 Hollywood came "totally out." In fact, the Academy Awards in early 2000 seemed to be like a three-and-one-half-hour infomercial for the homosexual agenda. Hillary Swank won Best Actress for *Boys Don't Cry,* in which she played a transgendered person, a girl who dresses up as a boy and is eventually murdered in a so-called hate crime. In her acceptance speech, she gave an impassioned plea for tolerance and for transgender rights, stating, "His legacy always lives on through our movie to remind us to always be ourselves, to follow our hearts, to not conform."[58] On the same night, the film *American Beauty*, written by an open homosexual, and which denigrated marriage, promoted statutory rape, full teenage female nudity, and homosexual behavior, won Best Picture.

In 2004, actress Charlize Theron won the Best Actress Award for playing a lesbian in the movie *Monster*. And, at the 2004 GLAAD Movie Awards, Sharon Osbourne, the wife of rocker Ozzy Osbourne, said, "My only regret in life is that none of my children are gay." Singer Alanis Morissette stated that she was becoming a licensed minister via an online course so she could indulge in her "fantasy" to "marry some of my gay couple friends." At the awards ceremony, GLAAD announced its new campaign to promote same-sex "marriage."[59]

Where does this constant drumbeat promoting homosexual behavior lead? The natural conclusion is what we reported earlier in this chapter: that more and more Americans are engaging in homosexual behavior, especially young people.[60] Just as Hollywood glamorized smoking back in the 1930s and '40s, and then promoted illegal drug use in the '60s and '70s, it is now making homosexual behavior the in thing to emulate. In both of the previous cases, Hollywood eventually was repudiated for its positive depictions of these behaviors, as people died of lung cancer and kids overdosed on drugs.

Will the same thing eventually happen with the portrayals of homosexual behavior, as people die early from sexually transmitted diseases and generations of children grow up sexually confused? Based on the evidence so far, we doubt it. Hollywood has been relentless in its promotion of high-risk behavior that, in many cases, leads to early death.[61]

An entire book could be written on the subject of the entertainment industry's promotion of homosexual behavior, but it is our goal to give you a brief overview of each subject so that you understand the number of cultural fronts in which the homosexual agenda is being pushed. We need to go back to words of Kirk and Madsen who stated that a media campaign would be the linchpin for their efforts to desensitize Americans to homosexual behavior. As we have seen in this chapter, that campaign has been relentless, and many of the gains made by homosexual activists to promote their agenda and restrict religious freedom have been made in movies, television, and other entertainment media.

In the next chapter, we will look at what is perhaps the most alarming front in this battle: the promotion of homosexual behavior to impressionable school children.

CHAPTER THREE

"Stupid" Parents, "Enlightened" Kids

*The fear of the religious right is that the schools of today will be
the governments of tomorrow. And you know, they're right.
If we do our jobs right, we're going to raise a generation of kids
who don't believe the claims of the religious right.*

—Speakers at the 1999 Gay, Lesbian, Straight Educational Network conference

One day, during his biology class, Kyle's teacher stated that homosexual behavior was genetic. Kyle immediately raised his hand to disagree. The teacher, a self-professed bisexual who had testified in support of civil unions in Vermont, immediately ridiculed and humiliated him in front of the entire high school class.

"What's the matter, Kyle?" she said mockingly. "Are you unsure of your sexuality? Did you know that the people who scream the loudest turn out to be gay themselves?"

The other students in the class, who had been subjected to homosexual indoctrination for years, laughed at him.

A few weeks later, in the middle of a discussion on genealogy, the teacher again digressed into the subject of homosexual behavior. Kyle asked again what homosexuality had to do with the subject.

The teacher again questioned his sexuality and implied that he might be covering up the fact that he was a homosexual. Kyle stood up and denied the accusation, stating that he had a girlfriend.

The class snickered at him. One classmate went as far to suggest that the girlfriend was a cover-up and that Kyle was a closet homosexual.

Devastated and humiliated, Kyle's grades dropped from a 3.70 grade point average to 2.10 in the months following the incident.[1]

This is war, so plan accordingly.
—Homosexual activist
Chuck Jones

That story is only one of numerous examples of how the homosexual agenda is being pushed in public schools and how those who don't toe the line are being humiliated and punished.

Every fall, millions of parents drop their children off at taxpayer-funded public schools, assuming that their children's education will provide what they need to be successful in life: strong academics, civility, and responsibility.

Unfortunately, many of these same parents have little or no idea of what is happening to their children once they pass through the classroom door. Instead of learning the three Rs or how to be good citizens like many of us were taught, they are learning how to reject the common values that many of their parents have tried hard to instill in them, the values that built America. Sadly, many of these parents refuse to believe that this is happening, even when you produce evidence of how the radical homosexual activists are targeting children in public schools to accept, affirm, and be recruited into homosexual behavior.

On a daily basis, all across America (but more prevalent in some areas of the country than others), children as young as kindergarten are being told that their parents are "stupid" or "bigots" or "intolerant" if they do not accept and embrace homosexual behavior as normal, or even something to be celebrated. In some classes, children are even recruited to promote gay pride marches and events.[2]

For young children, the open promotion of homosexual behavior in the media and the classroom has led to preteen children announcing to their parents that they are homosexual. Why? Because they are taught that if you are a girl who doesn't like boys, you are a lesbian, and if you are a boy who doesn't like girls, you are a homosexual. Yet, for most eight-year-olds, members of the opposite sex have "cooties" or similar perceived afflictions. This is the time when children bond and form their identity as members of their own sex, and it is just a natural part of childhood. To introduce homosexual behavior at this stage of development is only confusing for children.

Finally, once they reach their teenage years, sexually confused teenagers are turned over to homosexual counselors who assist them in determining how they can come out to their families and friends.[3]

Homosexual activists know that the best time to reach children is during the earliest, most impressionable ages. Christian researcher George Barna has documented that the chance for an individual to make a personal decision to believe in Christ greatly diminishes after the age of fourteen.[4] Just as children are more receptive to the gospel and religious instruction at an early age, they are also more susceptible to homosexual indoctrination. Is it any wonder why homosexual activists and their allies have tried so hard to keep the gospel out of and get homosexual indoctrination into the public schools?

In their private meetings, homosexual activists boldly proclaim their goal to get children to reject their parents' beliefs. At a 1999 Gay, Lesbian, Straight, Educational Network (GLSEN) conference in Atlanta, the following comments were made: "The fear of the religious right is that the schools of today are the governments of tomorrow. And you know what, they're right"[5] and "If we do our jobs right, we're going to raise a generation of kids who don't believe the claims of the religious right."[6]

The Homosexual Activists' Willing Partner

A more than willing partner with the homosexual activists has been the National Education Association (NEA). While the NEA has been promoting the homosexual agenda for years,* its most blatant attempt was at its 2001 annual convention in Los Angeles. At that convention the NEA considered a resolution to implement promotion of full-scale indoctrination of children to accept and affirm homosexual behavior. The resolution read as follows:

The National Education Association recognizes the complex and diverse needs of gay, lesbian, bisexual, transgender, and questioning students; and gay, lesbian, bisexual, and transgender families and their children require the development of programs to promote a safe and inclusive environment:

A. Development of curriculum and instructional materials and programs designed to meet the needs of gay, lesbian, bisexual, and transgender students.

---

*The NEA has passed several resolutions dealing with the promotion of the homosexual agenda. They are available for review at http://www.nea.org/resolutions.html. Past resolutions include funds to "alleviate sexual orientation discrimination," support for "Gay and Lesbian History Month," and the inclusion of sexual orientation into sex education programs.

B. Involvement of gay, lesbian, bisexual, and transgender characters in developing educational material used in classroom instructions.

C. Dissemination of programs that support gay, lesbian, bisexual, transgender, and questioning students and address the high dropout rate, suicide rate, and health risk behaviors.

D. Recognition of the importance of gay, lesbian, bisexual, and transgender education employees as role models.

E. Accurate portrayal of the roles and contributions of gay, lesbian, bisexual, and transgender education employees as role models.

F. Dissemination of programs and information that include the contributions, heritage, culture, and history of gay, lesbian, bisexual, and transgender people.

G. Coordination with gay, lesbian, bisexual, and transgender organizations and concerned agencies that promote the contributions, heritage, history, health, and care of gays, lesbians, bisexuals, and transgender people.[7]

This resolution was loaded with land mines for people who oppose homosexual behavior and could have dire consequences for an entire generation of children. After pro-family groups, such as Focus on the Family, became aware of what the NEA was attempting to do, they blew the whistle, and a public backlash occurred. As a result, the NEA "tabled" the resolution and sent it to a committee for "study." This means the organization will quietly implement it without member approval. In fact, that is exactly what the NEA is doing, and similar resolutions are showing up as official NEA policy in school districts nationwide.[8]

Former NEA president Bob Chase* openly admits to this strategy, stating, "Let me make it clear . . . in no way is the NEA backing down from the important issues raised by this resolution. . . . Some critics want the public schools to be an agent of moral doctrine, condemning children and adults when they are not in accord with Biblical precepts."[9] Interestingly, Chase is on the board of directors for the Gay, Lesbian, and Straight Educational Network (GLSEN).

Think about that statement for a second. The NEA is condemning parents who object to homosexual behavior and believe that it should not be taught in public schools, accusing them of forcing

---

*Chase went on to work for GLSEN, the leading pro-homosexual advocacy group in the public schools.

their "moral doctrine" on children. And yet, groups such as the NEA, GLSEN, P-FLAG (Parents and Friends of Lesbians and Gays) and other pro-homosexual groups are trying to do just that. They are trying to push a doctrine of homosexual behavior on young children while condemning and ridiculing those, including parents, who hold to biblical principles and to undermine the beliefs they are trying to instill in their children.

The NEA helped to publish a booklet, along with the American Academy of Pediatrics (which subsequently endorsed homosexual adoption),[10] the American Medical Association, and the American School Health Association, among others, titled *Just the Facts about Sexual Orientation and Youth.* This booklet, which was written to "combat the religious right," effectively calls for the censoring of free speech rights of teachers and counselors who might be inclined to share the biblical perspective on homosexual behavior. It also calls for the wholehearted encouragement for schoolchildren to experiment with homosexual behavior. Consider this excerpt:

> Sexual orientation is one component of a person's identity, which is made up of many other components, such as culture, ethnicity, gender, or personality traits. . . . Someone does not have to be exclusively homosexual or heterosexual, but can feel varying degrees of attraction for both genders. . . . Many deeply religious people and a number of religious organizations are supportive and accepting of gay, lesbian, bisexual people. . . . *A guidance counselor in a public school may not attempt to persuade a gay, lesbian, or bisexual student of the religious belief that homosexuality is a sin, or otherwise seek to impose a negative religious view on being gay, lesbian, or bisexual on the student.* . . . School officials should be deeply concerned about the validity and bias of materials or presentations that promote a change to a person's sexual orientation as a "cure" or suggest that being gay, lesbian, or bisexual is unhealthy.[11] [emphasis added]

Therefore, according to the NEA, GLSEN, and other organizations, Christians and other people of faith—and perhaps even experts on public health issues who may be teachers or counselors in the public schools—will not only be unable to share their religious views about homosexual behavior, they won't be able to even mention individuals, such as John Paulk, who have overcome homosexual behavior. If this doctrine is imposed, more religious freedom of those teachers, counselors, and their students will be taken away. Tragically, millions of sexually confused children will be told they have no other choice but to accept the fact that they are homosexual.

"Questioning" Youth

Anyone who has ever lived through the teenage years knows that it is a time of a great deal of sexual confusion as bodies change and hormones rage. Many early adolescents go through this state of confusion regarding gender attraction and attachment. Almost all of them emerge as healthy heterosexual adults. The phrase "questioning students" specifically targets these sexually confused early teens, who, with the assistance of public funding, will be encouraged to pursue homosexual behavior.

Sadly, this is not a relatively new phenomenon. This has been happening for years, while millions of parents, including many Christian parents, have been blissfully ignorant about how radical homosexual activists are targeting their children in the public schools.

In 1993, *Newsweek* magazine ran an article titled "Tune In, Come Out." In the piece, writer David Gelman chronicled the sexual confusion of adolescents and how they were being encouraged to engage in homosexual behavior. He wrote, "At high schools around the country, multiculturalism has begun to embrace multisexualism . . . more students seem to be coming out, and they're coming out younger."[12]

Gelman continued:

> Some high schoolers are coming out homosexual, some bisexual. *Others are admittedly confused* [emphasis added]. "It's very hard to figure out what you are in the core of your belly," says one Boston teenager who thought she was a lesbian until she found herself enjoying a relationship with a man. Teens' eagerness to experiment made bisexuality almost "cool" in some schools. "From where I sit, it's definitely more chic," says George Hohagen, 20, a Midwestern market researcher not long out of high school himself. "It's trendy even to ask, 'Do you think I am?'" At meetings of Boston Area Gay and Lesbian Youth, support group leader Troix Bettencourt, 19, a public health intern, has seen an increase in teenagers who identify themselves as bisexual. They don't want to be penned into one type of behavior, he says. "It [saying you're bisexual] just says that you're not

yet defined and gives you some freedom." It's also easier. "After all, you've still got the straight part," says 18-year-old Jessica Byers . . . who came out as a lesbian.[13]

These quotes sadly illustrate what happens when teenagers are encouraged to question their sexuality and experiment. The teenage years are often a time of testing limits and experimenting with forbidden fruit. The lure of illegal drugs, alcohol, and pornography are extremely strong during these years.

Caitlyn Ryan, a researcher at San Francisco State University, added, "Now that community resources are in place and public acceptance [of homosexual behavior] has increased, it's more feasible for adolescents to come out during adolescence. What you're getting in the LGBT community is the power of youth. It's their expression and exuberance and energy and also their contribution to the culture."[14]

This phenomenon was documented by Laura Sessions Stepp in the January 4, 2004, edition of the *Washington Post:*

> Move over Ellen DeGeneres, and make way for the younger girls. Way younger, actually, and way different from what most people think of as lesbians . . . . You can see them in the hallways of high schools like South Lakes in Reston, Magruder in Rockville, or Coolidge in the District. In 2002 at Coolidge, a teacher got so fed up with girls nuzzling each other in class and other public places that he threatened to send any he saw to the principal's office . . . . A group of girls at a private school in Northwest Washington charge boys $10 to watch the girls make out in front of them . . . .
>
> So are these girls bisexual? Perhaps. But they prefer descriptions like "gayish," questioning, even "queer"—an umbrella description so broad . . . that it encompasses straights as well as gays . . . . "I like women only right now," says Cary Trainer . . . a self-defined lesbian since high school, "But who knows where I'll be in 25 years?"
>
> [David] Shapiro is head of the Edmund Burke School . . . in Northwest Washington. In 2002, Burke held a "diversity day" assembly in which students and teachers stood together in a circle. An adult leader took the group through various exercises, and in one of those, participants were asked to move inside the circle if they defined themselves as gay or lesbian.

One female teacher stepped forward, but no students did.

Then the leader called for those who thought of themselves as bisexual—the broadest label offered. Out of the approximately 60 pupils in the group, 15 obliged; 11 girls and four boys. Shapiro said he was "astounded" at the number of kids who stepped into the bisexual group. As he thought about it, he concluded that "kids today know the difference between behavior and orientation. They say, 'I may be behaving in this certain way, but I'll make up my own mind about who I am in my own time.'"

"Most of these girls aren't gay" [says one student] . . . "They're just doing it because their friends are doing it."[15]

Dr. Frances Scott, a professor of childhood development at Chicago's Erikson Institute, stated that teens are liable to experiment because they are still trying to figure out who they are. This problem is particularly pronounced for children who come from broken homes and do not have strong relationships with both parents. She said, "Teenagers are at that point in life where so many aspects of their identity are coming together. They're figuring out issues of sexual identity, occupational identity, and role identity. They're really asking the question, 'Who am I?'"[16] This is one of the main reasons why homosexual activists have made a concerted effort to get into middle schools and high schools—they know that teenagers are likely to be receptive to their message as they try to figure out who they are.

Sadly, too many lives have been destroyed by bad decisions made during the teenage years that had dire consequences for an individual's future. Many adults regret decisions they made during those years. And now, homosexual behavior has been added to the mix as well.

So what is the bottom line? According to the NEA and its allies, children must be taught that sexual orientation is fluid (which is an interesting contradiction since homosexual activists are intent on proving a genetic link to their behavior), that only "intolerant religions" do not affirm homosexual behavior, and that once you are entrapped in homosexual behavior, there is no escape. No dissenting views are permitted. Thus, the gospel is silenced, parental values are undermined, and an impressionable child is doomed to engage in behavior that will often result in his or her eventual self-destruction.

Targeting the Children

And how does this all play out in public schools? In some areas of the country where homosexual activists have had free rein for years, the indoctrination of children starts as early as kindergarten. At a Massachusetts GLSEN conference, there was a specific workshop on how to "incorporate gay, lesbian, bisexual, and transgender issues into the early elementary years."[17] On the GLSEN Web site, there are elementary school lesson plans featuring the themes "What Is Boy/Girl?" and "Freedom to Marry?" along with books with titles such as "Queering Elementary Education."[18]

In the article "Gay-Ed for Tots," Debra Saunders chronicled the full implementation of homosexual indoctrination in the San Francisco Unified School District:

> The San Francisco Unified School District has a lesson plan for teaching kindergartners and first-graders about homosexuality. It is called "My Family," and is disseminated through the district's Support Services for Gay, Lesbian, and Bisexual Youth Department. . . . The lesson includes definitions that are politically correct—and downright confusing to adults, never mind kids. Homosexuals are "people of the same sex who have feelings for one another in a romantic way." A family is a "unit of two or more persons, related either by birth or by choice, who may or may not live together, who try to meet each other's needs and share common goals and interests." . . . The lesson includes class exercises designed to reinforce the notion that all families should be validated . . . presumably including families with no dads, three dads, or a 14-year-old mom. . . .
>
> This year, the Buena Vista School District went way beyond "My Family." As it had in past years, the school invited gay parents into the classroom to talk to elementary students. In a first-grade class, a gay man read to the children the district-approved book, "Gloria Goes to Gay Pride." But this year, students also worked on a rainbow banner for the gay pride parade, and they did so during class time. As a school missive explained, kindergartners "designed" the red stripe, first-graders the "yellow," and so on up to fifth grade. The rainbow banner, the message boasted, "reflects the creativity, love, and appreciation for diversity as expressed by the children of Buena Vista."[19]

In such an emboldened climate as the San Francisco Bay Area, homosexual activists make no bones about telling Christians and others who object to homosexual behavior to "get lost." For example, when asked about those parents who might have moral objections to the promotion of homosexual behavior in San Francisco schools, Lynn Lavin of the Gay-Lesbian Parents Group at Buena Vista school flippantly said, "If there are people who don't feel comfortable with [pro-homosexual] policies, they shouldn't be in public schools."[20]

In her conclusion to the article, Saunders tied the indoctrination of schoolchildren to the argument used by the secular left that religion or equal access for Bible study or prayer groups should not be allowed in public schools because children are "easily persuaded." Saunders wrote, "Those who support pressing young children into making a gay banner have insisted that there is nothing political about it or the city's gay pride parade. Instead, they have equated the gay pride parade with Martin Luther King Day. That Buena Vista's proselytizing, forced on kids who aren't old enough to think critically, might be the equivalent of public school prayer, doesn't compute with them."[21]

As we mentioned before in our discussion of George Barna's findings on children and faith, it is quite obvious that homosexual activists and their allies have no problem with the indoctrination of children. It is a child's exposure to traditional religious teachings on issues of sexuality and marriage that gets in the way of their objectives. It is that, according to homosexual activists and their allies, that must be eliminated during a child's formative years. Therefore, while they might make the statement that parents who believe homosexual behavior is wrong have no place in the public schools, it frustrates them to no end when parents come to that realization and either place their children in private schools or home school them. Thus, according to NEA resolutions, they want control over the curriculum parents and private schools teach.[22] Their fear of not being able to get to these children is best summed up by a first-grade teacher in Madison, Wisconsin (another pro-homosexual hotbed): "If parents are allowed to have their children opt out of gay and lesbian units, what will happen when we teach about Dutch culture or African-American history? It scares me."[23]

(In fact, homosexual activists in California have begun to come up with ways to force private schools to adopt pro-homosexual curriculum. In September 2001, former Governor Gray Davis signed a bill that forces private schools that wish to compete with public schools in interscholastic sports to have an anti-discrimination policy that includes sexual orientation.)[24]

If you're thinking of moving your family north of the border to escape all of this, don't. The situation is worse in Canada. At a recent convention, the Elementary Teachers Federation of Ontario voted 50-1 in support of introducing pro-homosexual curriculum into elementary school classrooms. The motion, according to the *Canadian Press*, "allows the union to 'encourage' school boards to establish funding for schools, upon request, for 'materials for student use which reflect lesbian, gay, bisexual, and transgender realities.'"[25]

GLSEN: The Gay, Lesbian, and Straight Educational Network

One of the most vocal pro-homosexual groups is the Gay, Lesbian, and Straight Educational Network. Its efforts to indoctrinate children are relentless. On April 10, 2002, GLSEN staged a Day of Silence in public schools nationwide.* Students were encouraged to remain silent throughout the day and not respond to their teachers or school administrators. If asked to speak, the students were told to hand their teachers a card that read: "Please understand my reasons for not speaking today. I am participating in the Day of Silence, a national youth movement protesting the silence faced by lesbian, gay, bisexual, and transgender people and their allies. My deliberate silence echoes that silence, which is caused by harassment, prejudice, and discrimination. I believe that ending that silence is the first step toward fighting these injustices. Think about the voices you are not hearing today. What are you going to do to end the silence?"

Organizers of the event told children that they should "brainstorm" a list of people "who are likely to stand in your way." Those people included teachers, counselors, and administrators who have "denied you their support in the past, or who've expressed bias against (lesbian, gay, bisexual, and transgendered) people." It is also suggested that the list include other children, school board members, people in the community, and *relatives* "who have shown intolerance" of homosexuality. The organizing manual notes that "people who oppose you on your issue are known as, you guessed it, your opponents."[26†]

---

*GLSEN called on students nationwide to participate in "Transgender Remembrance Day" on November 20, 2002.
†In 2003, U.S. Congressman Eliot Engel (D-NY) introduced a resolution calling on Congress to "recognize the efforts of students nationwide who will be organizing and participating in the Day of Silence." GLSEN set its 2003 "Day of Silence" for April 9, 2003. See "Day of Silence in Congressional Spotlight Thanks to Rep. Eliot Engel," GLSEN Press Release, March 11, 2003.

So, GLSEN is telling little children that their relatives are the "enemy" if they oppose homosexual behavior. Our question (and we are afraid of the answer): Does "relatives" include Mom and Dad? Indeed, we will see that this is exactly what GLSEN means. *It does mean Mom and Dad.*

It was not just Catholics and evangelical, conservative Christians who were outraged by GLSEN's Day of Silence. Rabbi David Eidensohn of the National Non-Sectarian Council of Pro-Family Activists said, "This is an assault on our school system by terrorists. The financial damage due to lost school time throughout the country will be enormous. We cannot, however, talk about money alone. The disruption of a school atmosphere, especially towards the end of the year, when discipline in schools is a challenge, could kill a year of learning for many students. Precisely when students should be concentrating on finals, they are told by GLSEN homosexual activists to refuse to speak in class and to disrupt school with activism. Students who should be learning to get along with others are making a 'hit list' of teachers and students who are Biblical or who refuse the homosexual agenda."[27]

However, to radical homosexual activists, the pushing of their agenda trumps academics. Keith Jennings, the executive director of GLSEN, told a church audience in New York City on March 20, 2000, about GLSEN's plan to deal with those who have biblical objections to homosexual behavior: "Twenty percent of people are hard-core fair-minded [pro-homosexual] people. Twenty percent are hard-core [anti-homosexual] bigots. We need to ignore the hard-core bigots, get more of the hard-core fair-minded people to speak up, and we'll pull that 60 percent [of people in the middle] . . . over to our side. That's really what I think our strategy has to be. We have to quit being afraid of the religious right. . . . I'm trying to find a way to say this. I'm trying not to say, '[Expletive deleted] 'em,' which is what I want to say, because I don't care what they think! Drop dead!"[28]

Jennings also talked about GLSEN's strategy in a speech at a 1997 conference: "I'd like five years from now for most Americans when they hear the word GLSEN to think, 'Ooh, that's good for kids.' . . . Sane people keep the world the same [expletive deleted] old way it is now. It's the [crazy] people who think, 'No, I can envision a day when straight people say, "So what if you're promoting homosexuality?" or [when] straight kids say, "Hey, why don't you and your boyfriend come over before you go to the prom and try your tuxes on at my house."' . . . If you believe that can happen, we can make it happen.

The only thing that will stop us is our lack of faith that we can make it happen. That is our mission from this day forward."[29]

GLSEN, at its conferences like the one that Jennings spoke at above, is very overt when it comes to its goal of indoctrinating even the youngest of schoolchildren. At a 1997 GLSEN regional conference, New York teacher and GLSEN activist Jaki Williams taught a workshop entitled "Inclusive Kindergartens." Here is just a sample of what she said: "Children in the kindergarten age are 'developing their superego.' . . . That's when the saturation process needs to begin. . . . Five-year-olds are very interested in the big questions. They're very interested in sex, death, and love, and they ask those questions, and they talk about them. And we want to help them find the answers . . . on their level."[30]

Williams added that she read to her class books such as *Heather Has Two Mommies* and *One Dad, Two Dads, Brown Dads, Blue Dads.*

At a 1999 conference, a retired lesbian gym teacher talked about how she discussed her sexuality with her kindergarten gym class. Peter LaBarbera, then with the Family Research Council and currently with Concerned Women for America, who witnessed her talk, filed the following report:

> [She] explained that at her school she was "out" as a lesbian to the principal and to most of the teaching staff, and that it was important for her to be "authentic" about her sexual identity. According to [her], one day a student in her gym class asked if she had a husband. She said no, and then another student asked if she had a boyfriend. [She] said no, "As a matter of fact . . . I have a girlfriend." After some of the children said, "Ohhhh!" as if shocked, they asked if she kissed her girlfriend. [She] said she did.
>
> [She] responded: "Some people think it's OK, and some people think it's not OK." . . .
>
> Then the gym teacher asked one of the boys in her class, "Do you ever kiss your father goodnight?" He replied, "Yes." [She] asked one of the girls, "Do you ever kiss your sister to show her that you love her?" "Yes," the girl responded. [She] then used the analogy between those kisses and her lesbian kisses as she told the children, "Some people will tell you that you shouldn't love some people [but] . . . your heart tells you who to love." . . .
>
> "This was a very teachable moment. . . . I was not in any way going to lie to my students," [she said of her

conversation with the kindergarten gym class]. "At the elementary school level, the teachable moments are the really critical ones."[31]

GLSEN put out a student organizing manual titled "Make It Real," to be used for the implementation of California's AB537, the California Student Safety and Violence Prevention Act of 2000, which does not obligate schools to inform parents about classroom instruction that conflicts with their religious or moral beliefs, nor allows parents to opt their children out of such instruction. Here are just a few excerpts from the manual:

> Imagine a school where two girls or two guys can hold hands, dance together, or even make out, and nobody notices.
>
> Ask your principal if he or she will respect students' wishes not to notify parents. . . . Some parents force them to undergo "therapy" to "change" them. . . . Once they are educated about the risks as well as their legal obligations, many principals will understand and respect a student's legal right to keep complaints confidential from their parents.
>
> Here's how you can use testers in your school: train pairs of students to pretend to be couples . . . . Half of the couples should be same-sex couples, and half of the couples should be opposite-sex couples. Create a list of public displays of affection (holding hands, hugging, walking arm-in-arm, dancing together, kissing hello, or goodbye, making out) and be very clear about the limits at each level. Try to include a variety of places, so that the widest number of people might potentially react. Make sure you definitely list a place where a school administrator is likely to view the display of affection.
>
> Anyone with two or more parents or stepparents understands the time-honored strategy of carefully choosing which parent to ask which question. If one parent is paranoid about your driving, ask the other if you can borrow the car. This is a basic form of ally building.[32]

From this manual, it is quite clear that GLSEN believes teenagers should conceal information from their parents and undermine parental authority by playing one parent off another. Parents, to GLSEN, are just something else to be manipulated to reach their goal of recruiting impressionable youth into homosexual behavior.

Soon after the Massachusetts State Supreme Judicial Court decision finding a new "right" to same-sex "marriage," GLSEN jumped at the opportunity to push their agenda even further in the public schools. Even before the decision was reached, GLSEN had prepared a curriculum guide that featured lesson plans that discussed the "historical parallels" to same-sex "marriage," (equating the legitimate struggle for civil rights by black Americans to the effort for same-sex "marriage"), books about homosexual behavior, and asked students to "consider" what it would be like to be in a same-sex "wedding."

The curriculum also states, "When discussing this issue, help students to move past preoccupations with the 'rightness' or 'wrongness' of same-sex coupling or homosexuality in general. Place the debate over marriage within the context of human rights, thereby expanding the dialogue beyond the realm of morality."[33] As in other instances, GLSEN is undermining parental authority and coercing children to reject the beliefs of their parents.

At a GLSEN conference for educators in Massachusetts, workshops such as "Ask the Transsexuals," "Early Childhood Educators: How to Decide Whether to Come Out at Work or Not," "The Struggles and Triumphs of Including Homosexuality in a Middle School Curriculum," "From Lesbos to Stonewall: Incorporating Sexuality into a World History Curriculum," and "Creating a Safe and Inclusive Sexuality in Elementary Schools" were held. The last workshop is described as providing the "rationale of integrating GLBT [gay, lesbian, bisexual, and transgender] issues in the early elementary years."[34]

It's Elementary?

In addition to its conferences, GLSEN, working with lesbian activists and filmmakers Helen Cohen and Diana Chasnoff, has developed and promoted the video *It's Elementary* to train teachers and administrators on how to push the homosexual agenda in public schools.* The video openly promotes homosexual behavior and ridicules and defames anyone who would object to it. One fifth-grade boy, who has obviously had years of homosexual indoctrination already, says in the video, "Some Christians believe that if you're gay, you'll go to hell, so they want to torture them and stuff."[35] There is no rebuttal. An eighth-grade girl defends the

---

*The producers have now come out with a second video titled "That's a Family!" endorsed by actor Robin Williams, that is designed to teach first graders through third graders about homosexual families.

teaching of homosexual behavior, stating, "If kids are too young to be taught about homosexuality, then they are too young to be taught about heterosexuality. . . . [If] children are reading Cinderella then they should read about a prince and a prince, or a princess and a princess."[36]

But perhaps the most alarming portion of the video involves a teacher lavishing praise on an essay written by an eight-year-old girl about her lesbian "parents." The teacher encourages the little girl to read her essay to her entire class, and the girl states that those who believe what the Bible has to say about homosexual behavior are stupid. The teacher then announces at the end of the class that this essay has won an award![37]

We don't know about you, but if we had characterized someone's sincere beliefs as stupid in an essay we had written during our school days, we probably would have been disciplined or at least forced to write the essay over again. But this is the perfect example of how children are being taught disdain for biblical values in our public schools.

It May Be Happening in Your Child's School

Here are just a few more quick examples of how the homosexual agenda is being pushed to elementary school children:

- In Boulder, Colorado, a new curriculum has been proposed that would require students to "demonstrate" their acceptance of homosexual behavior. Students would have to show they can "provide peer support" for homosexual classmates and demonstrate they can "advocate for a school environment free of . . . homophobia." Other standards require students to explain the health consequences of "heterosexism."[38]

- A southern California prep academy hosted a forum entitled "A Queer State of the Union." The school, Crossroads School for the Arts and Sciences, is attended by numerous children of Hollywood celebrities. The school has a "sexual orientation curriculum" that instructs kindergartners through fifth-graders about how "there are different kinds of families, which include families with two mommies and two daddies. The school also staged a play, "Everything Possible: A Gay Odyssey," that featured two teenage boys kissing. Faculty member Adam Behrman said, "One thing I'm starting to notice in the last year or two . . . which is really, really cool, not just at Crossroads, but other places, that it's becoming more and more OK for people who are probably largely toward the straight end of the spectrum to really think about, 'You know, maybe I'm bisexual . . . maybe I don't have to limit myself, what I am shutting myself off to?'" Behrman went on to add that 13- and 14-year-olds are "exploring bisexuality."[39]

- In Ithaca, New York, school officials are requiring that first and second graders be graded on tolerance. The kids will receive grades based on how well "they respect others of varying cultures, genders, experiences, and abilities." The grade will appear on their report cards under "Lifelong Learning Skills," before social studies, science, writing, and reading.[40] Thus, how a child views homosexual behavior is more important than the fundamentals he or she will need to succeed in life.

- In Provincetown, Massachusetts, the school board voted to begin teaching pre-schoolers about homosexual behavior and backed affirmative action for "sexual minorities." "We are on a trailblazing path," said Susan Fleming, superintendent of Provincetown schools.[41]

- In St. Louis, Missouri, Debra Loveless requested her right to exempt her daughter from a GLSEN seminar at her daughter's public school. Her request was granted, but she also wanted to see what was being presented at the seminar. When she arrived, an armed security guard told her that school officials wanted her to leave the school grounds. An ADF ally has come to the defense of her right to view what is being taught at the seminar, stating that school cannot prohibit parents from viewing the content of school seminars, whether or not their child is attending.[42]

- In Ann Arbor, Michigan, a local high school held a so-called Diversity Week that included student speeches on the topics of race, religion, and homosexuality at an all-school assembly. When one student wished to give a talk on the biblical position with regard to homosexual behavior, school officials censored her speech, claiming that her religious view toward homosexual behavior was "negative" and would "water down" the "positive" religious message they wanted to convey. That "positive" message was that homosexual behavior and religion are compatible and that homosexual behavior is not sinful. School officials also created written guidelines that prohibited "targeting" someone's "sexual orientation."[43]

When a religious view is to be presented in the public schools, it is a liberal version that affirms homosexual behavior* (however, if a conservative view were being presented, you can be assured that the squawk of "separation of church and state" would be loud and clear). One of the Alliance Defense Fund's allied attorneys testified to an example of this occurring in Los Angeles public schools: "We are arguing the case of *Park v. Los Angeles Unified School District.* This is a class action suit challenging the school district's policy of inviting pastors into the schools to teach from the Bible. The pastors invited for assemblies during Gay and Lesbian Pride Month every June preach from the Bible that God approves of homosexuality. [Note: Los Angeles city schools have turned an entire month over to the promotion of the homosexual agenda.] They cite various Scripture verses supporting their sermons and distribute booklets citing Bible verses with the conclusion that homosexual behavior is not a sin. Additional materials posted for display to the students (elementary through high school) include full frontal and female nudity . . . explicit descriptions of sexual acts between homosexuals and claims that Abraham Lincoln and King David were homosexuals."[44]

Harking back to the NEA brochure "Just the Facts about Sexual Orientation and Youth," it is not the promotion of a religious viewpoint on homosexual behavior that is offensive to the NEA and homosexual activists. It is the promotion of the wrong viewpoint that does not affirm homosexual behavior that is problematic for the NEA. Thus, the NEA promotes the religious freedom of those who affirm homosexual behavior, but it advocates censoring the religious freedom for those who would disagree. One viewpoint is "enlightened," the other, in the words of the fourth-grade girl in *It's Elementary,* is "stupid."

Where the Homosexual Activists Are Strongest

We could go on and on with numerous other examples of how homosexual behavior is being promoted in elementary schools, but it is time to turn our focus to middle schools and high schools, where the indoctrination by radical homosexual activists is even more intense.

*We will discuss this perspective further in chapter 6.

While homosexual activists have made inroads in practically every state of the country, they have made the most progress in states such as Massachusetts and California, where the left-leaning political environment, coupled with large homosexual population centers and the lack of traditional religious influences, has led to public schools that seemingly do little else but teach about homosexual behavior.

Massachusetts has thrown open the school doors to sexual activists and then has locked the doors to keep parents out. They have let homosexual activists have carte blanche to advance their agenda. Teachers and counselors have received special state-funded training for dealing with gay and lesbian students, school libraries are stocked with books and films on homosexual issues, and support groups for sexually confused adolescents are conducted to convince them they are homosexual.[45]

For example, in Framingham, Massachusetts, students were forced to answer a questionnaire that openly challenged the validity of their heterosexuality. Here are some of the questions they were asked:

1. What do you think caused your heterosexuality?
2. When did you first decide you were heterosexual?
3. Is it possible heterosexuality is a phase you will grow out of? [Of course, the flip side of this question is not asked: Is it possible that homosexuality is a phase you will grow out of?]
4. Is it possible you are heterosexual because you fear the same sex?
5. If you have never slept with anyone of the same sex, how do you know you wouldn't prefer it?
6. To whom have you disclosed your heterosexuality? How did they react?
7. Why are heterosexuals so blatant, always making a spectacle of their heterosexuality? Why can't they just be who they are and not flaunt their sexuality by kissing in public, wearing wedding rings, etc.?[46]

Notice how heterosexuality is portrayed as the abnormal behavior? If you substituted the words *homosexuality* and *opposite sex* into many of the questions, there would be a howl of protests from radical homosexual activists and their allies.

This questionnaire is just the beginning . . . it gets worse.

- In Newton, Massachusetts, the homosexual rainbow flag is flown proudly at many schools. Many of the same schools have chosen to ignore the Massachusetts law that the American flag be displayed on school grounds.[47]

- In Silver Lake, Massachusetts, a freshman health text says: "Testing your ability to function sexually and give pleasure to another person may be less threatening in your early teens with people of your own sex. . . . *You may come to the conclusion that growing up means rejecting the values of your parents*" [emphasis added].[48] This statement blatantly acknowledges the agenda of the radical homosexual activists: convince early teenagers to experiment with homosexual behavior and to reject the values of their parents. The students who received this text were told that they could not take it home.[49]

- In another instance, a parent removed a child after discovering the content of a four-day "sexual harassment" program dealt with homosexual behavior (it replaced algebra). The teacher told the student to return, stating: "Your parents don't have to know."[50]

And what happens when children start to reject their parents' beliefs after being indoctrinated in the public schools? After a week of mandatory Homophobia Week assemblies in Beverly, Massachusetts, a fourteen-year-old girl told her father that he was a homophobe.[51]

In their efforts to keep parents out of the public schools, homosexual and safe-sex advocates are doing everything they can to lock kids in. In Chelmsford, Massachusetts, high schoolers attended a mandatory assembly called "Hot, Safer, and Sexy" held by AIDS "educator" Suzi Landolphi. Parents were not notified about this assembly that was filled with graphic sexual information.

Landolphi started the assembly by telling the students, "What we're going to do is to have a group sexual experience here today. How's that? Is that good? With audience participation!"[52] Cheryl Wetzstein, in the *Washington Times*, described the rest of Landolphi's performance:

> She giggled and she strutted. They laughed and they cheered—especially when Dr. David Evans [of the American Medical Student Association] blew the condom on his head into King Kong proportions. . . .

The students [who filed the lawsuit] . . . were offended when she "simulated masturbation," used lewd and lascivious language for body parts and excretory functions, and closely inspected a male student's "butt," according to the court papers . . . . For example, Miss Landolphi asked a student to participate in a demonstration, and, holding a condom on one hand, she handed another condom to him. She licked the condom and asked him to do the same. Then, saying, "I don't want to waste this condom," she invited a teen-age girl to come down. Miss Landolphi told the boy to kneel and instructed the girl to take the condom and place it over the boy's head.[53]

The performers continued to attack Christianity stating: ". . . you are gay—that is your sexual orientation, and you happen to be proud of it. My name is not God. I was never given the right to judge another human being . . . . And I'll be [profanity] if I'll judge anyone by their . . . gender, their religion or their sexual orientation."[54]

One teenage girl, who had attended the session, stated, "This was definitely the best assembly in four years. She wasn't lecturing us like a parent. She was telling us something we need to hear. . . . Parents don't realize that the message she was getting across is important."[55]

The Alliance Defense Fund helped two former Chelmsford High School students in an appeal of their unsuccessful challenge to the school district over the performance. Unfortunately, the U.S. Supreme Court eventually rejected an appeal from the U.S. District Court of Appeals for the First Circuit, which had ruled against the students.[56]

At a special session for teenagers at a Massachusetts GLSEN conference, two officials from the state Department of Education and an AIDS educator taught a seminar titled "What They Didn't Teach You about Queer Sex and Sexuality in Health Class." The three adults took questions from the audience. When one of the students inquired about "fisting" (a practice in which a person inserts his or her hand and forearm into the rectum of a partner), the AIDS educator demonstrated to the teens the proper hand position for the act. One of the Department of Education officials chimed in, stating that fisting was "an experience of letting somebody into your body that you want to be close and intimate with."[57] The AIDS educator then urged the teens to consult their "really hip" Gay/Straight Alliance adviser at school for hints on how to "come on to a potential sex partner."[58] While one of the Department of Education employees was fired for the presentation, she was quietly rehired later after a decision in her favor by an arbitrator—with back pay dating to May 2000.[59]

This is just the tip of the iceberg in regards to the graphic sexual information that was shared with the teen audience. The conference was sponsored by the state of Massachusetts and was reportedly underwritten by corporate donations from American Airlines, Levi Strauss, and Eastman Kodak.

What comes through loud and clear in Massachusetts and in California is the wholesale encouragement for children to reject their parents' and America's common values. No dissent to the homosexual agenda is allowed, or if it is, it is severely limited and pushed to the fringes.

Consider this account from an attorney of what happened at Santa Rosa High School in Santa Rosa, California (where Craig graduated from high school more than two decades ago).

> Santa Rosa High School is one place where this [homosexual education] agenda has been fully implemented. I was privileged to be one of a panel of experts opposed to the "gay" agenda who had been allowed to make one 50-minute presentation during the first day of Diversity Week at school.
>
> The principal, Mr. Waxman, considers this single slot sufficient to provide "balance" in a weeklong program that included more than 20 hours of pro-homosexual indoctrination of students. The requirement of balance had been imposed on the school by the school board following a parental revolt the prior year, when a single "Day of Diversity" at another high school in the district failed to include opponents of the homosexual political agenda.
>
> What I learned during the course of that day [the first day of Diversity Week at Santa Rosa High School] was astonishing, even to a veteran pro-family leader like myself. We [concerned parents and the attorney] discovered a comprehensive program for promoting homosexuality to the student population, complete with a taxpayer-funded staff facilitator and the approval of the administration.
>
> The paid facilitator is a veteran "gay" activist named Jim Foster . . . [who] runs an off-campus community center called "Positive Images" where "gay" teens can mingle with older homosexuals. . . . This week's schedule included at

least four sessions on "homophobia," and many additional hours devoted to gender issues, transsexualism, and other topics dear to the "gay" movement. . . . I took the opportunity to sit in on a "Panel on Homophobia." It was worse than I expected. Seven or eight people sat in rows or tables at the head of the room and addressed a standing-room only crowd of their peers. The young activists took turns giving personal testimonies about how joining the "gay" movement has changed their lives from misery to bliss. Each one began by reciting his or her credentials as a victim of "homophobia," then explained how he or she had "come out" as "gay," lesbian, bisexual, or transgendered. Each finished by reciting how much he or she now felt loved and accepted in the "gay" movement. Frankly, the only comparable experience I have ever had to this has been in the church settings where people have testified as to how Christ changed their lives. Only here, the "savior" was identified as the "gay" community. . . .

I was confronted by a teenage girl who announced that she was head of the "Gay-Straight Alliance" club on campus. Her overt purpose in addressing me was to gloat that the new club had over 40 members and was making huge strides in converting students to the "gay" cause. She searched my eyes as she told me and was visibly pleased that I was pained by the news. As she walked away, one of her companions said aloud, "I hope he dies." Later, as I was leaving the campus, one of the parents called to me from across the parking lot and gestured over to a car parked near the office. As I approached, I saw that its license plates read "Pos Imag." It was Jim Foster's car. "Look at the seat," said the parent. There, as if placed to be noticed by passersby was a black and white poster. It was a picture of young boys around the age of puberty sitting together on some front porch steps. In big block letters at the bottom of the page read the message, "INCITE QUEERNESS."[60]

Despite ever-present denials by homosexual activists, the link to child sex (adults promoting sex with young boys) and homosexual behavior is alarming. At a 2002 Columbia University conference (sponsored by the New York City Department of Health) for "Lesbian, Gay, Bisexual, and Transgender Youth," one of the workshops was titled "Adult/Teen Sex." This seminar was described as follows: "This workshop is a discussion that will address adult-teen relationships and the controversies surrounding the issue. Some questions that the workshop will attempt to answer: Why are teens attracted to older adults? Why are older adults attracted to teens? What does the law say? What are some gray areas in adult-teen relationships?"[61]

We will read in a subsequent chapter about pedophilia and how it is now being promoted in the academic world as just another alternative lifestyle that is in some ways "beneficial" to children. In addition, we will look at the issue of adult/teen sex in the context of the controversies surrounding the Catholic Church and the Boy Scouts of America. This is the dangerous path that many radical homosexual activists are taking us, and our children, on.

In Visalia, California, not exactly an urban center like San Francisco or Los Angeles, the school district agreed to implement anti-harassment programs conducted by GLSEN and aimed at all students and staff, after being sued by the ACLU. The settlement called for mandatory training for all school staff and high school students. The student training was described as being "peer to peer," meaning students who do not agree with homosexual behavior will be pressured by their fellow classmates to comply. In addition, the district will name "compliance coordinators" to "help parents, students and teachers with incidents of discrimination."[62] Big Brother is alive and well in Visalia, California, and he is watching you and your kids.

The Influence Is Pervasive

The indoctrination that takes place in our public schools has definitely had an effect in shaping teens' attitudes toward homosexual behavior. In 2001, Zogby International released a poll that found that 85 percent of high school seniors thought homosexual men and lesbians should be accepted by society; 68 percent said homosexual couples should be allowed to adopt children; 88 percent supported so-called hate-crimes legislation, which in many of its forms has nothing to do with "hate" at all; and two-thirds thought same-sex marriage should be allowed. Even 80 percent of evangelical Christian students supported hate-crimes legislation, which in its many proposed forms, will be used to silence religious speech about homosexual behavior.[63] The researchers also were surprised that some of the most liberal views on homosexual behavior came from Catholic students. For instance, 80 percent of Catholic students supported homosexual marriage,[64] despite the Roman Catholic Church's unequivocal position in opposition.*

As if indoctrinating children isn't enough, radical homosexual activists are busy re-writing history, with little or no evidence, to support the assertions that they pass along as absolute truth to impressionable schoolchildren to convince them that scores of significant people, including biblical figures such as King David and the apostle Paul were homosexual. With the NEA resolution on homosexual behavior being quietly implemented into school curricula nationwide, more and more children will be taught these distortions of biblical and world history.

For example, some activists have declared that Leonardo da Vinci was homosexual.[65] In addition, they have also added Eleanor Roosevelt,[66] Alexander Hamilton,[67] and even Abraham Lincoln to their list.[68] In Lincoln's case, they claim that he shared a room with a man for a two-year period, thus that automatically made him homosexual.[69] If that is the case, every college freshman who has shared a dorm room or an apartment with someone of the same sex is homosexual as well! Yet such nonsense goes unquestioned. In fact, as mentioned earlier, many Los Angeles city schools devote an entire month of the school year to teaching gay history, which includes items such as this.[70]

While children are being told that Abraham Lincoln is homosexual, they are not learning true American history.† A recent poll of American high school students found that 22 percent believed that we fought the Revolutionary War against France, 13 percent said that we battled England in the Civil War, 15 percent had no idea of what happened on July 4, 1776, and 10 percent did not know that George Washington was the first president under the Constitution.[71] Educators are more concerned about Honest Abe's sexual orientation than they are of the significance of the Civil War.

The Teen Suicide Myth

Why has such indoctrination and rewriting of history taken place? One reason is that homosexual activists have been enormously successful in convincing educators and the general public that homosexual teenagers are more susceptible to dropping out of

---

*We will discuss the catechism of the Catholic Church and its stance on homosexual behavior in chapter 6.
†The National Park Service produced a video (now under review after public outcry) for the Lincoln Memorial that states that Lincoln would have supported homosexual "rights." See Marc Morano, "Park Service Seeks to 'Modify' Controversial Lincoln Video," CNSNews.com, March 4, 2003.

school and committing suicide because they are "harassed." However, this argument turns out to be a Trojan horse to get educators to open the doors for homosexual activists.

Marilyn Elias, in *USA Today,* wrote:

> Gay and lesbian teenagers are only slightly more likely than heterosexual kids to attempt suicide, contrary to past studies that suggest gay youths have about triple the rate of trying suicide, says a Cornell University psychologist. . . . Studies finding that about 30% of gay adolescents have attempted suicide exaggerated the rates because they surveyed the most disturbed youngsters and didn't separate thought from action, says Ritch Savin-Williams. Nearly all research on this topic has drawn teens from support groups or shelters, where the most troubled gather, and has taken at face value the claim of a suicide attempt, he says. Savin-Williams' own two studies . . . focus on 349 students ages 17 to 25. When they said they had tried to kill themselves, he asked what method they used. He also separated out the small minority who attended support groups. . . . Over half of reported suicide attempts turned out to be "thinking about it" rather than trying anything. . . . The other study of 266 college men and women found that gay youths were not significantly more likely than straight classmates to have tried to take their own lives. Again, the homosexual students were more likely to report "attempts" that further questioning revealed as thoughts. . . . Poorly designed studies that exaggerate the suicide risk "pathologize gay youth, and that's not fair to them," he says.[72]

Please let us make it clear that any act that takes a promising young life, whether it is suicide or murder, is tragic and grieves God. However, to deliberately manipulate such a tragedy for political gain and to entrap more children in a dangerous behavior is reprehensible. Radical homosexual activists use many questionable research methods to push their agenda (like the much-disputed and widely discredited claim of Alfred Kinsey that 10 percent of the adult population is homosexual). This ties directly into Madsen's and Kirk's policy that it makes no difference whether such claims were truth or lies, as long as the lies work to promote their political agenda.

P-FLAG (Parents and Friends of Lesbians and Gays) received a $250,000 grant to push homosexual indoctrination in public schools, based on the unproven claim that homosexual teens are far more likely to commit suicide.[73] GLSEN is given full access to school facilities (which many Christian groups are still denied despite Supreme Court decisions to the contrary) to set up so-called safe zones for "questioning" youth, and to promote their agenda without question.[74]

So what can a parent do? How can families protect their children when they have no other option than the public schools for their children? It is not easy, because homosexual activists have learned that intimidation and stonewalling work wonders in helping them to achieve their aims.

Mary Clossey, who had children in the Newton, Massachusetts, public schools, illustrates the problem. When her son brought home *The Perks of Being a Wallflower,* she was alarmed at the graphic homosexual content. She decided to complain to school officials and to the mayor of Newton. She found that the mayor's office refused to return her call. When she called school officials, she experienced "arrogant disrespect for parents." With the support of other furious parents, she went to the local prosecutor, who had been warned that she was coming. As a result, the receptionist would not allow her to see him, and she was continually stonewalled by other public officials when she tried to air her objections to the book.[75]

Back in the late 1980s, a young woman, who was Craig's friend, worked in the public policy division at Focus on the Family. "Linda" (a pseudonym) stood up to the homosexual activists in Los Angeles City schools as they attempted (and eventually) succeeded in implementing their agenda into the school system. Linda had to deal with her car being vandalized while she was attending school board meetings, as well as enduring death threats from radical homosexual activists.

However, we cannot allow the intimidation of homosexual activists to silence Christians in the public schools. While many Christian families have chosen to either home school or enroll their children in private schools (at great personal expense) to avoid the indoctrination of their children by radical homosexual activists, public schools remain the only option for millions of Christian families. If you have a child in public schools, *it is vital* that you know what is going on. It will require great diligence on your part, but your efforts are crucial if the radical homosexual activists are to be stymied. You will need to review curriculum, especially anything that falls into the categories of "family life education," "diversity," or "respecting differences." This will not be easy. You may be stonewalled, you may face threats, and you may be labeled a troublemaker. *But it is your right as a parent to know what is being taught to your child.* Your chances are also better if you are organized with other concerned parents, rather than fighting the school administration alone. Network with other Christian parents in your child's school. Then, when something troublesome comes up, you can go as a group to protest to the school board and administration. There is strength in numbers.

An example of this happened in Fairfax County, Virginia, where a large group of parents objected to the implementation of a new so-called anti-discrimination policy that included sexual orientation. More than two hundred parents rallied before the school board vote on the new policy, and their actions blocked the door's opening to pro-homosexual curriculum in their public school system.

And, if you still find yourself stonewalled, you can call the Alliance Defense Fund at 1-800-TELL-ADF or send an e-mail to info@telladf.org, and we will be able to provide you with information on the legal recourse you may have with your local school district to force it to show you what your child is being taught.

Finally, if your school system continues to persist in offering a pro-homosexual curriculum, you may need to pray for the Lord's direction in seeking an alternative from the public schools for your children. As difficult as this may be for some, it may be the only recourse to save your children from homosexual indoctrination.

One of parents' key religious freedoms is the ability to raise their children to accept Jesus Christ into their lives and to train them to hold biblically based beliefs. In our public schools today, this religious freedom is under daily assault. Sad to say, large numbers of children may have already been lost to the pro-homosexual efforts that have been quietly implemented in our public schools over the past decade. But harm to future generations can still be prevented. Confused children can still be redeemed. However, it is going to take an army of parents, not just one individual here and there, who will rise up in righteous anger over what is happening to our children. If concerned parents are educated and organized, rather than just being stray voices in the wilderness against the onslaught of homosexual activism, they will have a greater chance of not only stopping the advancement of the homosexual agenda in public schools, but of reversing it as well.

To talk about everything that is happening in the public schools regarding the homosexual agenda would require an entire separate book, but hopefully this chapter has given you a glimpse of how children are being taught to reject biblical values and embrace homosexual behavior. The day when we can trust our public school system to affirm America's traditional values is over. It is time to take back our schools from the radical homosexual activists for the sake of our children.

CHAPTER FOUR

The Lavender Tower

> We have had more challenges to our basic right to exist on
> campus settings during the past two years than in the previous
> fifty-five combined. It's not just us—this is hitting Catholics and
> Muslims and others. What we are seeing is a growing challenge
> to religious free speech.
>
> —Steve Hayner, former president of InterVarsity Christian Fellowship

In the early 1980s at the University of California–Davis, Craig witnessed firsthand how radical homosexual activists used intimidation to force a college administration to bow to their demands, at the expense of other students and legitimate academic programs.

In spring 1982, the university faced the possibility of making some budget cuts. One of the first places it looked was the so-called women's studies department that consisted of a group of about thirteen lesbian students who followed a charismatic leader named Merline. As Craig walked around the campus, he would often run into this group. They would be holding hands and listening breathlessly to every word Merline had to say.

When the university announced it would be eliminating Merline's position from the budget, one would have thought that it was calling for the elimination of the college's prestigious veterinary school. The lesbians chained themselves around the area where the school administration building was located, unfurled posters, attacked the administration in the campus newspaper, and eventually staged a sit-in in the dean's office. How dare they cut Merline's position! By the time the students were finished, one would have thought that Merline was Joan of Arc. The administration caved in, restored Merline's position, and eliminated the Mass Communications department.*

About six months later, Craig started graduate school at California State University–Sacramento, about twenty miles east of Davis. Who did he run into almost immediately? Merline and the same group of lesbians! She had found a way to get herself on the payroll there as well and she and her following bounced back and forth between the two campuses.

> The thing about this scholarship is that it could benefit any student in any program, as long as the student identifies him or herself as gay, lesbian, bisexual, or transgendered.
>
> —Eva Gaffney, Bridgewater State College spokeswoman

As sad as this story already is, it would take a tragic turn.

One day, a sweet girl named Laura came to Craig's InterVarsity Christian Fellowship group on campus. Laura was hurting when she came to the fellowship; but the group welcomed her with open arms, and she quickly heard about the healing power in Jesus Christ. Laura accepted Christ, and one of the more mature Christian girls in the chapter started to mentor her.

About two weeks later, Craig was walking around the campus when he ran into Merline and her group of lesbians. He was shocked to see that they had a new member: Laura. He expressed his concern to his friend who was mentoring her.

Unfortunately, neither Craig's friend nor anyone else in the chapter was aware of Merline and her Svengali type influence. The other members of his InterVarsity chapter expressed little concern over the matter. However, in a few weeks, Laura quit returning phone calls and coming to the group. Eventually, she disappeared completely.

About ten years later, a friend of Craig's from the InterVarsity group went into a small shop in downtown Sacramento, not knowing it was a lesbian bookstore. Before she left, she noticed the woman standing behind the counter. It was Laura. Her sweet face had been hardened, and her kind manner was nothing more than a memory. She was trapped in the lesbian lifestyle.†

---

*During Craig's time at the University of California–Davis, the homosexual activist groups staged a special week of "tolerance and understanding" for homosexual behavior. One of their requests was for all heterosexuals to refrain from any public expression of affection, such as holding hands, because such expression was "offensive" to those who engaged in homosexual behavior.

†One of the phenomena on some campuses is "LUGS" (Lesbians until Graduation). These are women who choose to engage in lesbian behavior during their college years but revert back to heterosexual behavior after graduating.

We share this story because it is an example of how pervasive homosexual behavior and its promotion are on our nation's university campuses. It is also a tragic reminder of what can happen when an individual looking for love and acceptance falls into the wrong company.

Queer Studies 101

Just as happens in the public schools, millions of Americans, at great sacrifice, send their almost-grown, very vulnerable children off to college campuses in search of the education they will need to succeed in life. Their expectations are that their sons and daughters will master calculus or history or literature. Yet, here is a small sample of some of the "courses" being offered on university campuses today:

* "Black Lavender: A Study of Black Gay and Lesbian Plays, and Dramatic Constructions in American Theatre" (Brown University).[1]
* "Discourses of Desire: Introduction to Gay and Lesbian Studies" (Columbia University).[2]
* "Science, Technology, and Queer Theory" (Yale University).[3]
* "Lesbian Communities and Identities" (Stanford University).[4]
* "Lesbian Novels Since World War II" (Swarthmore University).[5]
* "Queer Media" (Swarthmore University).[6]
* "Representations of Lesbians and Gay Men in Popular Culture" (Georgetown University).[7]
* "Lesbian/Bisexual Women's Theories/Lives/Activisms" (University of Arizona).[8]
* "Lesbian Lives in the U.S." (University of Iowa).[9]
* "Feminist Perspectives on Lesbian Studies: Crossing Erotic Boundaries" (University of Michigan).[10]
* "Gay Men and Homophobia in American Culture" (University of Minnesota).[11]
* "Lesbian/Queer Cultural Production" (University of Minnesota).[12]
* "Backgrounds of Homoerotic Literature" (Rutgers University).[13]
* "Issues in Lesbian and Gay Visual Representation" (University of California–Irvine).[14]
* "Queer Textuality" (University of California–Santa Barbara).[15]

While college students are being offered courses in "queer theory," they continue their ignorance of basic information, such as elementary level U.S. history. For example, at the top fifty-five secular colleges and universities in the United States, only 23 percent of the students knew that James Madison was a primary author of the U.S. Constitution and 40 percent of the students could not identify the correct fifty-year time frame in which the Civil War was fought.[16]

Why does this surprise us when the University of Colorado's English Department offers more than twice the number of multiculturalism and "gender" courses it offers on American literature?[17]

In addition, some college campuses are now going out of their way to recruit individuals who practice homosexual behavior, just like they would a star quarterback. For example, Bridgewater State College in Massachusetts announced that it was offering a special scholarship for homosexual students who were "cut off financially" from their parents because of their sexual behavior. College spokeswoman Eva Gaffney said, "The thing about this scholarship is that it could benefit a student in any program, as long as the student identifies himself or herself as gay, lesbian, bisexual, or transgendered."[18]

Judith Brown, director of the Lesbian Gay Bisexual Transgender Center at Tufts University, says, "Schools are inviting these students because they question the norms. They make people question their own assumptions, and that's a key to learning and growing as people."[19]

In a *Boston Globe* article, Patrick Healy wrote about admissions counselors at university campuses who believe that "the 'coming out' experience in high school can breed self-confidence, leadership abilities, cultural awareness, and other characteristics that colleges want."[20]

"All Animals Are Equal, but Some Are More Equal Than Others"

In their efforts to actively recruit individuals who practice homosexual behavior, many colleges now have a check-off box on their admissions forms for "sexual orientation."[21] Jibil Salaam, the associate director of admissions for inclusion and diversity at the University of New Hampshire, says, "If we truly want these students, it's vital to ask the question. . . . it will help us really tailor a message of support to them."[22]

For instance, the University of California at Los Angeles (UCLA) has received an endowment from the Charles R. Williams

Project on Sexual Orientation Law to develop the nation's first "think tank" dedicated to the legal advancement of the homosexual legal agenda. The university received an initial $2.5 million gift that was described as "the largest donation ever given to an academic institution in support of a gay and lesbian academic program in any discipline."[23]

Some universities have gone as far as to throw all logic out the window by tailoring their student housing policies to support homosexual behavior and preferences. Gene Edward Veith wrote the following in *World* magazine: "Many universities now have co-ed dorms, with men and women living on the same floor. But some have taken the next step: co-ed dorm rooms. Not that these colleges are encouraging their students to have sex with each other. Quite the contrary. Having a man and a woman share the same sleeping quarters is just another way to make homosexuals feel more comfortable."[24]

Veith adds that at Swarthmore College and Haverford College, homosexual groups claimed that it was "heterosexist" to require roommates to be of the same sex. He continues, "The reasoning went like this: A girl forced to live with a man she didn't know would feel very uncomfortable. Besides, the straight roommate might be homophobic. In order to avoid sexual issues, gay men should be allowed to room with females."[25]

Another student, who identified himself as "homoflexible," said, "I live with straight guys now, and I definitely see the sexual tensions, which have made me very uncomfortable."[26]

Gamma Rho Lambda, the first "lesbian sorority," was created at Arizona State University after Sigma Phi Alpha, the first male homosexual fraternity came into existence there. Sam Holdren, a member of the male homosexual fraternity, said: "I think it's amazing. I love it; this campus is becoming so queer-friendly and supportive, it's wonderful."[27]

At Wesleyan College, students no longer have to identify themselves as male or female on their health forms. Instead, they are told to describe their "gender identity history." Wesleyan also eliminated the word *women's* from the female rugby team. Why? Because several of the girls have chosen to be identified as males. One of the girls said, "We don't want people yelling, 'Go girls.'"[28] Concerning the college that bears his name, John Wesley must be spinning in his grave.

Smith College students (all female) voted to eliminate female pronouns from the student constitution because "she" and "her" were "insensitive" to transgendered students. Gene Edward Veith wrote in *World* magazine, "Since the language only has two genders, some activists are calling for new pronouns. The most politically correct are using 'ze' instead of 'he' or 'she' and 'hir' instead of 'him' or 'her.'"[29]

Then there is the bathroom problem. The United States Students Association has urged the nation's colleges and universities to provide "gender neutral" rest rooms for transgender students, in order to "protect" them from alleged harassment and physical violence. USSA spokeswoman Kristy Ringor said, "If a person is not safe [in a rest room on a college campus], that person won't necessarily be able to go to college."[30]

The right of the homosexual to have housing that makes him or her feel comfortable trumps the right of a heterosexual young man and young woman to have housing that does not place them in either a sexually tempting or sexually compromising environment. In addition, those individuals who have religious objections to homosexual behavior and therefore would rather not live with someone who practices homosexual behavior are labeled "homophobes" or have their requests fall upon deaf ears. We are reminded of the words of George Orwell in his classic book *Animal Farm*: "All animals are equal, but some are more equal than others."[31]

For example, ADF has been involved in several cases regarding the rights of people with sincere religious beliefs to not be forced to live with someone who practiced homosexual behavior or other behaviors that violated their beliefs. In one case, *Rader v. University of Nebraska*, a Christian student wished to move out of the college-mandated student housing because of the anti-Christian behaviors of the other residents. In another case, two Orthodox Jewish students who objected to the immoral atmosphere in college dormitories were denied their request to live elsewhere besides student housing. Yet, while people of faith find themselves forced to put up with behavior that offends them, those who practice homosexual behavior are catered to, at the expense of everyone else. The University of Nebraska case was a victory that affirmed the right of Christian students, while the two Jewish students lost their case.

This begs the following questions: Are these universities willing to recruit students who are serious about their religious faith with the same zeal they recruit those who practice homosexual behavior? And, second, once homosexual behavior is accepted and affirmed on the university campus, what comes next? The answers are disturbing for those who cherish religious freedom and who seek to protect their children from those who would exploit them sexually.

Those who advocate the teaching of homosexual behavior on college campuses state that it is just a way of teaching students to think critically and independently. However, that is the last thing it is. Dennis Evans, the director of credential programs at the University of California–Irvine, made the following observation, "How is it, then, that the character and content of much of the work in gay and lesbian studies so often seems to originate with the author's need to defend, to rationalize, or to attack? The works are invariably crafted as a priori polemics, and, as such, their purposes are more political than academic, more rhetorical than scholarly. They certainly neither model nor promote independent or critical thinking."[32]

The main purpose of such "studies" is seemingly twofold: to academically affirm homosexual behavior with those who are already trapped in the lifestyle and to silence and attack anyone who disagrees (i.e., those who have biblical objections to such behavior).

Jeremy Beer, a former student at Purdue University, remembers the following remarks by his philosophy teacher during the first day of class: "While you are in this class, you will be expected to be an agnostic or atheist. Anyone with sincere religious beliefs will be expected to take off his 'religious hat' when he enters this class and replace it with an agnostic one. That's the only way philosophy can proceed. Does anyone have a problem with that?"[33]

Edmund White, a homosexual professor at Princeton University (which was founded by devout Christians), openly wrote about his hostility to Christianity: "It seems to me that the biggest enemy to homosexuality is Christianity . . . . I hate it when gays try to accommodate Christianity and create their own gay group . . . . Any self-respecting gay should be an atheist."[34]

At the University of Notre Dame, the school recently held its first "queer film festival." Nicholas Sakurai of the pro-homosexual United States Student Association said, "The landscape has changed. Young people are coming out in droves in high school since the '90s. They're now in college and challenging administrators who would deny them a place in campus life."[35]

Sadly, this same attitude is prevalent on other university campuses originally founded by Christians. Around every turn, those students who hold religious beliefs are ridiculed and vilified, and much of this can be attributed to the work of homosexual activists. While homosexual students are recruited, religious students are vilified and, in many cases, discriminated against.

At Tufts University in Massachusetts, the InterVarsity Christian Fellowship chapter faced expulsion from campus because it would not allow an avowed lesbian to hold a leadership position with the group. She appealed to the student senate, which took away the chapter's access to campus facilities and funding because it "violated" the school's anti-discrimination policy, even though the group made it very clear that the members believed homosexual behavior violated their organization's core biblical beliefs.

The chapter was allowed back on campus only after a public backlash. However, InterVarsity was put on probation for "intolerance." Eventually, it was allowed to include adherence to biblical teachings as a qualification for leadership.[36] Nevertheless, the chapter's leaders were subjected to campus "tolerance" education, described by Gregory Fung, the president of the chapter: "We did what they asked us to do. We went to their tolerance classes. You think the institutions that teach tolerance won't turn around and bite you. But they do. We thought the people who taught all the classes would be tolerant. No way. They were determined to cure us of our intolerance."[37]

So-called tolerance, as Gregory Fung found out, really means intolerance for any viewpoint that does not affirm homosexual behavior. What happened at Tufts University is just the tip of the iceberg when it comes to the suppression of religious freedoms of Christians and other people of faith on college campuses.

Steve Hayner, the president of InterVarsity, put it succinctly: "We have had more challenges to our basic right to exist on campus settings during the past two years than in the previous fifty-five combined. It's not just us—this is hitting Catholics and Muslims and others. What we are seeing is a growing challenge to religious free speech."[38]

The University of North Carolina and Rutgers University threatened to revoke university recognition of the InterVarsity chapters unless it modified its charter to allow non-Christians or those who practice behaviors contrary to Scripture to be leaders. At UNC, the administration finally agreed to not revoke the recognition of InterVarsity, but Rutgers held steadfast. Alan Kors, of the Foundation for Individual Rights in Education, said: "UNC couldn't defend in public what it wasn't willing to do in private. Everybody on campus would immediately see the absurdity . . . if an evangelical Christian who believed homosexuality to be a sin tried to become president of the university's Bisexual, Gay, and Lesbian Alliance. The administration would have led candlelight vigils on behalf of diversity and free expression."[39]

Talk show host Laura Ingraham agreed: "One can only imagine if a group of devout Christians tried to join a Rutgers lesbian student group. The Christian students would probably be brought up on disciplinary charges, accused of violating Rutgers' 'principle of community.' . . . Perhaps if it changed its name to InterVarsity Students for Intramural Sex, it would not be bothered by intolerant campus bureaucrats."[40]

On March 19, 2003, after an avalanche of negative publicity and the work of Alliance Defense Fund allied attorney David French, the Rutgers administration relented and allowed the InterVarsity group to set their own standards for leadership without facing expulsion from campus. The fact that a case as obvious as this took so much time to settle demonstrates the tremendous influence that those who oppose the gospel have on college campuses today.

In fact, ADF has been involved in defending free speech and freedom of association rights for Christian groups on numerous other college campuses. We have found that many of these so-called "anti-discrimination" policies evaporate once they are brought to light for examination and college administrators quickly back down.

At Harvard University, much speech that does not affirm homosexual behavior has been effectively silenced. For example, an employee at a dining hall on campus, who had come out of homosexual behavior and accepted Christ, was vehemently attacked in the *Harvard Daily Crimson*, which accused him of being intolerant and promoting homosexual self-hatred. When an admissions officer was asked if dissenting views were allowed on campus with regard to homosexual behavior, he said, "Well, it's not really something one can debate about."[41] At Harvard Law School's Pound Hall, there is a large oil painting that hangs in a place of honor to celebrate "Deborah A. Batts 1972: U.S. District Court Judge . . . and the first and only openly gay, lesbian, or bisexual member of the federal judiciary."

Even the American Red Cross has faced the wrath of homosexual activists on college campuses. Two "student legislators" at Western Oregon University launched an effort to ban Red Cross blood drives from the campus because the Red Cross (out of legitimate health concerns about the transmission of the HIV/AIDS virus) asked potential donors if they have engaged in forms of homosexual sex. Student senator Shauna Bates said, "By continuing to allow the Red Cross on campus, the university is telling all the gay, lesbian, bisexual, and transgender students that we don't care about you."[42]

Yeshiva University is a private Orthodox Jewish college that adheres to traditional Jewish teaching that homosexual behavior is sinful. Two lesbians who wanted to have access to married student housing for themselves and their partners sued the university after their request was denied. In what has chilling ramifications for the religious freedom for any person or organization that holds to a biblical view of homosexual behavior, the court has ruled against the university.[43]

This case could help establish a legal precedent to force private religious colleges to not only give homosexual partners the same housing as married couples, but to force them to violate their core beliefs. This is something that the radical homosexual activists and their allies are very much aware of and will most likely exploit in the future.

ACLU attorney Matt Coles said, "It's a fabulous ruling. I think the fact that it's a private organization helps make it clear that it's unfair for anyone to use marriage as a qualification for anything as long as gay people are excluded from same-sex marriage."[44] Thus, the radical homosexual activists and their allies got a double whammy in this case: forcing religious organizations to violate their beliefs while promoting legalized same-sex marriage as the solution to the problem.

Mandatory Funding

Two hundred years ago, Thomas Jefferson said: "[To] compel a man to furnish contributions of money for the propagation of opinions which he disbelieves and abhors, is sinful and tyrannical."[45] This tyranny is occurring on almost daily basis on university campuses through mandatory student fees to fund radical homosexual and other left-leaning organizations.

Homosexual activists on university campuses not only want to silence or even banish groups that do not affirm homosexual behavior; they want people with sincere religious beliefs in opposition to such behavior to fund their agenda. An example of this is the case of *Southworth v. Board of Regents University of Wisconsin System.*[46]

In 1996, Scott Southworth, who was then a second-year law student, was told to pay $331.50 to the University of Wisconsin for his mandatory student fee over and above his regular tuition. If he did not do so, he could not get his grades or graduate from the university. Scott paid up, but as a committed Christian, he wanted to know where his money was going.

After some investigation, he was outraged. A portion of his student fee was being used to fund groups that advocated homosexual behavior. Scott and other Christian students made repeated attempts to convince university officials to let them "opt out" of paying the mandatory fees, based on religious freedom and First Amendment grounds. The administration refused to budge.

Scott felt he was left with little choice but to take formal legal action against the university. God led Scott to ADF, which was able to connect him with Jordan Lorence, now an ADF vice president. Lorence is one of the leading constitutional lawyers in the country. At every court level, Scott won, but the university kept appealing the case.

The case finally made it all the way to the United States Supreme Court, which remanded (returned) the case 9-0 back to the U.S. District Court to decide one critical issue: Do University of Wisconsin student government leaders who allocate mandatory student fees do so on a viewpoint-neutral basis, or are some funded groups given preference over others?

The homosexual activists and their allies crowed throughout the media that they had won a decisive victory to continue the funding of their agenda by those who had sincere religious objections to homosexual behavior. But Scott Southworth and ADF were committed to keep up the fight.

On October 1, 2002, the U.S Circuit Court of Appeals for the Seventh District ruled that aspects of the University of Wisconsin's student fee system remained unconstitutional, and it did not vindicate the university's position on mandatory student fees that we have opposed for years.

The university had argued that it should not have to make any changes in its policy to protect the rights of students forced to pay mandatory student activity fees to fund groups opposed to their personal beliefs. In fact, because of the litigation in Southworth, the university changed many discriminatory policies. However, in this case, the university was hoping that the court would rule that it could return to its previous policy that discriminated against Christians and Christian groups. The previous policy denied funding to religious groups. On that point, the university lost.

Interestingly, the court upheld portions of the university's policy that had been changed only after the ADF-funded litigation. As a result, here's where things now stand:

- Student government members must vow not to discriminate on the basis of viewpoint in their decision-making.
- The ban on funding religious groups and political groups has been repealed.
- The university established an appeals process for groups denied funding.

- When the student government denies funding to an applicant group, the student government must record the vote and state in writing why they denied funding to a group.

The key point is that if the university does not follow these guidelines imposed by the court, students cannot be required to pay the mandatory student activity fee. At least those who oppose the use of their monies to promote homosexual behavior have some avenue of recourse.

Intellectualizing Disordered Sexual Behavior

Lately homosexual behavior on college campuses is taking a dangerous new turn—the promotion of sexual relations between adults and children, known as pedophilia.

We mention the new promotion of pedophilia in the context of talking about the influence of homosexual behavior on college campuses, because, despite all objections to the contrary, the two are often intrinsically linked.*

Psychologist Eugene Abel found that homosexuals "sexually molest young boys with an incidence that is occurring from five times greater than the molestation of girls."[47] A 1992 study by researchers K. Freud and R. I. Watson discovered that homosexual males are three times more likely than heterosexual males to engage in pedophilia and that the average pedophile has sex with 20 to 150 boys before he is caught.[48] A 1988 study in the *Archives of Sexual Behavior* found that 86 percent of pedophiles identified themselves as either homosexual or bisexual.[49]

And there is a definite link as well between child molestation and later homosexual behavior. In a 2001 study, it was found that 46 percent of homosexuals and 22 percent of lesbians reported that they had been molested by a homosexual during childhood, compared to 7 percent of heterosexual men and 1 percent of heterosexual women.[50]

While trying to downplay the link between pedophilia and homosexual behavior in the media, many homosexual academics proudly proclaim their support for sex with children. For example, *the* homosexual newspaper, the *San Francisco Sentinel,* wrote, "The love between man and boys is at the foundation of homosexuality."[51]

---

*The American Psychiatric Association's Diagnostic and Statistical Manual (DSM-IV-TR) defines *pedophilia* as "sexual activity with a prepubescent child (generally 13 years of age or younger)." We, however, use a broader definition to include postpubescent children.

An article in the *Journal of Homosexuality* added that parents should view pedophiles "not as a rival or competitor, not as a theft of their property, but as a partner in the boy's upbringing, someone to be welcomed into their home."[52]

A 1995 issue of *Guide* magazine (which also published the original homosexual manifesto by Kirk and Madsen) stated: "We can be proud that the gay movement has been home to a few voices who have had the courage to say out loud that children are naturally sexual [and] deserve the right to sexual expression with whoever they choose . . . . Instead of fearing being labeled pedophiles, we must proudly proclaim that sex is good, including children's sexuality . . . . We must do it for the children's sake."[53]

A shot across the bow in this area occurred back in 1998 when the American Psychological Association (APA) published a study by three academics that concluded that sex between adults and minors might be a "positive experience" for the child.[54] Ironically, the American Psychiatric Association, which provides guidelines for treatment of mental disorders, says: "These activities [pedophilia] are commonly explained with excuses and rationalizations that they have 'educational value' for the child, that the child derives 'sexual pleasure' from them, or that the child was 'sexually provocative' . . ."[55]

Congress and the mainstream media roundly denounced the APA study. The U.S. House of Representatives voted 355-0 to condemn the study.[56]

The promotion of pedophilia among college professors and other academics is nothing new. Consider the following examples:

- In 1996, San Francisco State University Professor Gilbert Herdt stated in an interview with *Paidika* (an academic journal that promotes pedophilia) that "the category 'child' is a rhetorical device for inflaming what is really an irrational set of attitudes against sex with children."[57]
- John Money, professor emeritus of Pediatrics and Medical Psychology at Johns Hopkins School of Medicine, wrote in his 1987 book *Boys on Their Contacts with Men: A Study of Sexually Expressed Friendships* that those who oppose pedophilia do so because of "self-imposed, moralistic ignorance."[58]
- The Institute for the Advanced Study of Human Sexuality in San Francisco (whose executive officer testified on the "educational value" of pornography as an "expert witness" on behalf of hard-core pornographers nationwide) published an article, "Sexual Rights of Children," which said that there

was "considerable evidence" that there is no "inherent harm in sexual expression in childhood."[59]*

- Penn State University hosted a conference on "Women's Health and Wellness" featuring Patrick Califia-Rice, an outspoken proponent of pedophilia and sadomasochism. Rice has stated, "Boy-lovers and the lesbians who have young lovers . . . are not child molesters. The child abusers are priests, teachers, therapists, cops, and parents who force their stale morality on to the young people in their custody. Instead of condemning pedophiles for their involvement with lesbian and gay youth, they should be commending them."[60]

John Leo, columnist for *U.S. News and World Report*, noted that he had seen a trend toward the promotion of pedophilia among academics as early as 1981.[61] Leo mentioned his earlier observation in a recent column dealing with a book published by the University of Minnesota in 2002 titled *"Harmful to Minors: The Perils of Protecting Children from Sex"* by Dr. Judith Levine. The book features an introduction by former U.S. Surgeon General Joycelyn Elders, who had advocated the teaching of masturbation and handing out condoms in public schools during her controversial term in the early days of the Clinton administration.[62]

In her book, Levine says that the Dutch age of consent law is a "good model" because it allows for sex between an adult and a child between the ages of twelve and sixteen if the child consents.[63] In a phone interview, she added, "The research shows us that in some minority of cases, young—even quite young—people can have a positive [sexual] experience with an adult. That's what the research shows."[64] Levine believes that the real danger to children is not pedophiles but parents who "project their fears and their own lust for young flesh onto the mythically dangerous child molester."[65]

The University of Minnesota published this book under the guise of "academic freedom," a rationale often used by homosexual activists to introduce the promotion of homosexual behavior on university campuses. Yet, whenever Christians or other people of faith seek to express views on an issue, they are not protected under the same academic freedom argument. They are, as we have already seen, either silenced by the school's "tolerance" or "diversity" speech codes

---

*Alan extensively cross-examined this "expert" on his views that even the most extreme forms of hardcore pornography could never be legally "obscene."

or claims of "separation of church and state," or they are thrown off campus entirely.

Professor Harris Mirkin of the University of Missouri–Kansas City published a study (funded with taxpayer money) that compared the "moral panic" about pedophilia to previous "panics" about feminism and homosexuality.[66] His article was supported by Sheldon E. Steinbach, general counsel for the American Council on Education, who said, "The appropriate place to debate the legitimacy of a professor's thought is in the marketplace of ideas . . . . *Today's heresy often becomes tomorrow's orthodoxy*" [emphasis ours].[67]

That last statement is extremely chilling but also very true. Just as homosexual behavior has now become accepted orthodoxy on many university campuses and Christians and Orthodox Jews have become the heretics, we are going down the same road with pedophilia. As the homosexual agenda continues to sexualize our culture, other once-forbidden behaviors are exalted as just more alternative lifestyles. The result is that the well-being of millions of children is at risk, along with the right of parents to protect their children from sexual exploitation.

The *Wall Street Journal* noted this when it wrote: "It is Dr. Mirkin's view, published in the Journal of Homosexuality, that the 'panic over pedophilia' is much like the way people once viewed female sexuality and homosexuality. Pedophilia, he notes, has been permissible or obligatory in some cultures in certain periods of history. We might point out that the same can be said of human sacrifice."[68]

We received a heartbreaking reminder of the dangers of the promotion of pedophilia and other deviant sexual behaviors from an e-mail we received at the Alliance Defense Fund. We must note up front that the pedophile in question here is a heterosexual (and pedophilia is not strictly limited to those who engage in homosexual behavior; however, it is prevalent). This e-mail shows how the promotion of pedophilia in academia poses a significant threat to our children, regardless of whether the abused child is a boy or a girl:

> I am writing to you today because I have had enough, and I am wondering if your organization can help! It is so hard as a parent to raise our child in a secular, increasingly sexual and violent society we live in. I am very disturbed and even angry about the trend today of publishing "scholarly" books about the topics of child-adult sex, and pedophilia. These books are published under the pretense

of furthering academic debate, yet the real goal is to legitimize sinful, deviant behavior.

I am particularly angry about the publication of *Harmful to Minors: The Perils of Protecting Children from Sex* by Judith Levine . . . . It advocates sexual relationships between children and adults. Ms. Levine says that children can handle sexual relationships, and it is the fault of the parents and the "religious right" that these relationships are not treated as healthy and natural.

One particularly disturbing thing I read in an interview with Ms. Levine discusses Internet predators. Ms. Levine claims that stories about pedophiles and sexual predators on the Internet have been overblown by the media and by parents. She claims that children can "handle the sexual chat" they might encounter online. I beg to differ.

Here in [our] area, we have had 3 children in the past 2 months who have been sexually assaulted by pedophiles first encountered on the Internet. Last night there was a tragic story on our local news about a 13-year-old girl from Katy, Texas, just outside of Houston. She met a 34-year-old man in a chat room. After a couple of weeks of what Ms. Levine would call "harmless sexual chat," this pedophile sent the little girl a one-way bus ticket to Seattle. He instructed the girl in how to remove her computer hard-drive so no one could find them together. Unfortunately, the girl chose to make the trip to Seattle. Ms. Levine would say the girl should be allowed to make this decision for herself as a sexual being. I wonder if she condones what happened next. Tragically, this girl was brutally sexually assaulted and raped over a period of five days. When she was finally able to call for help, the police rescued her. Now, police in Seattle have learned that he assaulted at least 2 other girls, 12 and 13, and was attempting to lure an 11-year-old girl to his apartment.

This little girl got on the bus of her own free will. However, I do not believe for one second that she was able to comprehend the consequences of her decision. Sick people like Ms. Levine want to push the idea that sex between a minor and an adult can be a good thing. This poor little girl will be scarred for life because of this terrible experience . . .

My greatest fear is that more pedophiles and sexual predators will use material in this book to justify their evil plans to harm children. They will say, "Look, this scholarly review says that what I am doing is OK . . . ."

This tragic story is an example of what happens to the most innocent members of our society, when homosexual behavior, pedophilia, and other sexual disorders are not only seen as normal, but are given credence by those in academia. This is where the path of acceptance of homosexual behavior in our nation's universities and academia as a whole is leading. And just as college campuses have been the first wave in societal change, what is being promoted there today will become orthodoxy in our culture tomorrow.

Therefore, not only is the religious freedom to share and live the gospel, as well as freedom of conscience, either under attack or totally denied on college campuses, the freedom for parents to protect their children from sexual predators is under assault as well. What has occurred in academia is just a microcosm of the greater goal of homosexual activists: to use the power of the government to silence and punish those who do not affirm homosexual behavior. And just as the anti-war radicals of the 1960s found their ways into the corridors of power in the 1970s and beyond, the radical homosexual activists on university campuses today have and will continue to take greater and greater roles in determining American public policy for the future.

CHAPTER FIVE

The Family under Attack

The storm that will break over America after but a single vote legalizes gay marriage will surely be a moment of decisive social reckoning. In the wake of the first legalization, the battle over gay marriage will be characterized by rapidly escalating confrontation, followed by a radical, nationwide resolution . . . As soon as even a single state legalizes same-sex marriage, the nation will be plunged into a furious legal, political, and cultural struggle. The bitter and ongoing polarization in even an exceedingly liberal state like Vermont is a clear foreshadowing of the conflict to come. As legal and political battles over traveling couples spread from state-to-state, the chaos will multiply and the courts, already inclined to mandate same-sex marriage, will grow increasingly receptive to arguments that the Full Faith and Credit Clause demands national gay marriage. And the even stronger arguments for nationally mandated gay marriage under the Constitution's equal-protection clause will also find favor in the courts.
—Stanley Kurtz, writing in National Review

What Stanley Kurtz warned about happened on November 18, 2003. When the Massachusetts Supreme Judicial Court, in a 4-3 decision, citing the Provincial Court of Ontario as a source for legal precedent, ruled that same-sex couples have a newly discovered legal right to "marry," the court radically redefined marriage for the citizens of the Commonwealth—ignoring nearly four hundred years of state and national history and stripping marriage of its core purpose of uniting men and women as the basic unit of the family. *One judge's vote has* *changed the course of history.* America's moment of reckoning had come.*

As Jeff Jacoby wrote in the *Boston Globe*, "This job of the judiciary is to interpret the law, but this was no mere interpretation. It was a wholesale rewriting of the law to make it say and mean things it had never said or meant before."[1]

Why is this battle so important? Because it goes to the very heart of God's plan for marriage and the family. When anyone tinkers with that plan, the emotional, physical, and spiritual well-being of future generations is put at severe risk.

For instance, in Europe a generation of children is growing up with no idea of what a traditional family is like. In countries such as Norway, Sweden, Iceland, and Denmark, it has been decades since many children have known what it is like to live in a traditional family with a mother and a father. More than half of the children in Europe are born to unwed mothers. In Sweden, 54 percent of all children are born out of wedlock. In Norway, the figure is 49 percent, in Denmark, 46 percent, and in Iceland, it is over 65 percent.[2] In northern Norway, the illegitimacy problem is so bad that in 2002 an astonishing 82.27 percent of children were born out of wedlock.[3] And, in America, 26.7 percent of children born to white mothers and 68.8 percent of children born to black mothers are out of wedlock.[4] Over 43 percent of all children born in America will live in a single-parent home sometime in their childhood.[5]

Why has this occurred in Europe and why is it beginning to grow in America? Much of it has to do with the years of government subsidization of single parents and now the new push for "domestic partners" for homosexual couples, which also discourages marriage for heterosexuals. According to Erik Kofod of Denmark, "Because of the social welfare systems in Scandinavia, a woman has to be stupid not to realize that she has a better situation if she is not married. It's an appalling system that motivates people to do things that are unhealthy for society and for children."[6]

But it is not only the social welfare system that has caused this problem. Same-sex "marriage" or its equivalents have increasingly cheapened marriage. The situation in Europe is important because the homosexual agenda is seeking to send us down that same path. With the growth of domestic-partner ordinances, civil unions in Vermont, and the attempts to change laws elsewhere (such as the recommendation of the American Law Institute, which played a major

---

*The same court ruled on March 21, 2004, that the state's law against incest did not apply to stepparents.

role in bringing "no-fault" divorce to state law as a great "solution" to "archaic" divorce laws), marriage is being increasingly cheapened to the point that it could soon become irrelevant.

Stanley Kurtz, who holds a doctorate in social anthropology from Harvard, has commented on this frequently. He says, "Gay marriage is part and parcel of a whole new stage of marital decline—a stage still relatively unfamiliar in the United States. In this new stage of marital decline, couples don't just cohabit before they become parents. Couples cohabit after they become parents. Because gay marriage helps to break apart the ideas of marriage and parenthood, it is closely associated with this advanced stage of marital decline."

> We can win the
> freedom to marry.
> Possibly within
> five years.
> —Evan Wolfson, Lambda
> Legal Defense and
> Education Fund

Kurtz adds,

The National Swedish Social Insurance Board recently convened a panel in which two legal experts recommended changes in Swedish family law. One invoked same-sex parenting to argue for legal recognition of three- and even four-parent families. According to this scholar, the antiquated two-parent standard virtually forces lesbian couples to find anonymous sperm donors, rather than form a more complex family with, say, gay sperm donors with whom they feel close. The polyamory movement has reached Sweden, and there are now Swedes who would seize on triple or quadruple parenting to usher in legalized polyamory . . . . With so many dissolved cohabitors and gay parents, why not do away with the two-parent standard altogether? So as Sweden combines formal gay marriage with adoption rights for same-sex couples, the dawn of quadruple parenting and polyamory looms. So much for [the] claim that formal gay marriage will reinforce the link between marriage and parenthood.[7]

Marriage and the family are under attack by homosexual activists and their allies, both in America and internationally. At a conference at the University of London called "Legal Recognition of Same-Sex Marriage: A Conference on National European and International Law," one of the main themes of discussion was whether marriage should exist at all. The attendees laid out strategies to circumvent each nation's democratic process via the judicial system to force their governments to sanction and accept same-sex marriage. There was also discussion about ultimately abolishing marriage so adults could be free to pursue any sexual relationship they want with no legal restrictions whatsoever.[8]

Parts of Europe have already proceeded well down the road to the abolition of marriage. Same-sex marriage is already legal in the Netherlands,[9] and many other European countries have some sort of formal recognition of same-sex couples. In January 2003, Belgium joined the Netherlands to officially recognize same-sex marriages.[10] In April 2004, Spain's new socialist government announced that it also plans to legalize homosexual "marriages."[11]

In Norway, the nation's finance minister, Per-Kristian Foss, "married" his homosexual partner via a "partnership," which means that they have "almost the same legal rights as married heterosexual couples" but not the title.[12]

In Germany, a similar partnership law was passed. The first lesbian couple to take advantage of the law, Angelika and Gudrun Pannier, dressed themselves in black tuxedos and white bow ties. They exchanged rings and ended their ceremony with a kiss. Angelika said, "It is a great honor to be Germany's first lesbian couple to have a legal partnership. It is very exciting. It is also very important to have my family beside us on this great step for civil and human rights . . . . There is still a lot more to do, but it is the first step."[13]

Finally, Europe's top court recently ruled that all laws that do not recognize transsexual marriages are in violation of European law. The court's decision applies to all members of the European Union.[14]

These steps are just a precursor to the wholesale destruction of marriage. Domestic-partner polices and partnerships eventually weaken the institution of marriage for heterosexuals. In 1999, David Frum wrote vividly about how "civil solidarity pacts" had undermined marriage in France. His words have chilling repercussions for America as we start to head down the same path:

> [France created] a new legal status for homosexuals, analogous to marriage, but not exactly the same, called a "civil solidarity pact." Couples linked in civil solidarity pacts would file joint tax returns, receive all the welfare and employment benefits of spouses, and enjoy the inheritance rights of husbands and wives. . . . To qualify for all of these advantages, a couple would need only to appear before a court clerk and sign on the dotted line. Either partner could end the pact by providing three months' notice in writing. . . .
>
> Such pacts are obviously very convenient things, and it rapidly became evident that one way to mitigate political opposition to them was to make them available to just about everybody. After two years of haggling, the benefits

of the pacts have been extended to cohabiting heterosexual couples, to widowed sisters living together, even to
priests and their housekeepers. The French have crafted a
grand new alternative to marriage, one that offers almost
all of marriage's legal benefits and imposes many fewer of
its legal obligations. Given French society's already growing distaste for the institution of marriage (about a million
French heterosexual couples live together unwed), there is
every reason to expect the new pact gradually to crowd out
and replace marriage. It's a familiar story in the history of
the evolution of law. Once upon a time, a contract became
a contract only if it was sealed with wax in an elaborate
ceremony. Then courts began to recognize less formal written and oral contracts as nearly equally binding, and soon
the old form disappeared.

In this case, however, the disappearance of the old form
imposes consequences on innocent third parties: children.
Already, 40 percent of France's children are born outside
marriage. The cohabiting couples who have these children may imagine that they are providing their children a
home just as stable as that provided by marriage, but they
are deluding themselves. In France, as everywhere else, the
average cohabitational relationship lasts about five years.
Apologists for cohabitation praise it as a less burdensome
alternative to marriage; the truth is that it is a near-certain
prelude to fatherlessness.

What has all of this to do with gay marriage?
Everything. The argument over gay marriage is only incidentally and secondarily an argument over gays. What it is
first and fundamentally is an argument over marriage.
Unless a government is sufficiently powerful and disdainful
of religion to crush the objections of the local churches—
and few governments are—gay marriage will turn out in
practice to mean the creation of an alternative form of legal
coupling that will be available to homosexuals and heterosexuals alike. Gay marriage, as the French are vividly
demonstrating, does not extend marital rights; it abolishes
marriage and puts a new, flimsier institution in its place.

The gay marriage argument is only the latest round in
an argument over marriage and the family that began some
35 years ago. It pits defenders of marriage against those
who condemn it as stultifying and oppressive. It pits the

wishes of adults against the needs of children, the urgings
of the self against the obligations of family. As such, the
argument is a much more evenly matched battle than a
gay-straight fight would ever be. The battle has been lost in
France and Scandinavia. It is well on the way to being lost
in Britain and Canada. And it is very much in danger of
being lost in the United States.[15]

Radical homosexual activists recognize that domestic-partner policies, civil unions, and so forth will eventually destroy the institution of
male-female marriage. Chris Crain, writing in the homosexual newspaper the *New York Blade,* acknowledged this: "In
the English-speaking world, the faux marriages
have been called 'domestic partnerships.' In
France, they're called *Pacte civil de solidarite,* or
PACS . . . . The effect on 'traditional marriage' has
been dramatic. In France, where PACS first
became available in 1999, some 14,000 couples
signed up the first year, and almost half of them
heterosexual . . . . Back in the States, many heterosexual couples are also choosing domestic
partnership [DP] over marriage for many of the
same reasons."[16]

> *For the children, it*
> *makes no difference*
> *whether their*
> *parents are married*
> *or not. Traditional*
> *family values are not*
> *important to us*
> *anymore. They are*
> *something we do*
> *research on,*
> *like a fossil.*
>
> —Ebba Witt-Brattstroem,
> Stockholm University
> professor of comparative
> literature

France is not the only country that has seen
this trend. In 1970, less than 5 percent of live
births were outside of marriage. When the first
court challenge to traditional marriage occurred
there, the rate was approximately 12 percent. In 1991, when same-
sex couples were allowed to symbolically "register" as "married" couples, the rate was still approximately the same. Then rates started to
skyrocket. In 1997, Dutch same-sex couples were allowed to officially "register" with the state. At that point, approximately 18 percent of all births were to unwed couples. Three years later, same-sex
"marriage" was legalized, and the rate had risen to approximately 25
percent. In the three years after the legalization of same-sex marriage,
the rate increased from approximately 25 percent to 31 percent.
There is a trend happening here.[17]

Syndicated columnist Suzanne Fields asked the rhetorical question, "Will heterosexuals consider civil unions, too? It's difficult
enough for the confirmed bachelor to commit to a woman already.
Might he seek a lesser commitment as something desirable, avoiding
the expensive divorce courts where half the marriages end?"[18]

Gene Edward Veith, who writes for *World* magazine, summed up the consequences for American society if marriage continues to be redefined and devalued:

> Under the emerging framework, there will be no difference between a married couple, a homosexual couple, or a couple in a temporary sexual relationship. As many advocates are putting it, "What difference does it make to the government or an employer whom you are having sex with?" This sort of reductionism—a spouse is nothing more than a sex partner, so a sex partner is the same as a spouse—misses the point of what marriage is and what its role in society amounts to. . . . So far, governments are resisting same-sex marriages. But instead, marriage is being defined down. As marriage becomes unnecessary—not just for job benefits but for adopting children, inheriting property, and being socially acceptable—the whole nation will be "living in sin."[19]

Radical homosexual activists readily acknowledge that the redefinition of marriage is just a tool in their greater agenda to reorder society. While they will not admit it, children are just pawns to be used as they strive for total acceptance of their behavior. Consider this quote from Evan Wolfson, former president of the Lambda Legal Defense and Education Fund, a leading lobbying and legal action group for homosexual marriage: "We can win the freedom to marry . . . . We can seize the terms of the debate, tell our diverse stories, engage the non-gay persuadable public, enlist allies, work the courts and the legislatures in several states, and achieve a legal breakthrough within five years. I'm talking about not just any legal breakthrough but an actual change in the law of at least one state, ending discrimination in civil marriage and permitting same-sex couples to lawfully wed. *This won't just be a change in the law either; it will be a change in society. For if we do it right, the struggle to win the freedom to marry will bring much more along the way*" [emphasis added].[20]

George W. Dent Jr., writing in *The Journal of Law and Politics*, writes that once same-sex marriage is affirmed, then other forms of "marriage" will quickly be affirmed as well, such as polygamy, endogamy (the marriage of blood relatives), bestiality, and child marriage.[21] In fact, the policy guide of the American Civil Liberties Union calls for the legalization of polygamy, stating, "The ACLU believes that criminal and civil laws prohibiting or penalizing the practice of plural marriage violate constitutional protections of freedom of expression and association, freedom of religion, and privacy for personal relationships among consenting adults."[22]

Acting in lock-step with homosexual activists, the *New York Times*, *St. Louis Post-Dispatch*, and *Boston Globe* recently agreed to add announcements of same-sex "unions" to their wedding announcement page. According to the Gay and Lesbian Alliance Against Defamation (GLAAD), more than 135 papers now run such announcements.[23]

Once marriage is redefined for same-sex partners, it opens the Pandora's box to be redefined for any assortment of individuals. After all, if two men or two women have the right to be married, why not two men and three women, or two men, one woman, and a dog and a chimpanzee?

Redefining Monogamy

The argument to redefine *monogamy* is already being advanced by Marvin Ellison, a so-called "gay theologian" at the United Church of Christ's Bangor (Maine) Seminary. Ellison, an ordained PCUSA pastor, states that threesomes and foursomes should be considered for "marriage," as well as bisexuals. In fact, he ventures that perhaps marriage should be abolished all together (which we will see later is the ultimate goal of radical homosexual activists).

Ellison, who was married to a woman but then left her for a homosexual partner because in his words his marriage was not "user-friendly," says, "How exactly does the number of partners affect the moral quality of a relationship? Could it be that limiting intimate partnerships to only two people at a time is no guarantee of avoiding exploitation?" He adds that it is "troubling" that ethicists would see "marriage is a necessary social control mechanism to tame men's sexuality."[24]

One of the first recipients of a same-sex "marriage" license in Massachusetts, Joseph Yarbrough openly proclaimed his "open marriage," saying, "I think it's possible to love more than one person and have more than one partner, not in the polygamist sense. In our case it is, we have, an open marriage."[25]

University of Chicago law professor Elizabeth Emens has stated that our country should "rethink" its opposition to multiple sex partners as equal to marriage. In her book, *Monogamy's Law: Compulsory Monogamy and Polyamorous Existence*, she states that resistance to polyamory (loving more than one person in a multiple person group) "may merely be an artifact of historical associations with patriarchal polygyny . . ." She adds that we should rewrite our marriage laws dealing with adultery to permit consensual extra-marital relationships. Emens has done pro bono work for the Lesbian and Gay Immigration Rights Task Force.[26]

The *San Francisco Chronicle* reported that polyamorists are already jumping on the same-sex "marriage" bandwagon to push for marital rights of their own. "Polyamory is never having to say you've broken up," said Sally Amsbury, who shares her sex life with her husband and what she called her two "significant others." Amsbury added she is bisexual, her husband is heterosexual, and her two "significant others" are bisexual. One of her "significant others" lives in West Hollywood with his boyfriend, and the other, named Conly, lives in Santa Rosa, California. "I wear a wedding ring for my husband and a bracelet for Conly," she explained.

Jasmine Wallace, president of Unitarian Universalists for Polyamory Awareness, added, "Polyamory is not an alternative to monogamy. It's an alternative to cheating. For some of us, monogamy doesn't work, and cheating was just abhorrent to me."[27]

In Utah, a civil rights attorney has filed a lawsuit challenging the state's ban on polygamy. The ACLU's Utah executive director said that the state would "have to step up to prove that a polygamous relationship is detrimental to society . . . the model of the nuclear family as we know it in the immediate past is unique, and may not be necessarily the best model. Maybe it's time to have this discussion."[28]

The polygamists' attorney added, "It doesn't bother anyone, (and with) no compelling state interest in what you do in your own home with consenting adults, you should be allowed do so (engage in polygamy)."[29]

These examples show one place homosexual activists and their allies want to go with the redefinition of monogamy. The concept of marriage for many homosexuals is radically different from what God designed and what many Americans have held as the commonly held view of how one is to conduct oneself in a marital relationship. Lesbian writer Camille Paglia, hardly a friend of those who hold biblical values, wrote the following about monogamy and same-sex marriage: "After a period of optimism about the long-range potential of gay men's one-on-one relationships, gay magazines are starting to acknowledge the more relaxed standards operating here, with recent articles celebrating the bigger bang of sex with strangers or proposing 'monogamy without fidelity'—the latest Orwellian formulation to excuse having your cake and eating it too."[30]

Openly homosexual author Andrew Sullivan has admitted that most homosexuals' "understanding of the sexual commitment in a marriage is considerably broader that what nearly all heterosexual couples would tolerate."[31] He added that homosexuals have a "need for extramarital outlets" and therefore same-sex marriage will make adultery more acceptable for all married couples.[32] So every heterosexual husband who has ever been tempted to stray can argue, based on this logic, that he was just practicing "monogamy without fidelity" and meeting his "need for extramarital outlets" and therefore did not violate his marriage vows when he committed adultery.

In a study done by researchers at the University of Vermont (funded by the pro-homosexual Gill Foundation), this redefinition of marriage comes into sharper focus. In the study, conducted by UVM psychologists Dr. Esther D. Rothbaum and Dr. Sondra E. Solomon, of married heterosexual couples, homosexual couples who had entered into a "civil union," and homosexual couples that had not entered into such a union, they found the following: While 79 percent of married heterosexual felt that non-monogamy was wrong, only 34 percent of homosexual men not in civil unions and 50 percent in civil unions thought it was wrong to engage in non-monogamous sexual behavior. More than 50 percent of civil union couples said that they entered into the union to make a political statement. One other interesting note: lesbians in the study made $15,000 more than married heterosexual women in the workforce.[33]

In an ADF-funded case over child custody between a Christian heterosexual mother and her former spouse, an activist homosexual and his partner, the homosexual testified that he was "monogamous." On cross-examination he explained this as meaning that he and his partner were committed and faithful to each other, but Thursday night was "date night" when they would go to locations such as a bar and seek out a casual sex partner for that one evening, one time.

As one observer of the homosexual movement has warned, "Gay activists are sexual Marxists. Legitimizing same-sex unions is a warm-up act. Ultimately they want to eliminate any barriers, any signposts, that limit or channel the exercise of human sexuality."[34]

It actually seems that the more radical the homosexual activist, the more blatantly honest they are of their goals. They do not necessarily want marriage so that they can take advantage of its benefits. They want marriage so they can take a wrecking ball to the institution itself.

For example, homosexual activist William Eskridge says that he hopes gay marriage "will dethrone the traditional family based on blood relationships in favor of families we choose."[35] Michelangelo Signorile has told activists "to fight for same-sex marriage and its benefits, and then, once granted, redefine the institution of marriage completely . . . to debunk a myth and radically alter an archaic institution. . . . The most subversive action lesbians and gay men can undertake . . . is to transform the notion of 'family' entirely."[36] This means marriage will be no better than anonymous sodomy in a bathhouse.

The first bond of society is marriage.
—Cicero

Lesbian activist Barbara Cox wrote, "Yes, we must be aware of the oppressive history that weddings symbolize. We must work to ensure that we do not simply accept whole cloth an institution that symbolizes the loss and harm felt by women. But I find it difficult to understand how two lesbians, standing together openly and proudly, can be seen as accepting that institution? What is more anti-patriarchal and rejecting of an institution that carries the patriarchal power imbalance into most households than clearly stating that women can commit to one another with no man in sight? With no claim of dominion or control, but instead equality and respect. I understand the fears of those who condemn us for our weddings, but I believe they fail to look beyond the symbol and cannot see the radical claim we are making."[37]

In his excellent article, "The End of Marriage in Scandinavia," Stanley Kurtz talks about the observations of Danish homosexual social theorist Henning Bech and Norwegian sociologist Rune Halvorsen. According to Kurtz, "Bech, perhaps Scandinavia's most prominent gay thinker, dismisses as an 'implausible' claim that gay marriage promotes monogamy. He treats the 'conservative case' (that same-sex 'marriage' will bring stability and monogamy to homosexual relationships) as something that served chiefly tactical purposes during a difficult political debate. According to Halvorsen, many of Norway's gays imposed self-censorship during the marriage debate, so as to hide their opposition to marriage itself. The goal of the gay marriage movements in both Norway and Denmark, say Halvorsen and Bech, was not marriage but social approval for homosexuality."[38]

In fact, as homosexual couples staged rallies in support of same-sex "marriage," more radical homosexual activists expressed disgust at the actions of their colleagues. They would rather see marriage abolished all together. James Wagner, a longtime gay activist, said,

"Marriage is a way that government exerts social control. I'm uncomfortable supporting it. I'm interested in changing society, not assimilation."[39] Another homosexual activist, named William Dobbs, added, "Our movement has become about lusting for weddings and lavender picket fences. It's so embarrassing. I feel like turning in my gay card."

Patrick Moore, another homosexual writer, said: "Marriage is a problematic goal in terms of gay sexuality . . . the monogamous ideal enshrined in marriage is a challenge regardless of one's sexual orientation. . . . Careful polling would help answer the question of whether marriage is even a widely shared goal within the gay community . . . . In redefining what it means to be gay in America, the gay community itself is on the verge of marginalizing those who refuse to conform to a system of heterosexual morality."[40]

In New York State, Assemblywoman Deborah Glick (D-Manhattan) introduced legislation that would remove all references to marriage from the state Domestic Relations Law and turn all marriages into "civil unions." Glick said that religious and civil unions could still be called "marriages" under her proposed legislation, but the word *marriage* would no longer have any legal standing.[41]

Despite these dissident voices in the homosexual activist movement, the majority of homosexual activists continue to march to the same drum of pushing for same-sex "marriage." And once marriage and monogamy are redefined, they both become insignificant. It is the goal of radical homosexual activists to redefine both, and end up with a situation like parts of Europe where both marriage and the family have become meaningless.

Not surprisingly, one of the main benefits that homosexual activists see in getting married is the chance to get a "clean divorce." Jo Ann Citron, a Boston lawyer, said, "The single most important thing you get with marriage is divorce, a predictable process by which property is divided, debt is apportioned, and arrangements are made for custody and visitation of children."[42]

Meanwhile much of the Church of Jesus Christ remains either confused or apathetic. According to an April 2004 poll by Greenberg Quinlan Rosner Research, Inc., of Washington, D.C., 52 percent of evangelicals oppose a federal marriage amendment that would define marriage to be between one man and one woman.[43] They said that the matter of same-sex "marriage" should be left up to the states despite the fact that the Full Faith and Credit Clause of the U.S. Constitution requires that states honor marriages performed in other states, unless the state has passed a Defense of Marriage Act (DOMA). For example, if you were married in Arizona, you are also legally married in Colorado if you move there and are entitled to the same rights married couples enjoy in Colorado. DOMAs prevent homosexuals from exporting same-sex marriages (if legalized) created in one state to other states.

But homosexual activists know if a Federal Marriage Amendment is passed, the rest of their agenda is in trouble. Cheryl Jacques, the new head of the Human Rights Campaign, said, "If the Constitution is changed, then every arena where we're making progress—from the courts to corporate America—is shut down."[44]

Legal Attacks on Marriage

ADF trained attorneys have supplied legal assistance related to several state legislatures drafting and passing DOMAs. When homosexual activists make their claim that DOMAs are unnecessary, they are preying on people's ignorance of this constitutional provision. They will say things like "No one is trying to push for same-sex marriage in Ohio." But they know that once one state recognizes same-sex marriage, a same-sex couple can get married in that state and then can return to their home state. The home state will be forced to recognize the couple's union because of the Full Faith and Credit Clause. DOMAs are designed to prevent states from being forced to recognize same-sex marriages from other states or those entered into in a foreign nation. This is important because of Holland's and Belgium's legalization of same-sex marriage.[45]

Though there are many legal battles to redefine marriage, Christians have been able, by God's grace, to stymie many of the efforts. Here are just a few examples:

Alaska

When homosexual activists pushed for same-sex marriage in our forty-ninth state, ADF played a proactive role to stop their efforts. We brought together key lawyers and academics to formulate arguments to counter the demands put forth by the homosexual activist community. When the Anchorage Superior Court in Alaska handed down a decision in favor of same-sex marriage on February 28, 1998, an ADF trained and funded attorney, Kevin Clarkson, immediately filed on behalf of the Alaska Senate an appeal to the Alaska Supreme Court. Through his tireless efforts, Kevin and other family advocates were able to assist in preparing and supporting adoption of the legal language for an amendment barring same-sex marriage through the state's legislature. They then sued the lieutenant governor, who had tried to create ballot obstacles, and defeated the effort to keep the amendment off the Alaskan ballot (the ACLU and homosexual groups were unsuccessful in their lawsuits to get the amendment removed from the ballot). After a resounding 2-1 victory at the ballot box, ADF was heavily involved in post-election efforts to defeat legal challenges with which the homosexual activists and their allies attempted to thwart the will of the people.

After the Alaska vote, then ACLU executive director Ira Glasser showed his own personal contempt for the "will of the people" when it comes to objections to the homosexual agenda. He stated, "Today's results prove that certain fundamental issues should not be left up to majority vote."[46]*

Arizona

ADF represented a state representative in Arizona courts against an attempt by two homosexual men to have the state's DOMA declared unconstitutional. After a lower court ruling affirming the DOMA law, the two men appealed to the Supreme Court, which without comment, rejected their appeal.

Hawaii

ADF funded last-minute legal work before the November 1998 election to help defend traditional marriage in the Aloha State. After the ballot result allowing legislation in favor of traditional marriage, ADF played a key role in funding the postelection litigation to ensure that a "win remained a win" for those who believe in the traditional role of marriage between one man and one woman.

Indiana

Indiana law recognizes that marriage is only to be between one man and one woman. However, three same-sex couples who had obtained Vermont "civil unions" had come back to the state and demanded a marriage license.

Judge S. K. Reid of the Marion Superior Court Civil Division ruled that same-sex couples are biologically and legally different from one man-one woman unions and, therefore, the court cannot allow them to "marry."

---

*Sean Haley, executive director of the Boston chapter of GLSEN, has also added: "[Same-sex 'marriage'] is a tremendously sensitive issue. This is an area around civil rights and human rights that may not be appropriate for a majority vote." See Robert Bluey, "Massachusetts Court Set to Hear Homosexual Marriage Case," CNSNews.com, February 13, 2003.

The judge's decision affirmed traditional marriage by stating that:

- Traditional marriage between one man and one woman *"promotes the state's interest in encouraging procreation to occur in a context where both biological parents are present to raise the child. . . . Same-sex couples are not similarly situated with opposite-sex couples who cannot reproduce because same-sex couples can never reproduce on their own as a categorical matter."*

- Maintaining marriage between one man and one woman *"vindicates the related interest in promoting the traditional family as the basic living unit of a free society."*

- The court said that because of *"the history of traditional marriage as a critical component of Western Civilization, it is rational for the [Indiana] General Assembly to recognize opposite-sex marriage in order to promote traditional families as the bedrock of society. Same-sex marriage has not played a similar historical role."*

ADF staff attorney Glen Lavy, working with ADF's allied attorneys, provided important assistance on this case.

Vermont

While we cannot claim total victory in Vermont, many believe ADF's support was instrumental in keeping the Vermont Supreme Court from forcing same-sex marriage on the people of that state. ADF assembled the team writing the legal briefs and helped to fund appropriate private assistance in support of the state attorney general as he prepared the state's brief. We believe that without such assistance, the Vermont Supreme Court, or later the legislature, could have mandated the legalization of full-blown same-sex marriage. While we are far from pleased with the compromise the court reached—of ordering the legislature to adopt what became civil unions—the outcome could have been much worse without ADF's intervention.

Interestingly, as our lawyers predicted, most of the Vermont civil unions have not been for Vermont residents, but for out-of-state homosexual couples, who then hope to go back to their own states and try to force them to recognize their civil unions. As of October 13, 2002, there have been 4,371 civil unions, with the majority coming from outside of Vermont. Lesbians represent 66 percent of all unions to date. Sixty-three percent of civil unions "partners" have graduated from college.[47]

New Jersey

New Jersey, site of a 2003 challenge, does not have the protection of a DOMA. Homosexual activists have sued for marital rights in the state with the knowledge that the Supreme Court in that state is very sympathetic to so-called gay rights. (It is the same court that had ruled against the Boy Scouts.)

Sally Goldfarb, a professor at Rutgers University, said, "New Jersey has a long tradition of willing to be forward-looking and progressive, and looking to the state constitution to recognize new rights. The fact that New Jersey family law already recognizes same-sex relations as legitimate in several areas lends support to the position that there is no justification for denying same-sex couples complete access to marriage."[48]

Bill Duncan of the Marriage Law Project added, "There are a number of people who are very upset about what's going on [the legal push for same-sex marriage], but none of those people are on any of the courts in New Jersey."[49]

Unfortunately, the legal battle is not going well beyond America's shores. In Australia, a couple had their marriage declared valid by a family court after one of the individuals, a female-to-male transsexual, was declared a man by the court. The judge in this case said there was no pervasive reason to assume for the purposes of marriage that "if a person is male or female at birth, the person must be male or female at the date of the marriage."[50]

In October 2003, a lower court ruled in favor of traditional marriage, but the battle has just begun in New Jersey.*

Massachusetts

As mentioned earlier, the Massachusetts Supreme Judicial Court ruled in favor of same-sex marriage in the case of *Goodridge v. Massachusetts Department of Health*.[51] The writing on the wall is now clear: we can now expect a series of legal challenges from homosexual activists in every state to force same-sex "marriage" on the American public. And sure enough, same-sex "marriage" battles started to be waged across America after the Massachusetts decision.

One of the most outrageous aspects of this decision was the actions of Massachusetts State Supreme Court Chief Justice Margaret Mitchell. Mrs. Mitchell has been a friend of homosexual advocacy

---

*ADF was also successful in defending traditional marriage in Arizona when two homosexual men tried to use the U.S. Supreme Court's *Lawrence v. Texas* decision to legally impose same-sex marriage on the state. A lower court quickly ruled against them.

groups for quite some time. In 1999, she delivered the keynote speech (as an associate justice) to the Massachusetts Lesbian and Gay Bar Association. In her speech, she cited the "growing body of gay-friendly international jurisprudence," and in fact, *international law* (from the Canadian province of Ontario) was cited in the majority opinion in favor of same-sex "marriage."[52]

It is interesting to note that liberal groups have demanded that U.S. Supreme Court Justice Antonin Scalia recuse himself from numerous High Court cases because of speaking engagements he has done for conservative groups, but they are strangely silent when liberal justices address or socialize with homosexual advocacy groups.

The Election of 2004

November 2, 2004, was a great day for traditional marriage in America. In eleven states, citizens went to the polls to vote overwhelmingly to adopt state constitutional amendments that define marriage as between one man and one woman.* In all eleven states, the amendments passed, with margins of victory ranging from 86 percent to 57 percent.[53] ADF provided legal support in four states (Arkansas, Georgia, Ohio, and Oklahoma) to help stop homosexual activists and their allies from keeping these amendments off the ballot. Just weeks earlier, voters in two other states, Missouri and Louisiana (after ADF helped win court battles to keep the amendments on the ballot), voted by large margins for marriage. Advocates of homosexual behavior didn't want Americans to vote on the issue, and once they do, the radicals want to make their votes meaningless. ADF has been called upon to defend challenges to the amendments in several states.

Many secular commentators said that the same-sex "marriage" issue was pivotal in providing the margin of victory for President

> *And turning marriage into a free-form institution is good for children? Calling any relationship a marriage makes marriage less attractive by making it exclusive. We want men and women to marry because— after our 30-year experiment with single parenting—we understand that children need both a mother and a father. Even Heather with her 'two mommies' needs to know this is not the family society sanctions. The it-hurts-the-children argument is a smoke screen. Activists want their lifestyle validated regardless of the social costs.*
> —Don Feder, syndicated columnist

---

*The states were Arkansas, Georgia, Kentucky, Michigan, Mississippi, North Dakota, Montana, Ohio, Oklahoma, Oregon, and Utah.

Bush in Ohio—the state that ended up deciding the presidential election.[54] Many of these victories came despite the tremendous amount of resources spent by homosexual activists and their allies to defeat these amendments. In Kentucky, homosexual activists outspent pro-marriage groups by almost $300,000 and still lost by a 4-1 margin.[55] In Missouri, those who advocate homosexual behavior had outspent pro-marriage forces by a margin of nearly 40-1, and still lost 71 to 29 percent.[56]

Despite these incredible results, it is critical that those who believe in marriage as between one man and one woman stay engaged in the battle. Those who seek to redefine marriage are not going to give up and go away. They are already plotting strategies to "frame their issue" so it connects with "Middle America."[57] In addition, they will continue to file lawsuits challenging the will of the people, such as they did in Louisiana and Georgia almost immediately after the amendments were passed in those states.[58] Americans who believe in the sanctity of marriage between one man and one woman will need to remain vigilant and involved in the months and years ahead, as those who advocate same-sex "marriage" will not be deterred in their efforts to reshape the American family.

Beyond Our Shores

In England, it was reported that three members of the House of Lords had given permission to a male-to-female transsexual to appeal a court decision that had ruled that his marriage to a man twenty-one years ago was not valid. The *Scotsman* reported that Elizabeth Ballinger had taken his case to the House of Lords after his marriage had been ruled void by lower courts. Those courts had ruled that the terms "male" and "female," which are assigned at birth, could not be altered. Dame Elizabeth Butler-Sloss, head of England's Family Division, said that the case "highlighted a human problem" and the court was "very much aware of the plight of those who, like the appellant, are locked into the medical condition of transsexualism."[59]

In Ontario, Canada, the Superior Court ruled that prohibiting homosexual couples from marrying violated the province's Charter of Rights and Freedoms. Much like what happened in Vermont, the court suspended the decision for two years for Parliament to "remedy" the situation. Ontario Premier Ernie Eves clearly sided with homosexual activists when he said, "If two people decide that they want to be in a union, why would I interfere with that?"[60] Ontario's Commissioner of Human Rights has subsequently called for measures to force all private schools in the province to stop teaching that marriage is reserved for a man and a woman.[61]

In the Canadian province of Quebec, legislation was passed that created a civil union registry for same-sex and opposite-sex couples. The new law extends most marital benefits to unmarried couples and allows an easy withdrawal from the relationship, further cheapening marriage (only a notarized signature is needed).[62]

To illustrate the instability of same-sex "marriages," two lesbians filed for "divorce" less than a year after the Ontario court granted the "right" to same-sex "marriage." The couple "separated" just five days after their "marriage." Ontario Premier Dalton McGuinty said, "We certainly support same-sex marriages and logically what flows from that are divorces."[63]

All of this is empowering homosexual activists in the U.S. Evan Wolfson had this to say about Canada and its effect on our country: "The future is clearly the Canadian way. The United States cannot lag behind its major trading partner, the nation with the longest common border, its closest internationally. With the increasing trade and travel between the two nations, how can we avoid going the same direction?"[64]

Lambda Legal Defense and Education Fund has already attempted to force corporations in the United States to recognize same-sex "marriages" in Canada. When a retired Prudential Financial employee "married" her lesbian partner in Canada, Lambda challenged Prudential's decision not to extend medical benefits it provides to other retired employees to the "spouse." Lambda has also written a guide called "We Got Married in Canada, What's Next?" to equip same-sex "couples" to challenge corporations and local and state governments to recognize their "unions."[65]

The Pretense of Tolerance Is Over

In the days leading up to World War II, Winston Churchill, in a speech to the Royal Academy, said, "No large organization can long continue without a strong element of authority and respect for authority."[66]

On Valentine's Day weekend 2004, San Francisco Mayor Gavin Newsom, in open defiance of the rule of law, ordered his county clerk to issue "marriage" licenses to same-sex couples despite the state law Proposition 22, passed by the voters in 2000, that defines marriage as between one man and one woman. Eventually, nearly four thousand same-sex "couples" were issued "marriage" licenses and were "married" by government officials.[67]

If taken to its logical conclusion, this open contempt for authority and the rule of law could lead to social anarchy where no laws are worth the paper they are printed on. The words of Churchill would become prophetically real for America.

ADF and its allies immediately sprung into action to stop the unlawful actions of Mayor Newsom's county clerk. ADF attorneys were literally shuttling back and forth to San Francisco on an almost daily basis, as well as spending late night after late night as other open challenges to marriage—spurred on by Mayor Newsom's actions—started to rear their heads in Oregon, Washington, New Mexico, and North Carolina—to name only a few of the many states where homosexual activists went on a full-court press for same-sex "marriage."* After a series of frustrating setbacks in the courtrooms of San Francisco, ADF filed a direct action in the California State Supreme Court, on behalf of California taxpayers, and the High Court eventually halted—in a 7-0 vote—the issuance of the invalid licenses. They set a two-hour oral argument to determine the legal validity of the "licenses" on May 25, 2004.

On that day, ADF senior counsel Jordan Lorence appeared before the California State Supreme Court to defend state law and argue that the so-called "licenses" be declared invalid. Jordan noted that if an elected official can defy or ignore one law, then all other laws are in jeopardy. Within thirty seconds of her opening statement, opposing counsel Therese Stewart (a lesbian), the deputy city attorney for the city and county of San Francisco, found herself grilled by Chief Justice Ronald George on this very point. Even a liberal court in a liberal state was not going to buy the argument that an elected official can openly defy the law.

On August 12, 2004, the California Supreme Court agreed with Jordan's arguments, and in a 7-0 decision ruled that the mayor of San Francisco had overstepped his authority when he directed the city and county clerk to issue the "marriage" licenses. In addition, the court, in a 5-2 decision, declared the licenses that had been issued to be invalid because the mayor had no authority to issue them.

According to Newsom, his "marriage" decision was made on the spur of the moment when he heard President Bush express support for the Federal Marriage Amendment during his annual State of the Union address. As events in San Francisco continued to unfold, word got out that Mayor Newsom's illegal actions were staged for political

---

*Multnomah County, in Oregon, issued more than three thousand invalid marriage licenses until they were halted in an ADF legal action on April 20, 2004.

gain, well before the president's address even occurred. The *San Francisco Chronicle* reported, "From the minute Newsom lifted the curtain with his call for gay marriage licenses, to his cross-continental debate with President Bush, Team Newsom has done its best to manage the image coming out of City Hall. . . . From day one, the 'story' was about the gay couple next door—and not the mayor as gay-rights leader. . . . The Newsom people made sure that when the mayor came out swinging against Bush's backing for a constitutional amendment banning same-sex marriage, he was standing in front of an American flag. The overall goal was to make Newsom appear the earnest young politico who—whether you agreed with him or not— was willing to take the heat for doing something he believed in. . . . 'What you saw this week,' said former Newsom campaign manager Eric Jaye, 'was the catalyst for the entire Newsom operation from day one—control.'"[68]

Writing for *National Review,* Stanley Kurtz added,

> Defiance of the law is rapidly becoming the leitmotif of the gay marriage movement . . . it's foolish to put faith in laws that supposedly prevent gay marriage in Massachusetts from spilling over into other states. When it comes to same-sex marriage, it barely matters how the law is written. Again and again, gay marriage advocates have shown themselves eager to disobey any law that would prevent the spread of gay marriage from state to state. . . . It took only a single day of legal gay marriage to reveal the worthlessness of assurances about this experiment's confinement to Massachusetts. . . . Even though same-sex marriage is legal in no other state, [Massachusetts Attorney General Thomas] Reilly would only definitively rule out marriage as the union of a man and a woman. Reilly was vague about whether marriages would be denied to residents of other states.
>
> Next came the plans for civil disobedience. . . . Town clerks in Provincetown, Worcester, and several other Massachusetts cities announced they would issue marriage licenses to out-of-state couples. Then district attorneys in several localities said they would not prosecute clerks who violated the law. . . . The mayor of Sommerville explicitly welcomed out-of-state couples. More than a third of applications in Provincetown were from out-of-state couples. Some made it clear on their applications that they had no

intention of moving to Massachusetts. . . . Events have made it clear that on the question of same-sex marriage, it's going to be all or nothing. Either we are going to have same-sex marriage everywhere, or we are going to have a Federal Marriage Amendment."[69]

I don't think lesbian, gay, bi, or trans marriage, or whatever you want to call it, is that far off. I sure didn't think I'd see it in my lifetime . . . This is cutting edge stuff. If we can do this in California, it's going to sweep across this country, and that's why all the national organizations are looking to California to see how soon we can produce this [civil unions], because it's going to move like wildfire.

—Jean Harris, executive director of California Alliance for Pride and Equality

Other homosexuals were upset that their colleagues had pushed the envelope prematurely; in particular, activists and their allies started to ignore the rule of law in San Francisco, Oregon, and other places—creating a public backlash against same-sex "marriage." Bruce Carroll, writing in the homosexual newspaper *The Washington Blade*, wrote, "The backlash over gay marriage . . . doesn't come as a surprise to me. . . . Since two-thirds of Americans oppose gay marriage, and the same percentage support legal protections for gays in the workplace, then why, I asked, are the radical gay groups forcing marriage down the throats of America at this time? . . . it wasn't the 'religious right' or President Bush who started this round in the culture war. It was us . . . we get Rosie O'Donnell who says she's getting married in front of TV cameras merely because President Bush says he's opposed to it. Well, that's one sure way for opponents to question the sincerity of the true commitment to gay marriage, isn't it?"[70]

John Derbyshire, writing for *National Review Online*, added, "Opinion pollsters only get a bare majority of respondents favoring legal homosexual *relationships*, never mind marriages. Last July (2003), for example, in a CNN/*USA Today*/Gallup poll . . . the numbers broke 48-46 on the statement: 'homosexual relations between consenting adults should or should not be legal.'"[71]

Still, homosexual activists push for same-sex "marriage," despite documented public opposition to it. It is more evidence that for many homosexual activists the pretense of "tolerance" is over. Radical homosexual activists and their allies are determined to ignore the will of the people and impose same-sex "marriage" on the American public—either through the judiciary or through the open defiance of law.

These activists are banking on an eventual wearing-down (as discussed in chap. 1) of the American public. They will keep coming back and coming back until the public is worn down, and then will get what they want. Sheila Kuehl, an openly lesbian California state senator, says, "My analysis is that the closer we get to anything that looks to people like marriage, the more reluctant they are to jump on board. But that will change. And until then, we'll just keep moving step by step on the rights we've already won."[72]

In the Best Interests of the Child?

Besides marriage, radical homosexual activists have the family, and particularly innocent, vulnerable children in their sights as well. This has been accomplished by demanding the right to adopt children. They have presented their efforts as "being [in] the best interests of children," but it is hardly that. As Don Feder said, "the best interests of the child" is a smoke screen for another way to have homosexual behavior blessed by the state.[73]

And that is exactly what is happening. The Pennsylvania Supreme Court has ruled that homosexual partners have parenting rights over their partner's children. In a 5-2 decision, the court ruled that a woman had the right to seek shared custody of and visitation rights with a child who had been born to her former lesbian lover. The ruling gave a non-parent homosexual "partner" the same right as an actual parent to have child custody and visitation after the dissolution of their relationships. Stacy Sobel, executive director of the Center for Lesbian and Gay Rights, said about the decision, "Our courts should recognize the significant role of gay and lesbian non-biological parents raising children today. . . . The court made the right decision to support the child's best interests in this case by allowing the child the opportunity to continue a relationship with both parents."[74]

In Florida, lesbian comedienne and talk show host Rosie O'Donnell lobbied for the overturning of a state law banning homosexual adoption. The cover of *Rosie* magazine proudly proclaimed, "The anti-gay law that made Rosie speak out for children," as though she was Saint Rosie coming to rescue innocent children from slaughter. An article in the magazine dealt with two homosexual men who wanted to adopt children in Florida.[75] O'Donnell's real motive? She wanted to spend some time in Florida and take her three adopted children with her from New York. And she got the all-too-willing media to go along, saying: "I called [Diane] Sawyer and said if you do an investigative piece on these two men, I would talk about my life and how it pertains to me."[76]*

O'Donnell's coming out and advocacy of homosexual adoption helped homosexual activists to move the ball several yards downfield in their quest not just for tolerance, but for acceptance and a total reordering of society as well. After her interview with Diane Sawyer, ABC News reported a new poll that showed that *for the first time* more Americans supported homosexual adoption than opposed it.[77]

But is this all in the best interests of the children? Well, according to the American Academy of Pediatrics, which has endorsed homosexual adoption, it is.[78] However, many of the pro-homosexual conclusions have again been based on sloppy research and undocumented facts.

In the book *No Basis: What the Studies Don't Tell You about Same-Sex Parenting,* researchers Robert Lerner and Althea Nagai† have refuted many of the so-called studies used to promote same-sex parenting. After analyzing forty-nine studies, they found:

- A majority of the studies examined (59 percent) failed to produce a testable hypothesis, therefore being unable to produce any sort of dependable conclusions.[79]
- Any form of academic research must have a "study group" and a "comparison group." This means that one group must study children raised in homosexual homes (i.e., the study group) and children raised in heterosexual homes (i.e., the comparison group). Yet in the forty-nine studies examined, only one used a proper study/comparison group method. Lerner and Nagai wrote: "At an absolute minimum, a study of whether parent sexual identity affects child outcomes needs a study group and a comparison group. If an independent variable is the sexual orientation of the parent, there must be at least two groups of parents, homosexual and heterosexual. Otherwise it is impossible to draw any conclusions about the possible effects of parental sexual orientation . . . 21 studies (43 percent) had no heterosexual comparison group at all. This makes them scientifically

---

*In the days following her public "coming out," the so-called Queen of Nice went on a rampage trashing everyone in her path. The publishers of *Rosie* magazine saw sales of the magazine plummet after O'Donnell's announcement but were afraid to pull the plug on the magazine in fear of Rosie screaming "homophobia." Source: Richard Johnson with Paula Froelich and Chris Wilson, "Mag Suits Fear Rosie Revenge," *New York Post,* August 12, 2002.

†Robert Lerner and Althea K. Nagai received their doctorate degrees from the University of Chicago in sociology and political science, respectively. They are currently partners in Lerner and Nagai Quantitative Consulting, a social-science research and consulting firm.

invalid from the outset."[80] In fact, one study of thirty-seven clinical cases of children raised by transsexual and homosexual parents lacked even one heterosexual comparison group.[81] Lerner and Nagai commented, "These 49 studies were conducted with control methods that are so inadequate that they cannot be relied upon for either scientific conclusions or public policy reforms."[82]

• The studies also had serious sample problems. According to Lerner and Nagai, "Publications and newsletters were also a major vehicle for recruiting homosexuals but not heterosexuals. Seventeen studies relied on gay-lesbian or feminist publications for the homosexual parent samples. In contrast, one heterosexual sample was obtained from an advertisement in a feminist newsletter (which would be sympathetic to the homosexual viewpoint) which is likely to minimize rather than maximize differences between homosexual and heterosexual respondents."[83]

Anyone who has ever taken an undergraduate class on statistics or polling of public opinion learns about the principles of proper sampling and study/comparison groups in the first two weeks. No study that does not employ these methods has any academic credibility. Despite this, these studies are dragged out time and time again to promote same-sex parenting in the legislatures and the courts.

In a column entitled "Homosexual Parenting Findings Based on Faulty Stories," syndicated columnist Maggie Gallagher challenges the assumptions and motives of advocates of homosexual adoption. In response to the American Academy of Pediatrics decision to endorse homosexual adoption, she wrote:

> Baby doctors of the world unite! The American Academy of Pediatrics has declared that same-sex parents are good for kids. . . . Are pediatricians just doing their public health duty? Are they reporting results of careful scientific studies that compare, say, health outcomes for children in the four states that permit second-person adoptions with outcomes for children in the other 46 states? No, of course not. The real issue here is not the well-being of children, but the sexual liberties of adults.
>
> What does this remind one of? Nothing so much as the urgent claims of divorce advocates in the '70s that "studies show" children of divorce do fine. An enormous amount of

damage was done before more careful research created a new scholarly consensus that in fact, marriage matters a great deal.[84]

Gallagher is right. Think back to the late 1960s and early 1970s when we were told that divorce was either beneficial for children or had little or no effect on them. Only twenty years later, in the groundbreaking studies done by Judith Wallerstein and others, did we find out the tragic results of our folly. We have now raised an entire generation of dysfunctional adults who have trouble committing to and honoring relationships because we as a nation embraced no-fault divorce.[85]

Robert Lerner, one of the authors of *No Basis*, made this parallel between homosexual parenting and the divorce movement of the '60s and '70s:

> When the divorce laws were liberalized (beginning during the late '60s, early '70s and extending through the next decade or so), it was claimed that scientific research showed that the children would not be harmed and therefore a high divorce rate would not be a problem but would free adults to self-actualize.
>
> When the findings from technically proficient studies began to appear, however, it appeared that the earlier results, which were in fact very sketchy, were totally wrong. Divorce can and does cause a good deal of harm for children caught up in it. Although this finding is now widely accepted, the new conventional wisdom does not help the many children who suffered because their parents were told that divorce was perfectly okay. Damage occurred that was not necessary and would not have occurred except for the acceptance of wishful thinking disguised as social-science evidence. In fact, the issue had never been properly studied, especially when the earlier guesstimates and summaries are compared with today's rigorous studies. If we are not careful, the same results are likely to ensue.[86]

Adults seeking to change the family and traditional sex roles to suit their own desires are using innocent children again. To intellectual elites, homosexual activists, and their allies, children are guinea pigs in a social experiment, instead of individuals that need love, care, discipline, and nurturing.

The no-fault divorce laws of the sixties and seventies left a trail of broken children. No-fault divorce did not mean "no harm." Then there were the radical feminists who tried to convince us that girls and boys were basically the same—it was the environment that made boys aggressive and athletic and girls feminine and domestic. The result? Sexually confused children who grew up to be sexually confused adults. Now, almost thirty years later, study after study, as well as good old common sense, has confirmed what God knew right from the beginning: that there are biological differences between boys and girls.[87] Obviously, we have not learned from our past mistakes. Social engineers and homosexual activists are using children as pawns again, just as those who promoted divorce and militant feminism, to push their own self-interests and agenda.

Political leaders, prominent entertainers such as Rosie O'Donnell, and the medical establishment incessantly repeat the mantra that homosexual parenting is just another form of family and is in the best interests of the children. In April 2002, a United Nations conference attempted to recognize families "in various forms" including cohabiting and homosexual couples.[88] Maria Sophia Aguirre, population and development expert at Catholic University of America said that the change would form three different types of families: nuclear, extended, and "re-organized." The last form would include homosexual couples.[89]

Former presidential candidate Al Gore and his wife Tipper donated $50,000 to the Human Rights Campaign to help its "FamilyNet" campaign promote homosexual adoption.[90] Their book, *Joined at the Heart: The Transformation of the American Family*, prominently featured homosexual "families."[91]

Dennis Prager probably put it best about the effect of these new families on children. He wrote:

This past year, *Los Angeles Family* magazine asked me to write an article making the case for the two-parent family. That a mainstream family magazine would commission such an article is quite a sign of the times. How has this happened? How has the nuclear family become controversial? It has happened because many groups and ideologies have a personal interest in denying that it is best for a child to be raised by, or even to start out life with, a father and a mother . . . . What do all these people and groups have in common? None of them is asking what is best for children. The rhetoric of rights (applied here to gays) . . . and of equality (applied here to gays and men-women) combined with a culture of not judging are all preoccupied with the adults involved, not the children. Compassion for children, a child's right to a mother and a father, their equality as human beings—these all get drowned in the sea of self-centeredness, moral confusion and misdirected compassion that denies them their right to a mom and a dad.[92]

In a later column, Prager would expand upon this argument:

Of all the arguments against same-sex marriage, the most immediately compelling is that it hurts children. If children have the right to anything, it is to begin life with a mother and father. . . . Only same-sex marriage would legally ensure that children are deprived from birth of either a mother or a father. Why, then, doesn't a child's right to begin life with a mother and father have any impact on the millions of people who either advocate same-sex marriage or can't make up their minds on the issue? Among gay activists the reason is narcissism. Though gays already have the right to raise children without an opposite-sex parent and the right to adopt children, gay activists want society to enshrine one-sex parenting with its highest seal approval—marriage. For gay activists, the fact that a child does best with a good mother and good father is of no significance (or worse, denied). All that matters is what is good for gays.[93]

Yet, in the name of rights, children continued to be used as pawns to push a radical social agenda. Here are a few examples (both international and national) of how children are getting trapped into various types of entanglements involving homosexual parents and alternative families:

- In New Zealand, the following was reported: "A lesbian told a court . . . her partner's son was better off in a two-women 'nuclear family' than with his homosexual sperm donor father. But the boy might be allowed to play footy [football] with his dad one day, the Family Court heard. The two-year-old boy is at the center of a court battle over his sperm donor dad's request to see him every second weekend and alternative holidays. . . . The mother's lesbian partner said an on-going, traditional father-son relationship was not in the boy's best interests. It would be a 'total reality change' for him to suddenly have a deeper relationship with his father, she said . . . . The mother said her son would be better off knowing his father as a donor rather than as a traditional dad."[94] The case was eventually resolved with the court giving the boy three parents—the biological mother, her lesbian partner, and the homosexual sperm donor.[95]

• In Great Britain, a study by a British think tank published a study titled "Broken Hearts: Family Decline and the Consequence for Society." It found correlations between family breakups and "child homelessness, drug abuse among the young, the physical abuse and neglect of babies and children, high rates of teenage pregnancy and a continuing cycle of broken relationships." The study was released while the House of Lords debated a bill that would have established "civil partnerships" to give homosexual and unmarried heterosexual couples the same legal rights as married couples. Report author Jill Kirby said, "We can see a sharp rise in children born out of wedlock in the U.K. The report also identifies that children born outside of marriage (including homosexual parenting situations) experience the break-up of their parents at a much faster rate than those born to married couples."[96]

• Also in England, a lesbian couple was given the same parental rights as heterosexuals after the couple's relationship had broken up. One of the women had one of the children with a man, so the child—like the young boy in New Zealand—now has three legal parents. One of the mothers stated, "To me, family is about cohesion, about bringing people up in a secure, loving, stable environment." The couple's attorney echoed the sentiment: "Family is a broad concept that has to take into account the reality of who is caring for the child, not the biology of the parents."[97]

• A deaf suburban Washington, D.C., lesbian couple said they did "everything possible" to make sure their newborn son was deaf by seeking a sperm donor for artificial insemination from a family with a long history of deafness. They wanted their family to have all the same characteristics and tried to design a baby to meet their own desires.[98] Where can this all lead?

• In New Jersey, a Sussex County Family Court ruled that two women can be listed as parents on the birth certificate of the baby that they were to give birth to in May 2003.

Homosexual activists trumpeted the decision as another victory for "the expanding definition of family."[99]

- In Canada, a lesbian couple asked a Canadian court to recognize the two of them, plus the biological father, as the legal parents of a young boy. Stanley Kurtz wrote in *National Review:* "The case . . . gives the clearest indication yet of the real impact that gay marriage will have on the American family . . . . Once parental responsibilities are parceled out to more than two people—even to someone living outside the household—it becomes that much easier for any one parent to shirk his or her responsibilities . . . . But the biggest danger here is that legalized triple parenthood opens the way to legalized polygamy or polyamory . . . . And just as gay adoption has set a legal precedent for gay marriage, so will group parenthood pave the way to group marriage . . . . Gay marriage means group marriage—which means no marriage."[100]

- In Sacramento, California, a lesbian couple created a child by combining one of the women's eggs with the sperm of an anonymous donor. The fertilized egg was then removed from the first lesbian and implanted in the other. The baby girl was then declared by a Superior Court Judge to have the two lesbians as her "natural parents." Shanon Minter, legal director for the National Center for Lesbian Rights in San Francisco, said, "Two people in a committed, monogamous relationship who are raising a child together is my definition of a family, regardless of gender. This is a new frontier."[101]

In England, homosexual and lesbian couples are teaming up to "share" babies. In one case, a lesbian named Sue decided that she wanted to have a child with her partner, Kim. Kim had had two children from a heterosexual marriage. The lesbian couple said: "We wanted the potential father to donate sperm and not have any other involvement, although we would send a photograph of the children now and then."

Sue and Kim met John, a homosexual doctor, who donated the needed sperm. Two weeks later, Sue was pregnant with a baby boy. The boy, Jack, is now two years old, and they have had a second child, a girl named Kate.

John changed his mind about being no more than a sperm donor after Jack was born. Now, John and his partner Paul have a shared custody arrangement with Sue and Kim. The children refer to John as "Daddy," Paul as "Daddy's partner," Sue as "Mummy," and Kim as "Mummy's partner." Sue concluded: "I don't think if you are brought up in a gay environment you are going to be gay. I think being gay is due to genetics. It would be interesting to see if either of the kids are gay when they grow up."[102]

Children have become pawns in a social experiment to see if they turn out deaf or if they turn out gay. The well-being of the child is denied, while the desires of the adults are exalted.

And not everything is peaches and cream in homosexual households, despite what activists would like people to think. In Akron, Ohio, two lesbian women allegedly beat their five sons, locked them in the closet, and forced them to eat animal feces. One of the boys said, "My entire life has been horrifying because of the abuse, neglect, and mistreatment that both of you have inflicted." Pictures showed the boys with ribs and collarbones protruding through the skin—while the couples' refrigerator and pantry were overflowing with food. While we readily acknowledge that horrible abuses such as this also regrettably happen in heterosexual homes, this is a side of homosexual "families" that rarely gets reported in the media.[103]*

The Alliance Defense Fund has already provided funding for a case involving child custody issues between a Christian heterosexual mother and a group of three men in various stages of sex transformation, who claimed to be a family. What concept of family will these children have once they are adults?

Then there are situations in which tolerant parents have deliberately tried to indoctrinate their children (and confuse them at the same time) with the homosexual agenda. Consider this alarming piece from *USA Today* by a tolerant parent (who writes for *Parenting* magazine and *The Sesame Workshop*) about his five-year-old daughter:

> Last spring I was sitting at the dining room table with my 5-year-old as she pondered her latest homework assignment. Bridgette's kindergarten teacher had cleverly combined a writing exercise with the class study of the calendar by asking students to draw and label pictures that rhyme with the word "May."
>
> Bridgette looked to me for help, so I began listing the possible "ay" words in the alphabet: "Ay, bay, cay, day, eay, fay, gay . . ."

---

*Posters on the Boston transit system, sponsored by the Gay Men's Health Crisis, read: "1 in 4 gay men are victims of domestic violence in their relationships."

Bridgette brightened: "Gay!" she announced. "That's it! And I know exactly what I'll draw."

Of the many times in which my young daughters have filled me with pride, this was clearly a standout. In a world that still instinctively blanches at the utterance of the word homosexual, it was uplifting to witness Bridgette, in her blissfully unjaded way, extract only joy from hearing "gay." Indeed, all she really cared about was the picture she intended to draw. And what a picture it was: two men standing side by side, both smiling wildly, with hearts drawn above their heads . . . .

I'd be falsely immodest here were I not to credit my wife and myself for trying to provide a more decent perspective for Bridgey on homosexuality. Since the beginning, Alene and I have made it a point to *stress love over gender* [emphasis ours] as the most important criterion in selecting a partner, neither omitting nor gratuitously focusing on same-sex relationships.[104]

The piece goes on to discuss her relationship with her homosexual relatives and how they are so good to little Bridgey. But the bottom line is this: What kind of view will Bridgey have of traditional marriage and gender roles if she has been taught to stress love over gender in the selection of a mate? Does that mean that if she loves her dog, she should marry it? After all, if love is more important than gender, is species really important?

As George Dent wrote in his article, "The Defense of Traditional Marriage" in *The Journal of Law and Politics*: "Some argue that love is the only valid requisite for marriage.[105] . . . Love takes many forms. C. S. Lewis distinguished family love, affection, erotic desire, friendship, and compassion.[106] All can be good, but compassion is not deemed a basis for marriage. Close relatives often love each other but cannot marry. One who is married may love a third party more than one's spouse, but one cannot marry the third party. Children can love but cannot marry. Many people love pets, but they cannot marry them. Hence, homosexual love is not the only love ineligible for marriage. Indeed, many forms of sexual love, such as pederasty, adultery, bestiality, and incest, are criminal even in states that permit homosexual acts."[107]

And what about the two children from England? What kind of image will they have of marriage, when multiple partners are raising them? These children will become increasingly confused, and the result will be even more sexual dysfunction when they become young adults.

Unfortunately, the indoctrination of schoolchildren (as discussed in chap. 3) and the continual push to force children into alternative families does not bode well for the future of marriage if these issues are allowed to go unchecked. The UCLA Higher Education Research reported that 57.9 percent of incoming college freshmen now support full recognition of same-sex marriage.[108]

It is not by coincidence that the very first thing that God created after the heavens and the earth was the family. It is his institution for the raising and nurturing of children. If we wreck what God has ordained, the generations that follow will reap the consequences of our actions. We have now learned, the painful way, that the divorce "reform" movement of the sixties started a cycle of dysfunctional relationships that is affecting future generations—leading to premarital sex,[109] out-of-wedlock births,[110] increased likelihood of dropping out of school,[111] early marriage and divorce,[112] poverty for many women, and so forth. In contrast, children who grow up well grounded in two-parent, traditional families are far more likely to have higher grades[113] and are less prone to substance abuse.[114] When the institutions of marriage and family are tinkered with, children are ultimately the losers.

Stanley Kurtz puts it best:

> In setting up the institution of marriage, society offers special support and encouragement to the men and women who together make children. Because marriage is deeply implicated in the interests of children, it is a matter of public concern. Children are helpless. They depend upon adults. Over and above their parents, children depend upon society to keep them from chaos. Children cannot articulate their needs. Children cannot vote. Yet children *are* society. They are us, and they are our future. That is why society has the right to give special support and encouragement to an institution that is necessary to the well being of children—even if it means special benefits for some, and not for others. . . . It [same-sex "marriage"] will, however, spell the end of marriage, and of the protection marriage offers to vulnerable children who cannot vote or articulate their interests. The number of children potentially endangered by the collapse of marriage is far larger than the number of gays or "polyamorists."[115]

And, if the indoctrination remains unchecked, another generation of children, following in the footsteps of generations that were socially engineered by divorce and radical feminism, will be damaged with little hope of repair.

CHAPTER SIX

The Silence (and Silencing) of the Church

[The Religious Right] is not about to admit that they just want to bash gays if they can . . . . You have to remember, Sunday after Sunday, millions of people come to church to hear their diatribes.

—Steven Green, spokesman, Americans United for the Separation of Church and State

It was a Sunday morning in early December 1989. The late Cardinal John O'Connor was just beginning his sermon in New York City's St. Patrick's Cathedral. Suddenly, shouts came from the congregation.

"You bigot, O'Connor, you're killing us," yelled one angry man. Others quickly joined him from the militant homosexual group, ACT-UP, who stretched themselves out in the aisles or chained themselves to the pews. O'Connor tried not to be flustered and went on with the service. As he continued, the police arrested forty-three protesters, carrying out on stretchers those who refused to stand. One irate individual made his way to the altar for Communion, took a wafer, and threw it on the ground.[1]

Flash forward to 1993 in Colorado Springs, Colorado. In November 1992, the voters of Colorado had passed Amendment 2 that would have denied those who practice homosexual behavior special legal privileges. The man who helped get Amendment 2 on the Colorado ballot, Will Perkins, was sitting in his normal pew at Village Seven Presbyterian Church. Just before the pastor got up to read the morning Scripture, more than a dozen radical homosexual activists leaped out of their seats among the congregation and bombarded the parishioners with condoms.[2]

In 2004, militant homosexuals—who call themselves members of the "Rainbow Sash Alliance"—attempted to block access to the Communion rail at Chicago's Holy Name Cathedral. The priests had refused to serve them Communion because of the church's biblical stand opposing homosexual behavior.[3]

These examples are just a microcosm of the war that radical homosexual activists have staged against the church. It has been a war in which the church has either totally capitulated on the issue and embraced homosexual behavior while rejecting biblical teaching, or found herself under increasing attack from inside and outside the sanctuary for taking a biblical stand on the issue.

What the Bible Says about Homosexual Behavior

Why is the battle so heated? Because for those who take their faith seriously, Scripture is very clear on this issue.

1 Corinthians 6:9–10: "Do you not know that the wicked will not inherit the kingdom of God? Do not be deceived: Neither the sexually immoral nor idolaters nor adulterers nor male prostitutes *nor homosexual offenders* nor thieves nor the greedy nor drunkards nor slanderers nor swindlers will inherit the kingdom of God" (emphasis added).

Matthew 19:4–5: "'Haven't you read,' he [Jesus] replied, 'that at the beginning the Creator "made them male and female," and said, "For this reason a man will leave his father and mother and be united to his wife, and the two will become one flesh."'"

Romans 1:24–27: "Therefore God gave them over in the sinful desires of their hearts to sexual impurity for the degrading of their bodies with one another. They exchanged the truth of God for a lie, and worshiped and served created things rather than the Creator— who is forever praised. Amen. Because of this, God gave them over to shameful lusts. Even their women exchanged natural relations for unnatural ones. In the same way the men also abandoned natural relations with women and were inflamed with lust for one another. Men committed indecent acts with other men, and received in themselves the due penalty for their perversion."

Leviticus 18:22: "Do not lie with a man as one lies with a woman; that is detestable."

1 Timothy 1:8–11: "We know that the law is good if one uses it properly. We also know that law is made not for the righteous but for lawbreakers and rebels, the ungodly and sinful, the unholy and irreligious; for those who kill their fathers or mothers, for murderers, for adulterers and perverts, for slave traders and liars and perjurers—and for whatever else is contrary to the sound doctrine that conforms to the glorious gospel of the blessed God, which he entrusted to me."

In addition to these verses, there is the passage in Genesis 19 about God's destruction of Sodom and Gomorrah (and it wasn't because of lack of hospitality as radical homosexual activists and theologically liberal churches argue) and how the men of the town attempted to have sexual relations with the angels the Lord had sent out to warn Lot of God's imminent judgment.

These verses are straightforward, and it is difficult to see how anyone could interpret them as anything different than condemning of homosexual behavior. However, as we will see shortly, theologically left-of-center churches are either in total denial about these passages or cook up theories such as the one cited above, to explain away their affirmation of homosexual behavior.

Before we launch into the issue of the church and homosexual behavior, we need to stop and make an important point. **There is no irrelevant sin in the Bible.** There is a long list of sins in the Bible, some more serious than others, but all wicked in the eyes of God who created us all to live without any sin. The Word of God is clear in its condemnation of adultery, false witness, theft, and murder, just to name a few sins. We are all sinners who deserve condemnation, and it is only because of the love and saving grace of Jesus Christ that we can be reconciled to our Father and have eternal life.*

Therefore we strongly disassociate from and condemn those who spew phrases such as "God hates fags" or picket the funeral of an AIDS victim. Such behavior is beyond contempt and only escalates the anger radical homosexual activists have for the church. Christ had compassion for the sinner, and for believers to show otherwise would be spitting on the grace that he has offered to all of us, who are sinners, through his death and resurrection.

However, we also make his death and resurrection meaningless if we cannot point a hurting individual to the love, mercy, and grace

---

*Romans 3:23–24 says, "For all have sinned and fall short of the glory of God, and are justified freely by his grace through the redemption that came by Christ Jesus."

of Christ. When Christ loved someone, like the woman caught in adultery, he did not condemn her but expressed compassion for her. He also gave her the loving admonition to "go now and leave your life of sin" (John 8:11). As followers of Jesus Christ, we cannot sit idly by while someone is trapped in sinful behavior that separates him or her from God (John 8:24). We must be able to show people their need for a relationship with Jesus Christ, which only comes through illuminating the sinfulness of their behavior that separates them from their loving God.

There is no activist movement that exists worldwide today (yet?) to legalize theft, adultery, or lying. But there is a mobilized movement that challenges God's truth on a daily basis in regard to homosexual behavior.

Affirming Everything but the Scriptures

Unfortunately, just as some in the church have shown a total lack of grace, the theologically liberal church has gone the other direction and totally capitulated on the issue without ever dealing with the sin and sorrow. Rather than helping those engaging in forbidden behavior to turn from their sin by pointing them to Christ, the theologically liberal church is providing "spiritual" cover that enables their actions and the terribly destructive results.

For a vivid example of this, consider this excerpt of an article from Great Britain:

A [British] government minister has launched an outspoken attack on church leaders in a new collection of prayers written for homosexuals. Ben Bradshaw, the Foreign Office Minister, accuses Christian leaders of "hostility" to homosexuals in a forward to a controversial anthology, which includes contributions by Church of England clergy. One prayer in the book is addressed to "the wife of my lover," another prays that the next Pope "shall be young, colored, and gay" and one contributor argues that Jesus was a homosexual. Mr. Bradshaw, who is himself gay, said that the new book would "provide strength and inspiration for those who want to celebrate their God-given sexuality in the face of continuing rejection and hostility from church leaders." There are prayers in the book for same-sex "marriages," sex changes, and "fantasy and fetish."[4]

This may seem extreme, but this is what often happens when the church chooses to affirm homosexual behavior. The result is that the Bible is rewritten, as well as the liturgy, and the church itself becomes one big celebration of homosexual behavior. The liberal church in America is well down the same path as the Church of England. Here are just a few examples:

- Liberal United Methodist ministers in Northern California held a mass wedding for same-sex couples in Sacramento.[5] Despite the fact that this is a direct violation of the church's book of discipline, Bishop Melvin Talbert (who is supportive of same-sex "marriage") turned the other way and chose to ignore the direct disobedience by these clerics to church teaching.[6]

- Another United Methodist minister refused to conduct legal marriages in her sanctuary until the denomination's ban on same-sex "marriages" was overturned. Her church describes itself as "a community of faith of about 200 members from diverse backgrounds exploring together the many ways of understanding God . . . celebrating the gifts of all persons regardless of sexual orientation or gender identity. . . . We honor a diversity of theological expression, and use both feminine and masculine images of God. . . . [Our creed is a] diversity of theological expressions: traditional Christianity, an appreciation of other sacred texts, concern for ecological dimensions of the creation and planet, Liberation theology, Native American spirituality, and a critique of patriarchal religion and hierarchy. Diversity means reflecting both feminine and masculine images of God."

> *Religion is often at the core of why people hate us . . . . People often get their views from their religions, so we don't want the pulpit saying that being gay is wrong.*
> —Cathy Renna, Gay and Lesbian Alliance Against Defamation

This particular church was honored by its local government for flying the homosexual rainbow flag and providing "a venue to discuss homophobia in faith communities." The pastor has gone as far as to endorse a "transgender anti-discrimination" bill that was passed by the New York City Council and amended the city's human rights ordinance to include "gender identity or expression" and grant civil rights protections to "transgender" or "variable gender" persons.[7]

- Drew University, the major Methodist university (located in Madison, N.J.) in the Northeast, was chosen as the "most gay friendly university" in the country. [8]
- The Rev. Howard Edington, the pastor of the successful First Presbyterian Church of Orlando (the fourth largest church in the PCUSA) was forced to retire under pressure from some members of his congregation and the Central Florida Presbytery because of his vocal opposition to the ordination of homosexual pastors, same-sex marriage, and preaching a sermon against the city's sexual orientation anti-discrimination policy. Rev. Edington was also part of the Presbyterian Coalition, a group of pastors opposed to homosexual ordination. Rev. Jim Henry of the neighboring First Baptist Church said: "We have lost a voice of conviction that spoke eloquently calling us to the high ground of morals and values. We have lost one of the best communicators of the good news of hope in all the land."[9]
- United Methodist minister Richard Zomastny went on voluntary leave in 1999 to undergo a sex-change operation and become Rebecca Steen. He/she was subsequently approved to serve in the pulpit in the Baltimore-Washington United Methodist Conference.[10] In his/her defense, the Reverend Chip Aldridge of the pro-homosexual group Reconciling Ministries Network said, "When persons simply say that the Bible views homosexuality as a sin, they're dealing with a specific, narrow interpretation of the Bible. And there are many astute Bible theologians who dispute use of those limited number of Biblical references to interpret how ministry should take place with gay and lesbian people in 2002."[11] Mr./Ms. Steen finally surrendered his/her credentials to be a minister; however, Bishop Felton Edwin May of the Baltimore-Washington conference said that the issue of transgender clergy would be brought up at the denomination's 2004 general conference. The Reverend Gayle Annis-Forder said, "It's time [for transsexual clergy]."[12]
- When the minister of Woodland Park (Washington) United Methodist Church came out and publicly stated that he was a "practicing gay man," a denominational committee dismissed any ecclesiastical charges against him after asking him only one question, which he refused to answer.[13] Another pastor, Karen Dammann, declared to her bishop that she was a practicing lesbian. A church trial occurred,

and thirteen pastors acquitted her—despite[14] the fact that the denomination's Book of Discipline forbids pastors from engaging in homosexual behavior. Her attorney said, "Karen has chosen not to live the lie. She has invited the United Methodist Church to come out of the closet with her and live a life of open honesty."[15]

- The United Church of Christ already ordains practicing homosexuals.[16] In August 2001, the Evangelical Lutheran Church of America voted to study the blessing of same-sex unions and ordaining homosexual ministers.[17] This is despite that fact that Martin Luther wrote, "The heinous conduct of the people of Sodom is extraordinary, inasmuch as they departed from the natural passion and longing of the male for the female, which was implanted by God, and desired what is altogether contrary to nature. Whence comes this perversity: Undoubtedly from Satan, who, after people have once turned away from the fear of God, so powerfully suppresses nature that he beats out the natural desire and stirs up a desire that is contrary to nature."[18]

- In Philadelphia, an Episcopal priest was defrocked for stating that the church had become too liberal on issues such as the ordination of women and the recognition of same-sex "unions."[19]

- In Canada, an Anglican church diocese agreed to bless same-sex unions. The result was that a number of conservative Anglican churches voted to split from the diocese. At a conference of the dissident churches, Archbishop Yong Ping Chung of Southeast Asia said that the church needed to adhere to biblical teaching with regard to homosexual behavior, stating: "The world is confused and chaotic without the Bible. The value and moral state of life, or lack of it, is forever changing according to what's seen to be the latest trend or fashion."[20] What is happening in the Anglican church is happening in other mainline denominations as well: the acceptance and affirmation of homosexual behavior is causing them to implode.

- The leader of Americans United for the Separation of Church and State, an ordained United Church of Christ minister, claimed during a debate on homosexual behavior that the Roman centurion commended by Jesus for his faith had a male sex slave kept with Jesus' approval (Matt. 8:5–13). He then compared Jesus to homosexuals, stating "was he not

engaged fundamentally in an unnatural relationship"
because he never married, comparing celibacy and homosexuality as equivalent. After the debate, this individual tried
to suppress the distribution of the tape even though he had
previously agreed to allow it to be made available.[21]

* A liberal Southern Baptist pastor in Wedgewood, North
  Carolina, Dr. Chris Ayers, preached a sermon titled
  "Homosexuality Is Not a Sin: The Christian
  Education of a Baptist Minister." Wedgewood
  Baptist, the church Ayers pastors, left the
  Southern Baptist Convention several years ago
  because of the SBC's biblical stand on homosexual
  behavior. The pastor cited the work of theologian
  Walter Wink, rather than a biblical discussion of
  why he felt that homosexual behavior was not
  sinful. According to Wink, those who condemn
  homosexual behavior are guilty of "pick and
  choose" theology, discarding some Bible verses
  while hanging on to others. Ayers said that even
  Jesus was guilty of engaging in "pick and choose"
  theology. Yet, in his sermon, Ayers never discussed any of the New Testament verses that deal
  with homosexual behavior.[22] It is interesting to note that those
  who advocate homosexual behavior "pick and choose" which
  Scriptures they choose to abide by and which they choose to
  ignore.

> *There has been a
> radical cultural shift
> in the past ten years.
> Attitudes toward
> gays and lesbians
> have changed in the
> workplace, schools,
> and other civic
> entities. For the
> church to continue to
> stall seems archaic
> and irrelevant.*
>
> —Unnamed
> homosexual "pastor"

* Boston College, a Catholic University, has granted official
  recognition to a gay-straight student alliance, even though
  homosexual behavior is incompatible with the church's
  teachings.[23]

* United Methodist theologian Rev. Theodore Jennings Jr. and
  Dr. Morton Smith of Columbia University said that there is
  "irrefutable evidence" that Jesus was bisexual if not homosexual. Dr. Rollan McCleary (who is homosexual) of the
  University of Queensland in Australia said that he "discovered" that three of the disciples were homosexual. Jennings
  says that the references to the "disciple Jesus loved" in the
  Gospel of John refers to his "gay boyfriend." Smith says that
  he found a manuscript at a monastery near Jerusalem that
  refers to Jesus having a homosexual relationship with a
  young boy. McCleary adds that Christianity was founded on
  "gay principles." Homosexual activist Peter Tatchell com-

mented, "Since there is no proof of the heterosexuality of Jesus, the theological basis of Church homophobia is all the more shaky and indefensible."[24]

- The New Hampshire Episcopal Diocese elected Rev. Canon V. Gene Robinson, an openly practicing homosexual, to head the diocese. He quickly embraced his "partner" when he heard the news.[25] He later won the consent of the General Convention and accolades from the national media.
- Vermont's Episcopal Diocese has developed a liturgy for same-sex "marriages." Stan Baker, the lead plaintiff in the Vermont "civil unions" case and the senior warden of St. Paul's Episcopal Church, said, "There isn't another diocese that has this complete a policy, with the theological background supporting it, the liturgy itself and the resources for the couple."[26]
- Homosexual activists have developed a plan with left-leaning mainline churches to argue that the proposed Federal Marriage Amendment limits the free exercise of religion—claiming that the amendment might ban pro-homosexual clergy from performing same-sex "marriages." It is their hope to "co-opt" the marriage issue from religious conservatives.[27]
- Historic churches in Cambridge, Massachusetts, have hoisted large posters on their exterior that say, "Support Marriage Equality—We Do!"

To see how the radical homosexual agenda can permeate an entire church to the point where the church stands for nothing but the affirmation of homosexual behavior, consider this excerpt from the March 20, 2000, issue of *Newsweek*:

> When Sylvia Kunst and Linda Meeker met in a Detroit church five years ago, it felt like both a blessing and a curse. For years the two deeply religious women had denied their sexuality. Linda stayed in a heterosexual marriage for thirty years. Sylvia became born again and convinced herself she was "cured" of her lesbianism. Be with God or be gay, that's what they were always taught. It seemed an impossible choice to make. "We knew that we loved one another but we also loved the Lord," says Meeker . . . "We prayed and prayed for an answer."
> The couple gave up finding a church until they saw a listing in a gay circular for Fellowship United Methodist, "a

diverse and welcoming church." . . . Tucked off the road, in
a prim upper middle-class neighborhood in Troy, Michigan,
the tiny church looked very traditional. The congregation
consisted of mostly older, button-down and carefully
coiffed married couples and widows. But the pastor wore a
rainbow stole, a symbol of diversity.[28]

The article proceeds to describe the very same path that has led
to the "homosexual liturgy" emerging in the Church of England. The
Michigan church compromised once, hiring a homosexual choir
director. That, in turn, led to the appointment of a pastor who
preaches seemingly nothing but total acceptance of homosexual
behavior.

According to the article, the Reverend Marjorie Munger "acces-
sorizes her pastor's garb with iridescent gay-pride stickers, includes
lessons on homosexuality in her sermons and lists the church in gay
magazines."[29] Munger has also protested the church's position on
homosexual behavior at the denomination's annual conference, stating, "Right now the church is intricately involved in creating a climate of spiritual violence. If you don't say anything at all, then you
allow the voices of hate to be the dominant voices."[30]

It must be interesting to see how the Reverend Munger interprets
the Scriptures that deal with homosexual behavior. The most likely
is probably the same dodge used in the past by radical feminists and
others who have tried to reshape the church and the gospel in their
own image. That dodge can be best summarized as "the Bible has to
be interpreted in the context of the time it was written and therefore
that passage is no longer relevant today." That mind-set has opened
the church and seminary doors to radical feminism,* (including god-
dess worship),[31] the rewriting of God's Word into "gender-inclusive"
language,[32] and in the most liberal examples, praying to "Mother and
Father God" or "that great cosmic force in the sky."†

---

*Craig attended a seminary in southern California that is renowned worldwide for its supposedly con-
servative, evangelical teaching. In the early eighties, the seminary had compromised on the issue of
inclusive language, issuing a policy that a paper would automatically be given a failing grade if masculine pronouns were used for God and "mankind" was used instead of "humankind." By the late eighties, the head of the "women's study" department at the seminary proudly posted the following signs on
her office door: "Not the church, not the state, only I will decide my fate" (the credo of militant abortion supporters), "Lesbian Rights Now," and "My Karma Ran Over Your Dogma." Alan briefly attended
another nationally acclaimed seminary where he was taught on the first day that the Bible was nothing
but a book of myths and fables and that Pharoah's army drowned in "less than a foot of water" if there
was anything to such a tale.
†Craig grew up in a Methodist church in northern California during the 1970s that became increasingly
liberal over the years. By the end of the decade, the church was praying to "Mother and Father God"
and to "O Cosmic One." The associate pastor at the church eventually left his wife (who was also a pastor) for another man.

The Metropolitan Community Church

The Metropolitan Community Church was founded by an openly homosexual former Baptist minister named Troy Perry, and it now claims more than seventy-seven thousand members. According to the church's Web site, members believe the following:

• The Bible is full of errors that have resulted from being copied, recopied, and translated over and over again.
• Homosexual behavior is not a sin in God's eyes. Instead, the teaching that homosexual behavior is sinful is the result of twisted teaching of "homophobic" men.
• The references to homosexual behavior in the Bible really don't mean what they say.
• Sodom and Gomorrah were destroyed *not because of homosexual behavior* but because the people there ignored the poor and needy.
• Jonathan and David were homosexual lovers.
• Ruth and Naomi were lesbian lovers.
• As we mentioned before, Christ lived an alternative lifestyle and he loved other men besides John.
• Christ wore a purple robe to the cross as a connotation of his homosexuality.[33]

Another method of denial is to change the definition of being a Christian. Consider this piece, "On Being Christian and Gay," featuring a lesbian "family" and posted on the Web site of the pro-homosexual Human Rights Campaign:

My partner and I have spent a lot of time talking about organized religion and what does and what does not constitute a "Christian" person or family. [This topic] has something that has become a bit of a thorn in the side of our family. Although we do not attend a church or claim an organized religion, Sonya and I consider our home to be a loving, Christian home in which we raise our son. We have tried and tried to find a church that will accept us as a family here in our area. We have found several that have told us we were welcome to attend but they would openly state that homosexuality was a sin. How could we attend a church that taught our son that we were sinners? . . . Sonya and I were raised in different faiths with one common belief. We were taught to believe that God is a loving God. God does not hate or condemn anyone. . . . In our beliefs, a Christian would be defined as someone who is kind and giving to others. . . . A Christian treats all people equally and does not judge others for being different, but instead embraces and learns from diversity.[34]

Sadly, these women have a skewed notion of what a Christian is. Yes, as Christians we are called to love one another and to be kind and giving to one another. However, that is only one part of the equation. We are called to obey as well, and as we have already discussed, the practice of homosexual behavior is clearly not obedient. Obedience is a natural result of a personal relationship with Jesus Christ. Using their definition of being a Christian means that you can practice any kind of sin you want, and as long as you are loving and kind to others, you are fine.

Their statements are an indictment of the churches we have described above as well. When the church no longer preaches the gospel or takes the teachings of the Bible seriously, then it does not matter what you believe or what actions you engage in because the only basis for membership is being civil to one another rather than calling sinners to repentance and new life in Jesus Christ.

In addition, the comment about their son learning that his family members are sinners goes right to the struggle between homosexual behavior and religious freedom. *The two are incompatible.* The goal of the radical homosexual activists is to make sure that no church can say that homosexual behavior is sinful, lest they feel stigmatized. The only church they want is one that either affirms their behavior or merely exists for potluck dinners and bingo tournaments or for the advancement of leftist causes.

As one homosexual activist said about the issue of same-sex "marriage": "Ultimately I think it is religion, the liberal faith traditions, that are making the issue [of same-sex "marriage"] possible because they have already said, from Judaism to the United Church of Christ, that gay and lesbian couples can marry."[35]

Columnist Dennis Prager, a conservative Jew, probably put it best when it came to the spiritual confusion of pro-homosexual churches and synagogues. He wrote,

> There is nothing in mainstream Christianity or Judaism that supports same-sex marriage. There is nothing biblically supportive—and there is much biblically opposed—and there was not one major religious leader or thinker in Jewish or Christian history prior to the present generation who argued for same-sex marriage. Religious supporters of

same-sex marriage have either substituted their own feelings for God, for the Bible, and for religious law, or they
have simply attached a cross or a yarmulke to their leftist
politics. Clergy and laypeople who stand the Bible on its
head, no matter how well-intentioned they may be, are
thoroughly distorting Judaism and Christianity. Intellectual
honesty demands that they either support same-sex
marriage solely from a secular standpoint or create a new
religion from which to do so. If Judaism and Christianity do
not stand for man-woman marriage and the father-mother
family, they stand for nothing.[36]

Spiritual Apathy

But it is not only pro-homosexual churches and synagogues that
are empowering the advancement of same-sex "marriage" and the
homosexual agenda. Many evangelical Christians are unwittingly
doing so as well by treating the issue of same-sex "marriage" and
other aspects of the homosexual agenda with little more than a
shrug of the shoulders. Many have either thrown up their hands in
a "what's the use" attitude, are ambivalent about the effect on same-
sex "marriage" on their children and grandchildren, or are fearful of
being seen as "intolerant."

The *New York Times* reported the following on February 28,
2004: "[D]own in the pews of Western Michigan, a major center of
evangelical Prostestantism, not everyone is sure that the proposed
[federal marriage] amendment matters so much. 'For me personally,
even though I have a strong religious belief, who am I to say?' said
Grant Reed . . . a member of the non-denominational evangelical
Ada Bible Church in Ada, a suburb of Grand Rapids. . . . 'I think we
have bigger things to worry about than whether two men or two
women want to get married.'"

The article goes on to quote Jeff Manion, pastor of Ada Bible
Church: "Though the church, and though I, have firm convictions
about sexuality, our ministry is primarily about people's spiritual life
and not about pushing a political agenda."[37]

Unfortunately, like many others in the evangelical community,
this pastor is unable to connect the dots between same-sex "marriage" and people's spiritual condition. How can one minister to
someone's spiritual life when the government openly sanctions and
enables the very behaviors that trap him and that will ultimately
lead to his eternal destruction? Secondly, what about the spiritual

life of future generations, who will be taught that same-sex "marriage" is as normal as heterosexual marriage—and will be further indoctrinated in either pursuing homosexual behavior or have their ability to live and proclaim the gospel seriously impaired? Christian commentator Chuck Colson summarized this spiritual ambivalence succinctly: "What's our excuse for staying silent? I think some [Christians] don't really believe this is such a critical battle. To them I say—wake up and pay attention. The issue has the potential to redefine and, ultimately, to destroy the institution of marriage in this country—and with marriage goes the family. . . . But there are other Christians who recognize the importance of this battle over same-sex "marriage" but are still not speaking up. For many of them, I think the problem is a lack of faith. . . . A lot of Christians—even some of our most prominent leaders—seem to have succumbed to the 'what's the use?' attitude. They believe that the cultural climate has turned so much against us that we'll never be able to stop the advance of same-sex 'marriage.'"[38]

As Dennis Prager wrote, if the church is silent on this issue—or embraces the promotion of same-sex "marriage" and homosexual behavior—then what does the church stand for?

The Campolos

In addition, several individuals who would describe themselves as "evangelicals" also have promoted much of the homosexual agenda. Like Lot in Genesis 19, they have chosen to associate themselves with the radical homosexual movement and have focused on love without repentance.

Tony Campolo and his wife Peggy have spent the last ten to fifteen years touring the country and weaving part of the homosexual agenda into many of their presentations at unwitting churches and Christian organizations. Tony has done wonderful things in ministry for the poor and should be commended for his efforts in that area. He also has had a wide following on college campuses and is extremely influential with a major college ministry. His extremely charismatic personality has had a tremendous, and life-changing, impact on many young adults.

However, in the mid-to-late 1980s, the Campolos started to edge toward the promotion of much of the homosexual agenda.*

---

*Peggy Campolo is a national leader of the Association of Welcoming and Affirming Baptists, a homosexual friendly caucus in the American Baptist Denomination.

In 1987, Tony was invited by a committee of evangelical pastors and leaders in the Sacramento, California, area to conduct a crusade at Arco Arena, the home of the Sacramento Kings basketball team. Craig was on staff at one of the churches that invited Tony to the event.

While Tony thought the crusade was a smashing success and that the committee believed he was great,[39] that was not necessarily the case.*

The last night of the crusade, Campolo convinced the crusade organizers to do a "media ploy" and have the offering go to a local AIDS group. It was his thought that the sight of evangelicals giving money to an AIDS group would garner media attention for the crusade.[40] While we would agree that many Christians acted callously toward AIDS victims in the 1980s and that we must minister (by living and sharing the gospel) to those who are dying a sad, painful, but preventable, death, Campolo used the incident in his book *20 Hot Potatoes Christians Are Afraid to Touch* as a launching pad to castigate Christians, saying, "I hope that we will see church people show as much love for AIDS victims as has been shown by actress Elizabeth Taylor, who has worked relentlessly on their behalf."[41]

> *Apartheid is a sin. Racism is a sin. Sexism is a sin. Heterosexism is a sin. . . . How God created us to love is not sinful.*
>
> —Rev. Susan A. Minasian, pastor, Disciples United Community Church, Lancaster, Pennsylvania

Yet, is it love to work as Elizabeth Taylor has in the promotion of "safe sex" and special privileges for homosexuals, which only enable the harmful behavior, or is it love to share the full, uncensored gospel with those who are in desperate need?

Peggy Campolo has gone even further in the promotion of the homosexual agenda. She has stated publicly that she believes Romans 1 does not apply to monogamous, "loving," homosexual relationships.[42] She also has stated support for same-sex marriage. While Tony has argued on behalf of homosexuals in the military[43] and extending federal civil rights protections to practicing homosexuals,[44] he does not go as far as Peggy in these areas and has stated publicly that he does disagree with her interpretation of Romans 1 and with her stance on same-sex marriage.

Despite this, many conservative, evangelical Christians remain unaware of the Campolos' support for the homosexual agenda in the church and welcome them into their ministries with open arms.

---

*At a staff meeting later that week the pastor of the church that Craig worked in said that the committee would never invite Campolo back again.

The actions of the Campolos and other evangelicals who have given aid and comfort to radical homosexual activists reminds us of the story of Sodom and Gomorrah, in which Lot refers to those who seek to engage in homosexual behavior. On one hand, these evangelicals say, "Don't do this wicked thing," and yet call homosexual activists "my friends" and attack those who are trying to take a stand for righteousness.

Mel White is the founder of Soulforce, an organization dedicated to the silencing of the church with regard to homosexual behavior. His organization pickets the Southern Baptist Convention on an annual basis because of that denomination's biblical stand on the issue.[45] White has written a book justifying homosexual behavior and regularly receives positive press coverage about his pleas for "understanding."

White also staged a hunger strike in light of Focus on the Family's support of Amendment 2, which attempted to prohibit cities in Colorado from granting special legal privileges to homosexuals, and planned to stage a homosexual protest next to the ministry's campus.

One of White's assertions is that conservative Christians lack grace when dealing with those trapped in homosexual behavior. However, we need to look at the biblical understanding of "grace" as written by the apostle Paul in Romans 6. It is not something to be taken lightly:

> What shall we say then? Shall we go on sinning so that grace may increase? By no means! We died to sin; how can we live in it any longer? . . . Therefore do not let sin reign in your mortal body so that you obey its evil desires. Do not offer the parts of your body to sin, as instruments of wickedness, but rather offer yourselves to God, as those who have been brought from death to life; and offer the parts of your body to him as instruments of righteousness. For sin shall not be your master, because you are not under the law, but under grace. What then? Shall we sin because we are not under law but under grace? By no means! Don't you know that when you offer yourselves to someone to obey him as slaves, you are slaves to the one whom you obey—whether you are slaves to sin, which leads to death, or to obedience, which leads to righteousness? (vv. 1–2, 12–16).

Those who are trapped in homosexual behavior, just like those who engage in adultery or are addicted to hard-core pornography or other sexual sins, are slaves to that sin. Yet, while most in the church continue to take a fairly hard line on adultery, for instance, the same leaders have chosen, in many instances, to ignore the fact that homosexuals are also slaves to sin and are in need of being pointed to the way of obedience, which leads to righteousness.

Unfortunately, many evangelicals fear the *I* word (*intolerant*) and therefore seek appeasement with those who seek to undermine and silence the moral authority of the church and the gospel. It is much like Neville Chamberlain's going to see Adolf Hitler at Munich in 1938 and selling out his own country and its allies for the sake of "peace in our time."

The bottom line is that with radical homosexual activists appeasement is not enough. As we have seen, they are demanding total submission to their agenda. Therefore, with each compromise the church makes, another compromise is expected, until the church has nothing left to defend. That is the exact strategy developed by Kirk and Madsen in 1987, and much of the church has unwittingly fallen into their trap.

Attacks on the Church

Let us take a turn here from the appeasement of the church to the trench warfare being waged by radical homosexual activists and their allies in the media against the moral authority of the church. It is not much unlike Chamberlain being convinced that by appeasing Hitler he would avoid war with Germany, at the same time Hitler was lining up his troops to invade Poland.

The most vivid example of the type of warfare being staged by radical homosexual activists and their allies is the sexual abuse scandal in the Roman Catholic Church.

It has been documented that a cadre of homosexual priests has caused a large amount—if not virtually all—of this abuse. However, the radical homosexual activists, the media, and all others who despise what the church stands for, have seized the opportunity in an attempt to swing the church doors open wide for the practice of homosexual behavior, militant feminism, support for abortion, and so forth—all of which fly in the face of the basic tenets of the faith.

For two thousand years, the Roman Catholic Church has taken an unequivocal stand on the Scriptures' teaching regarding homosexual behavior and traditional relationships between men and women. From the writings of Saint Thomas Aquinas to the most recent version of the *Catechism of the Catholic Church,* homosexual behavior, adultery, and other sexual sins are condemned. Here are some excerpts that deal specifically with homosexual behavior:

*   "Lust is disordered desire for or inordinate enjoyment of sexual pleasure. Sexual pleasure is morally disordered when sought for itself, isolated from its procreative and unitive purposes."[46]
*   "Homosexuality refers to relations between men or between women who experience an exclusive or predominant sexual attraction towards persons of the same sex. It has taken a great variety of forms through the centuries and in different cultures. Its psychological genesis remains largely unexplained. Basing itself on Sacred Scripture, which presents homosexual acts as acts of grave depravity,* tradition has always declared that homosexual acts are intrinsically disordered. They are contrary to the natural law. They close the sexual act to the gift of life. They do not proceed from genuine affection and sexual complementarity. Under no circumstances can they be approved."[47]
*   "The number of men and women who have deep-seated homosexual tendencies is not negligible. They do not choose their homosexual condition; for most of them it is a trial. This must be accepted with respect, compassion, and sensitivity. Every sign of unjust discrimination in their regard should be avoided . . . ."[48]
*   "Homosexual persons are called to chastity. By the virtues of self-mastery that teach them inner freedom, at times by the support of disinterested friendship, by prayer and sacramental grace, they can and should gradually and resolutely approach Christian perfection."[49]

The Roman Catholic Church takes an uncompromising stand on the nature of human sexuality. The church's call for celibacy is meant to liberate its priests from sexual temptation. It is not meant to oppress them and force them to act out on so-called suppressed sexual desires, including homosexual behavior and pedophilia. The Catechism also stresses the need to have compassion for the individual trapped in homosexual behavior.

Despite what the catechism says, those who wish to remake the church in their image have attacked celibacy as the cause of the hor-

---

*Cf. Genesis 19:1–29; Romans 1:24–27; 1 Corinthians 6:9–10; 1 Timothy 1:10.

rible incidents that have occurred in the church. Rather than attack the root of the problem, seminarians and priests who have chosen not to live by the teachings of the church have adapted the world's view of sexuality and therefore have given themselves over (as in Rom. 1) to "shameful lusts."

Sad to say, because of the fear of ridicule and rejection for taking biblical stands, many in the Roman Catholic Church itself have played into the hands of those who seek to destroy it. George Weigel in his book, *The Courage to Be Catholic*, describes the tension that has occurred within the church from the infiltration of practicing homosexuals into the priesthood. Many Catholics, in fear of already being "politically incorrect" and the object of secular scorn on the issues of abortion and the ordination of women, try to do anything possible to make themselves look politically liberal and tolerant. (This is also a trend that is seen among many evangelical Protestants as well.) Weigel writes,

> Many U.S. bishops, feeling stuck in politically and culturally uncomfortable company on the pro-life and women's ordination issues, were eager to look "liberal" on as many other issues as possible . . . . This determination not-to-appear "conservative," which fit neatly with what bishops had absorbed from the therapeutic culture, seems to have created a fear of appearing "judgmental" and "homophobic" in dealing with cases of clergy sexual abuse. The bishop surely knew by the early 1990s that the overwhelmingly majority of cases of abuse had to do with the abuse of teenage boys and young men by homosexual clergy. Yet they were slow to act? Why? The determination to appear liberal on social issues other than abortion and euthanasia, and the fear of adding "homophobe" and "misogynist" in the standard American high-cultural vocabulary of put-downs of the Catholic Church, may well have blunted the bishops' ability to deal vigorously with the breakout of the scandal of clergy sexual abuse.[50]

Before we continue with our discussion on the attack on the Catholic Church by radical homosexual activists and their allies, we need to make it clear that we are not condoning the cover-up of, or the terrible sexual abuse that has unfortunately occurred. We have great compassion on those who were abused as children by sexual predators who disguised themselves as men of God.

However, despite the abhorrent nature of what has occurred, we cannot remain silent about how radical homosexual activists and their allies are exploiting this tragedy for their own personal, political, and legal gains.

Paul Likourdis, writing in *The Wanderer,* properly described the exploitation of this tragedy when he observed, "Catholics who thought there might be some reticence on the part of gay activists in the face of the Church's current homosexual scandals, can see now how homosexual misconduct and crimes actually advance their agenda, just as the AIDS disease was exploited, spun, and twisted to enormously advance public support for homosexual acts and homosexuals, exemplified by the AIDS activists' slogan, 'AIDS Is Our Power!'"[51]

So-called progressive Catholics (who perhaps should not call themselves Catholic since they oppose every basic tenet of the faith), like Frances Kissling of Catholics for a Free Choice and the homosexual Catholic group Dignity,* have used this unfortunate scandal as a wedge issue in their drive to remake the church the way they want it to be. Writing for *National Review Online,* Michael Novak explains their agenda:

> According to Tom Fox, long-time publisher/editor of The National Catholic Reporter, the flagship publication of "progressive" Catholics, a new wind is blowing, a new surge of energy, and the moment has come for charging into the breach in the thick walls of the Church, just blasted by the current scandals, in order to install at last the once-deferred new "progressive" church.
>
> That dream has two essential parts. . . . The second part consists in changing the sexual teachings of the Church, to make it conform to current understandings and practices . . . not only to welcome a homosexual ordination as a good [thing] but also to accept (as long as they are loving and respectful of the other) homosexual acts, to acquiesce in the naturalness of premarital sexuality, to permit divorce and remarriage, and generally to extend a warmer and more poetic acceptance of sensual, erotic, and sexual experience. . . . In short, the Roman Catholic Church should become rather more like the Church of England. The cross can be taken down from the steeples and replaced with a weathervane . . . .

*Dignity has gone as far as to sue the Newman Center and Chapel (a Roman Catholic meeting center) in Minneapolis, Minnesota, because the center did not renew Dignity's lease because of legitimate biblical differences. Dignity had wanted to conduct a mass on the church property. The Newman Center was initially found in violation of the city's Civil Rights Ordinance protection against discrimination on the basis of "affectional preference," and faced a civil fine of $15,000 plus other related legal costs. The Minnesota Court of Appeals overturned the decision.

The reason for this heightened optimism among the "progressives" is a sudden opportunity thrust upon them to defame the legacy of Pope John Paul II, which they had feared would extend far beyond their own lifetimes. Now, they sense, is their last opportunity to dismantle the church as we have known it.[52]

Kissling, who has made it her own personal crusade to get the Vatican kicked out of the United Nations because of its anti-abortion stand, has exploited the abuse tragedy to push her agenda. Kissling has called upon the United Nations to sanction the Vatican. Her mission and that of the radical homosexual activists? It is best summed up in the words of Austin Ruse, president of the Catholic Family and Human Rights Institute, "Their concern is not with the church. Their concern is with overthrowing the church."[53]

And sure enough the media is attacking with a vengeance the elderly and frail pope, who has taken courageous biblical positions on homosexual behavior and the sanctity of human life. In a virulent *New York Times* op-ed column titled "Is the Pope Catholic?" Bill Keller not only attacked the pope but the entire moral foundation of the church: "The uncomfortable and largely unspoken truth is that the current turmoil in the Roman Catholic Church is not just a sad footnote to the life of a beloved figure. This is a crisis of the Pope's making . . . . The distrust is the legacy of Pope John Paul II."[54]

And how was the pope responsible for the crisis, according to Keller? By abiding by the moral teachings of the church. He continued his diatribe:

> But the struggle within the church is interesting as part of a larger struggle within the human race, between the forces of tolerance and absolutism. . . . Implored by Catholics to consider,* at least, the lifesaving power of condoms in the age of AIDS, Pope John Paul II was unyielding. He actually grouped contraception with genocide in a litany of "intrinsically evil" acts that condemn sinners to hell for eternity . . . . In America, most Catholics ignore the Pope on this, as they do on divorce and remarriage, abortion, sex out of wedlock, homosexuality, and many other things that Rome condemns as violations of natural law. It seems fair to say that a church that was not

---

*Catholics such as Frances Kissling.

so estranged from its own members on subjects of sex and gender, a more collegial [i.e., tolerant] church, would have handled the issue of child abuse earlier and better.[55]

To follow this line of thought means that, in Keller's eyes, the church's problem (and these statements can be translated to every church that takes these biblical teachings seriously, not just the Catholic Church) is that it defends biblical morality by actually calling sinners to repentance. In his viewpoint, and those who call themselves progressives, the last thing the church should be doing is preaching moral absolutes but should instead allow homosexual behavior, along with other sexual sins, to run rampant through the church. Thus, the Catholic Church (and all other churches) would become like the tolerant liberal churches, i.e., not much more than a country club.

In response to Keller's vicious attack on the pope and the moral absolutes of the church, Pat Buchanan wrote, "That Keller would hail the salvific properties of condoms is also understandable when one realizes who he works for. According to its political correspondent Richard Berke, speaking to the Gay and Lesbian Journalists Association, 'Three-quarters of the people who decide what goes on the front page [of the Times] are "not-so-closeted" homosexuals.'"[56]

The duplicity of the argument ("Intrinsically disordered behavior caused the problem so let's open up the doors to more such behavior") put forth by radical homosexual activists and progressives boggles the mind. It is always interesting to note that they always demand that conservative, Bible-believing institutions reject their beliefs and embrace modern sexuality (which has brought us AIDS, teenage pregnancy, sexually transmitted diseases, to name just a few "benefits"). This is despite the fact that, in the case of the Catholic Church, it was a contingent of homosexuals violating their promises to celibacy in the priesthood that has caused the problem to begin with! In addition, there is never a link to the fact that while at the same time homosexual activists are attacking the church for allowing men who prey on teenage boys to infiltrate the priesthood, they are attacking the Boy Scouts for keeping the same individuals out!

This argument reminds us of the old adage "We need to destroy this city to save it." Jon Meacham wrote a prime example of this in the May 6, 2002, issue of *Newsweek*: "Some Catholic traditionalists are trying to manage the scandal's fallout by arguing that the sexual predation of children and teens by priests is largely a homosexual issue. Such a stance isolates the problem and, conservatives seem to hope, forecloses talk about the future of celibacy, married priests or, at the farthest edge, ordaining openly gay clergy and allowing same-sex unions. By pointing their fingers mainly at homosexuality, these church leaders are avoiding discussion of the questions that should be front and center: the roots and costs of a culture of sexual repression and secrecy."[57]

Meacham went on to call for the ordination of homosexual priests,* the open practice of homosexual and heterosexual sexual license in the church, and rejection of traditional marriage. He stated: "Being more open about sexual orientation might lead to less repression, and less repression—for heterosexuals and homosexuals—might well lead to a climate in which there is less destructive behavior." He adds: "Isn't the role of the church to encourage people to enter into stable relationships? [No, it is to preach the gospel. Loving, stable opposite-sex marital relationships flow naturally out of submission to Christ—the authors.] The purpose of marriage, or 'unions,' or whatever we want to call them, should be the establishment of a committed, loving family. Heterosexuals who do not produce children are no less 'married.' . . . We've changed the definition of marriage before, both to liberate women from being legal property and to allow people of different races to marry. Such an approach should encourage monogamy and bring homosexuals into the fuller life of the community."[58]†

In a very blunt column for Universal Press Syndicate, Ann Coulter exposed the shallowness of these arguments. She wrote:

> Since liberals categorically reject the notion that homosexual conduct is often correlated with homosexuality, they have responded to the gay sex abuse crisis in the priesthood by blaming Catholicism. In particular, liberals have identified the church's celibacy requirement as the root of the problem.
>
> There is absolutely no logic to this theory. It is nothing more than liberals reacting to the concept of sexual restraint like *The Exorcist*'s Linda Blair did to holy water. . . . When did celibacy become a gay magnet? . . . If celibacy is to blame,

---

*This is in despite of a 1961 Catholic Church document that bars the ordination of homosexuals to the priesthood. The document reads: "Those affected by the perverse inclination to homosexuality or pederasty should be excluded from religious vows and ordination."

†A top Vatican official announced on December 5, 2002, that the church must not bring homosexuals into the priesthood. Cardinal Jorge Arturo Medina Estevez wrote that ordination of "homosexual men or men with homosexual tendencies is absolutely inadvisable and imprudent and, from a pastoral point of view, very risky." See Nicole Winfield, "Vatican Aide Rejects Ordination of Gays," Associated Press, December 6, 2002.

this is a show-stopping, Nobel Prize winning discovery overturning years of liberal claptrap. In all other circumstances,
it is punishable by death to suggest that sexual behavior is
not determined at birth or that gays can be "cured." Now liberals are hawking the idea that gay priests could have been
cured by marriage! It's nice to see liberals becoming such big
marriage-boosters. Too bad their newfound respect for
marriage—an eminently dissolvable agreement, rescindable
by either party without cause or notice—is
limited to gays and priests.

> *I've never felt con-
> demned by God—
> it's just the church
> that's the problem.*
>
> —Mark Matson, a homo-
> sexual human relations
> director, Columbus, Ohio

Blaming celibacy is not only contrary
to various liberal dogmas, but contrary to
all known evidence about any vice. Total
avoidance, not limited temptation, is the
only hope for controlling weakness.[59]

Columnist John Leo, writing in *U.S. News and World Report*,
added that the increasing tolerance of homosexual behavior and
other sexual behaviors, inside and outside the church, played a significant role in the scandal.

The rise of the sexually active gay subculture among the
clergy didn't cause the horrors of priestly sex abuse. The
vast majority of gay priests would never prey on the young.
But did the subculture play the role of enabler in the scandals? *I think it did, expanding tolerance for the forbidden and
generating a sense of futility among the rule-keepers* [empha-
sis added]. Self-deception is infinitely expandable. One
man's justification for violating celibacy or the ban on non-
marital sex is another man's justification for "intergenera-
tional love," formerly child rape.

The way out for the church is not to hunt down and
expel every last gay priest, which would be impossible anyway. But it should restore the pressures to keep priests, gay
and straight, from acting out sexually, whether by shower-
ing with a mature friend or preying on a child. The key
principles are easily learned: Maybe celibacy will be
changed some day, but if you make a vow to stay celibate,
you ought to keep your word. And in the seminaries,
Catholic sexual morality should be taught by people who
actually believe it. Is this controversial?[60]

Sad to say, according to the homosexual activists and the media, it
is controversial for the church to actually teach and live out what the

Bible says about homosexual behavior. Therefore, while radical homosexual activists and their allies within the church are trying to reshape it into a modern-day Sodom and Gomorrah, others are attacking it from the outside in hopes of bringing the church to its knees. Both routes can lead to the church's eventual destruction. This is the strategic approach that radical homosexual activists use to achieve their agenda. They try to convince the media and the general public that they represent the "high road" while bombing their enemy incessantly. Here are just a few examples of this tactic:

- In California, a bill was introduced by Senate President Pro Tem John L. Burton of San Francisco (any coincidence?) that would lengthen the statute of limitations so adult victims could sue the Roman Catholic Church for damages. The bill passed a Senate committee unanimously.[61]

- A Saint Paul, Minnesota, attorney named Jeff Anderson, who has made a career out of clergy abuse cases, included the Vatican in a RICO (Racketeering, Intimidation, and Corrupt Organization) lawsuit. In RICO suits, defendants, if found guilty, have to pay triple the amount of court-ordered damages. The law, which was created for dealing with organized crime, is meant to bankrupt such organizations. Anderson said, "We filed a lawsuit naming several dioceses and bishops as racketeers in an ongoing conspiracy to conceal child sexual abuse. We also named the Vatican as in part responsible for the racketeering activity."[62]

- In San Francisco, openly homosexual district attorney Terence Hallinan asked the archdiocese there for seventy-five years of records related to sexual misconduct by priests.[63]

Regardless of claims to the contrary, the current sexual problem in the Catholic Church is primarily a homosexual behavior problem. As Rod Dreher wrote in the *National Review*: "The reluctance [to mention homosexuality] arises, no doubt, partly out of a fear of antagonizing homosexual anti-defamation groups, who resent the stereotype of male homosexuals as pederasts. It's much safer to focus inquiry on the question of mandatory celibacy, or the issue of ordaining women. Yet it defies common sense to imagine that an ordinary man, having made a vow not to marry, is therefore going to be sexually attracted to boys."[64]

To get a glimpse of why this is a homosexual issue, one need not look any further than the Reverend Paul R. Shanley, one of the most notorious priests caught in the scandal. He has been indicted in the

Commonwealth of Massachusetts for various crimes.[65] During his time in the priesthood, Shanley allegedly engaged in the following:

- While on "sick leave" in California, his payroll checks were sent to the Cabana Club Resort, a racy homosexual club in the Palm Springs, California, area. Shanley became an owner of the hotel along with another homosexual priest who was on sick leave as well.[66]

- He attended the 1979 meeting that created the North American Man-Boy Love Association (NAMBLA).[67]

It has also been well documented that many liberal Catholic seminaries have a gay subculture.* For example, it has been estimated that at one time homosexuals made up anywhere from 30 to 70 percent of the student body at St. John's Seminary in Camarillo, California.[68] R. Scott Appleby, a history professor at Notre Dame University, said, "People I know quite well have left the seminary either in disgust because people are not keeping their vows, or in alienation because they're not gay. In some cases, it's a serious problem."[69]

Joel Mowbray, a lifelong, practicing Catholic, put the problem this way:

> Male homosexuality is inherently promiscuous. In a heterosexual relationship, women moderate the innate, intense male sex drive. But in a homosexual conduct, there is no such check. In short, gay couples have two people with male attitudes about sex, which naturally leads to a more permissive view of sexuality. And when seminaries began filling up with homosexuals—both in terms of seminarians and in leadership positions—promiscuity inevitably followed. . . . So how does this relate to the sex abuse scandals? The generation of priests who are largely responsible for the rash of sexual abuse cases mostly entered the priesthood at an extremely early age, ushered into an ensconced environment where they never got a chance to grow up. Teenage boys are the natural objects of sexual desire for an immature homosexual who was enveloped in a promiscuous, homosexual culture in the seminary.[70]

---

*One of the more detailed books on this subject is *Goodbye Good Men!* by Michael Rose. He devotes an entire chapter to the homosexual subculture at Catholic seminaries. Other chapters include a detailed discussion of the impact of left-leaning theology and its application on two generations of prospective Catholic priests. Interestingly, he documents an increase in the number of seminarians and dioceses loyal to traditional biblical teaching on homosexual behavior, e.g., the Diocese of Omaha, led by Bishop Fabian Bruschewitz.

John Leo echoed these thoughts in *U.S. News and World Report*: "The church's 'pedophile priest' problem is actually two problems blurred into one. True pedophiles are rare. *Most sexual abuse victims of priests are teenage boys—perhaps 95 percent, according to one estimate.* A study of Chicago's 2,200 priests identified 40 sexual abusers, only one of whom was a pedophile. Abusers of teens are generally treatable. Pedophiles aren't. *But the church is reluctant to mention the distinction, most likely because opening up the issue of sexually active gay priests is itself explosive, even apart from charges of abuse.*"[71] [emphasis ours]

Father Donald B. Cozzens, author of *The Changing Face of the Priesthood*, asked the pointed question: "Why are 90 to 95—and some estimates say as high as 98—percent of the victims of clergy acting out against teenagers, boys? Why isn't there a higher percentage of teenage girls?"[72]

The Knights of Columbus ran an advertisement in the *Washington Times* that stated: "We speak of homosexuality, for this indeed is the problem. We all know the truth: The vast majority of the exposed scandals are cases of pedophiliac homosexuality, and thus a particularly heinous spillover of the more widespread problem of homosexuality. Large sectors of the media, however, choose to gloss over the homosexuality and highlight the pedophilia."[73]

In fact, while the media was concentrating so hard on the problem in the Catholic Church, homosexual priests and nuns within the church continued on as if nothing had happened. The National Association of Diocesan Lesbian and Gay Ministries had a conference in Cincinnati in September 2002 that featured seminars on "Creating a Welcoming Parish," "Catholics Respecting Youth in Sexual Minorities," and "Spirituality for Gay Men."[74]

The *New York Times, Time* and *Newsweek,* to mention a few, brought up the specter of homosexual priests but trod on that turf quite lightly, because they were aware that too much discussion of the issue might derail the homosexual agenda. Rob Dreher wrote, "For journalists, to confront the issue is to risk touching the electrified third rail of American popular culture: the dark side of homosexuality."[75]

The homosexual activist groups are well aware that this issue, which many hope to exploit to undermine the moral authority of the Catholic Church, could explode directly in their faces. Paul Bedard wrote in *U.S. News and World Report,* "Gay groups are freaking out over the progression in news coverage of the Roman Catholic Church sex scandal. What started as a story about a few bad men in black has moved to headlines about a subculture of gay priests, some of whom

sexually abuse altar boys, and others who may tolerate the crimes. . . .
Their worry: After making homosexuality acceptable in the media,
the fight might be back to square one."[76]

As secular news publications started to raise the specter of
homosexuality in the priesthood and its link to the sexual abuse of
teenage boys, the Gay and Lesbian Alliance Against Defamation
(GLAAD) and the Human Rights Campaign (HRC) put out the following "talking points" to members of the media in order to spin the
story away from homosexual behavior:

> Do not imply, suggest or allow others to suggest a
> cause/effect relationship between homosexuality and child
> sexual abuse. Attempts to insinuate that gay men—either
> within or outside of the priesthood—have a natural
> propensity to sexually abuse minors are baseless, defama-
> tory and calculated to fuel anti-gay sentiment among the
> general public. Please also note that priests who sexually
> abuse children are guilty of abusive exploitation that is not
> reflective of any healthy adult sexual orientation—gay or
> straight. . . . When your coverage touches on sexual orien-
> tation/identity issues, please broaden your resource base to
> include "openly gay Catholics." One of the "openly gay
> Catholic" groups GLAAD and HRC recommends [sic] for
> media people is Dignity/U.S.A.[77]

The radical homosexual activists know that this can either be a
golden moment to weaken the Catholic Church and further restrict
religious freedom, or a moment when people will see the dark side of
homosexuality and its link to pedophilia and other sexually disordered behavior. As Anthony DeStefano wrote in *USA Today*: "Their
[critics of the Catholic church] true aim is to hurt the church, to
damage its credibility in order to reduce its ability to work effectively
against the immorality of an increasingly godless society. . . . That is
the real meaning of the attacks on the church."[78]

And that is the point that needs to be made when it comes to the
homosexual legal activists, their allies in the media, and their attack
on the Catholic Church. It is hypocrisy, pure and simple. While they
attack the church for the pedophilia scandal, they promote homosexual sex with teenage boys on TV programs such as *Queer as Folk*
(see chap. 2). The Knights of Columbus in the advertisement we
mentioned earlier states: "This same media [that promotes homosexuality and pedophilia] has no qualms about unleashing a fero-
cious uproar against the Church, Her doctrine and morals."[79]

Chuck Donovan, former vice president of the Family Research Council and now president of the Family Action Alliance, also predicted this hypocrisy in the media, and from homosexual activists themselves, when he wrote,

> When homosexual activists marched outside of the House of Parliament several years ago, they carried signs saying "Stroppy queens [obstreperous homosexuals] demand sixteen." They were demanding, not asking, that the age of consent for homosexual relations be lowered to sixteen. Tony Blair's government gave in without hesitation. Are we really certain that all those 16-year-old boys thus liberated will make mature decisions to engage in homosexual relations when invited or pressured by older, more powerful, probably richer males? When a priest entices a 16-year-old boy, it is truly a scandal. But what will be the press response if a British banker, an Oxford don, or a member of the House of Lords seduces a teen? I suspect it will be a bemused world-weariness—unless the seducer is a prominent Catholic.[80]

And where does this all lead? To the persecution of the church for taking a stand against the problem! In Lexington, Kentucky, three priests who have taken a biblical stand on homosexual behavior received threatening letters warning them to stop "persecuting homosexual" priests in their diocese. The letters were purported to be from "The Gay Priests Association" and stated that one of the priests must get "under control and out of the country . . . That is if you would like to continue to receive a salary and keep your life intact." The priest said he was targeted because he teaches "Gospel values and Gospel principles." One of the other priests said to his parishioners, "So many people didn't believe there was a gay culture throughout the priesthood, and here it is right here. This is how far we have degenerated."

Interestingly, the former bishop of Lexington had resigned after three men had sued the church and accused him of sexual misconduct. Now these three priests are having their lives threatened for taking a biblical stand against the very behavior charged that caused the bishop to resign![81]

The Price for Taking a Stand

The reality is that radical homosexual activists and their allies are looking for any opportunity to attack and silence any church that takes a biblical stand with regard to homosexual behavior, regardless of denomination. The scenario being played out against the Catholic Church is just a small part of the persecution that many believers and other churches in homosexual enclaves, such as San Francisco, face on a daily basis. What these believers are experiencing now is a snapshot of what will happen to the church in America if it continues to resist the demands of radical homosexual activists. The heat is only going to get higher and the temptation to compromise the gospel in face of persecution is going to become more attractive. However, if the church fails to stand strong in the face of attack, then its very reason to exist (evangelization to spread the gospel) is compromised.

We have already briefly discussed what happened to Focus on the Family in the early 1990s after Colorado's Amendment 2 had passed. Craig was employed there at the time and can attest to the following:

- Rocks were frequently thrown through the windows of the ministry's then-downtown headquarters. In addition, pink triangles were frequently plastered on the walls of the building.

- Dead-animal parts and a casket were left on the ministry's front door after a homosexual teen committed suicide, and homosexual activists blamed his death on the passage of Amendment 2 and the "hostile" climate toward homosexuals in Colorado.

- On the light poles in front of the ministry's headquarters and throughout the downtown area, flyers were posted, calling for conservative Christians to be thrown to the lions.

- Focus on the Family employees were verbally assaulted in local restaurants by homosexual activists and their allies. As a result, employees were told for their safety to remove their name tags in public.

- Homosexual activists played a part in helping launch an expensive, time-consuming IRS audit of the ministry, which turned up nothing.

- Homosexual activists accused the ministry of conducting a witch-hunt against homosexual teachers. The rumor was quickly denied by the local school district. Despite this, homosexual activists continued to make this allegation, with no documentation to support it.

- Bomb threats were made on a regular basis to the ministry's headquarters.

- At the dedication of Focus on the Family's new facilities in 1993, a group named Lesbian Avengers attempted to stage a kiss-in and remove their tops to expose their breasts to the public. Craig was sitting in the same section as the Avengers and quickly summoned security before they were successful in their protest. The Avengers made sure that their eviction was videotaped and then tried to peddle the video to various news outlets.*

Focus on the Family and Dr. James Dobson are not the only ones to experience the wrath of angry homosexual activists. Three years ago, at a crusade in Charlotte, North Carolina, several homosexual members of the Seigle Avenue Presbyterian Church choir walked out in protest after Anne Graham Lotz, the daughter of Billy Graham, stated that homosexual behavior is a sin. To her credit, Lotz did not back down from her assertion.[82]

What Focus on the Family experienced in the days after Amendment 2, what the Catholic Church is experiencing in the sex abuse scandal, and what Anne Graham Lotz experienced at her crusade are only a small sampling of what sincere religious believers have faced when they have taken a stand against the affirmation of homosexual behavior. For example:

- Ron Greer, an eighteen-year veteran of the Madison, Wisconsin, fire department handed out a tract to his fellow firefighters and friends that outlined the biblical position on homosexual behavior. Greer was suspended without pay and ordered to attend diversity training. When he refused, he was fired.[83]
- In April 1996, Scott Southworth was scheduled to speak at a Madison, Wisconsin, church about homosexual behavior and the Bible. About one hour before the speaking event, roughly four hundred to five hundred homosexual activists gathered across the street from the church. They chanted things (all caught on video) like "Queer mob rule," "Hey, Hey, Ho, Ho, homophobia's got to go," "Go away," and "Two-four-six-eight! We don't want your Christian hate." One demonstrator repeatedly yelled, "Bring back the lions!" Other protesters carried flags and signs that read "Bigots are Perverse," "Gay Love is Divine," "Haters—Repent or Perish," "Hate is Not a

---

*Craig Osten was employed at Focus on the Family 1988–2001 and was an assistant to Dr. James Dobson, 1993–2001. He witnessed all of these events during his time there.

Family Value," and "God is Gay—He Loves Men." Eventually
the demonstrators found their way into the church and dis-
rupted the entire presentation.[84]

- Orthodox Presbyterian minister Chuck McIlhenny dismissed his church organist when the organist divulged that
he was a practicing homosexual. The organist sued the
church, tying up McIlhenny in five years of legal battles in
which he and the church ultimately prevailed. During that
time, he and his family received death threats, had their
residence firebombed, and were told by the San Francisco
Police Department that there was nothing they could do to
stop radical homosexual activists from threatening him and
his family.*

- Eugene Lumpkin was a member of San Francisco's Human
Rights Commission. He was also the pastor of a local Baptist
church. In the June 23, 1993, issue of the *San Francisco
Chronicle,* Lumpkin expressed his sincere religious beliefs
about the sinfulness of homosexual behavior. He was immediately fired from the commission and was quickly branded
a homophobe. A pro-homosexual group proclaimed, "It's
about time hate-spewing Christian priests got their bigoted
remarks 'corrected.' Let's hope this correction serves as a
warning to other homophobic religious bigots that their
intolerance just isn't going to be tolerated."[85]

- Also in 1993, the Hamilton Square Baptist Church in San
Francisco invited a well-known pro-family leader to speak at
the church. Radical homosexual activists stormed the church
doors, pounding on them and screaming, "We want your
children! Give us your children!" The church experienced a
great deal of vandalism, and again the San Francisco Police
Department said it could do nothing to stop the rampaging
homosexual activists. Dr. David Innes, the senior pastor, was
told: "You have to understand, this is San Francisco."[86]†

- Radical homosexual groups in Ferndale, Michigan,
attempted to have the city's police chaplain fired because he
expressed the biblical position with regard to homosexual
behavior. Rev. Tom Hansen of Bethel Missionary Church had
objected to the city hosting the state's largest annual gay

---

*The McIlhennys' long struggle against radical homosexual activists is chronicled in the book *When the
Wicked Seize a City* by Pastor McIlhenny and Frank York (Huntington House Publishers).
†A tape of the homosexual protesters later aired on Focus on the Family and is still available through
that ministry.

pride festival. Erin James, of Mel White's "Soulforce" group, said: "He [Hansen] believes the Bible condemns homosexuality . . . . Homosexuality is not a sin and not a sickness." A homosexual resident said: "Rev. Hansen's interpretation of the Bible is hurtful and divisive."[87]

- U.S. Senator Mark Dayton (D-Minn.), in a speech to the Rainbow Families Conference, said religious people who support traditional marriage show "only disgust and disdain while they spew hatred and inhumanity." He continued, "Jesus Christ didn't say, 'Love only thy opposite-sex neighbors.' Christ was silent on homosexuality even as he repeatedly condemned adultery and divorce." A group of pastors immediately sought an apology from the Senator, writing, "We are grieved by your name-calling of those who hold to a traditional view of marriage and we believe you owe the people of Minnesota a public apology for your harsh and intemperate attacks on people seeking to uphold basic Christian beliefs. You also stated that Jesus was silent on homosexuality. Jesus was also silent on rape and incest but we are not to interpret the lack of recorded comments as approval of such behaviors. Both the Old and New Testaments condemned homosexual behavior and Christians are obligated to uphold the Scriptures' teaching."[88]

- Two men were arrested in Dayton, Tennessee, for attempting to assemble two large wooden crosses during the city's "Gay Day" gathering. They were cited for disorderly conduct. One of the men, Michael Siemer, said, "This is the first time I've been arrested for being a Christian." The two men were *standing across the freeway* from the park where the "Gay Day" event was being held.[89]

- On April 28, 2004, the Canadian Parliament passed Bill C-250, which could make certain portions of the Bible that deal with homosexual behavior be classified as "hate speech" with criminal penalties. The Canadian Bible Society put out repeated warnings that the bill could have a chilling effect on religious freedom and evangelism in Canada. Janet Epp of the Buckingham Evangelical Fellowship of Canada said, "Pastors are afraid. They're afraid to preach on this subject. Nobody wants to have the police come to the door."[90] The bill, which added "sexual orientation" to Canada's hate-propaganda law, passed by a vote of 59-11. The bill reads, "Every one, who by communicating statements, other than in private conversation, willfully promotes hatred against an identifiable group, is guilty of an indictable offense and is liable to imprisonment for a term not exceeding two years."[91] Meanwhile, the author of the bill, openly homosexual Svend Robinson has stepped down after video surveillance cameras caught him stealing a $50,000 ring from an auction house.[92]

- When Christians met at a Calgary, Alberta, hotel to discuss the bill's implications, they were interrupted by a group called the "Gay Militia." The homosexuals beat sticks together, roared slogans, and drowned out a speech by Rev. Tristan Emmanuel on the increasing hostility to Christians. The homosexual men ignored both meeting organizers and hotel security personnel who asked them to leave. "Haters!" screamed the protesters. "Bigots! . . . what you are doing is a hate crime!"[93]

- An openly homosexual Canadian senator, Laurier L. LaPierre, sent an e-mail back to individuals who opposed C-250: "God! You people are sick. God should strike you dead! In a book [the Bible] that is supposed (sic) to speak of love and you find passages of hatred: You should be ashamed of yourself for reading such books! . . . If your god teaches you to hate and judge, then get another god." The senator did somewhat apologize, saying, "On February 7 I answered some e-mails in a less than Senatorial manner. I am apologizing for my vitriolic answers to two e-mails. [I] mistakenly let out months of frustration."[94]

- Officials in the Canadian province of Ontario fined a Christian mayor $10,000 for refusing to proclaim "Gay Pride Day" in his city. A Christian businessman was fined $5,000 for refusing to print materials for a homosexual rights group. Attorney Bruce Long, writing in the March 2004 issue of *Church Law Bulletin,* said, "Churches and religious institutions may want to consider . . . avoiding public criticisms of identifiable groups . . . limiting opinions to private conversations, and if targeted or investigated, rely on the constitutional right to remain silent."

- In England, an elderly evangelical Christian, who had been repeatedly assaulted for speaking out against homosexual behavior, was ruled to have been "properly convicted" by the British High Court of "breaching the peace." The sixty-nine-year-old man, who had passed away before the final judgment was rendered, had been fined 300 British pounds (approximately $550 American dollars) by a lower court for simply holding a sign that read "Stop Immorality. Stop Homosexuality. Stop Lesbianism" and featured a reference to Jesus. Despite the fact that the man had been repeatedly physically assaulted, the high court judges ruled that the restriction on Hammond's right to free expression was justified under the European Convention on Human Rights.[95]

*   Back in the United States, the Canyon Ferry Road Baptist Church in Helena, Montana, hosted a closed-circuit presentation of a rally to support the proposed Federal Marriage Amendment that was held in Colorado Springs. During the rally, petitions were circulated asking state legislators to place a constitutional amendment protecting traditional marriage on the Montana ballot—an activity that churches can legally engage in without jeopardizing their tax-exempt status. Homosexual rights groups and their allies complained that the church had not filed the "proper paperwork" and should have its tax-exempt status revoked as well as pay a stiff fine. An ADF allied attorney—working with ADF staff counsel Gary McCaleb—has intervened legally on the church's behalf.[96]*

This last item is something that many are warning will happen when evangelical churches refuse to perform same-sex "marriages." Raymond Flynn, a former U.S. ambassador to the Vatican (appointed by President Clinton) and mayor of Boston, believes that there is a "distinct possibility" that homosexual activists will try to force churches to redefine religious marriage or lose their tax-exempt, non-profit status. Flynn says, "The issue of legalizing same-sex marriages in Massachusetts and California raises the question: Does this mean there will be cases brought against the Catholic Church for discrimination? I think it is the next step."

Allan Carlson, president of the pro-family Howard Center and a distinguished fellow with the Family Research Council, adds, "I think there's vulnerability [to the tax-exempt status] there. If same-sex marriage is determined to be a fundamental human right, would churches still be allowed to ban such things and also claim a tax exemption? I don't know."[97]†

---

*In appendix 2 of this book, we include a letter from ADF staff counsel Gary McCaleb on what churches can legally do with regard to public policy matters without jeopardizing their tax-exempt, non-profit status.

†In appendix 1, we provide a detailed examination of how the U.S. Supreme Court's decision in the Bob Jones University case could conceivably be used by homosexual activists and their legal allies to revoke the tax-exempt status of churches that engage in "discrimination."

Nowhere is the fight for religious freedom more evident than in the assault of radical homosexual activists upon the church. Radical homosexual activists will not be satisfied until the church either becomes an advocate for their behavior, as we have seen in the Church of England and Marjorie Munger's church, or is silenced by intimidation or legal action—as we have seen in Canada. Some activists will exploit anything (as we have seen in the Catholic Church scandal) to achieve their aims. The ultimate goal is to not only restrict, but also to punish any speech that does not affirm homosexual behavior. As Cathy Renna of the Gay and Lesbian Alliance Against Defamation put it, "People often get their views from their religions, so we don't want the pulpit saying that gay is wrong."[98]

Renna is right on one point. It is religious belief that plays a major determining role in the acceptance of homosexual behavior. A 2004 Pew Research Center poll found that while 55 percent of Americans believe homosexual behavior is sinful, 76 percent of individuals with a high religious commitment believe so. Individuals with high religious commitment oppose same-sex "marriage" by more than a 6-1 margin.[99] That is why the silencing—or as we discussed earlier—the spiritual apathy of the church is so essential to the fulfillment of the homosexual agenda.

To take a look at what possibly awaits for the church, we need look no further than the past. As we stated in the first chapter, the radical homosexual activist community has adopted many of the techniques used in Nazi Germany.

The *Rutgers Journal of Law and Religion* recently published an article that summarized several documents from the World War II era. One of these documents was "The Persecution of Christian Churches" by the Office of Strategic Services (OSS), the intelligence agency that had been set up in World War II to spy on Germany and its allies.

The report reads as follows: "The Nazis believed that the churches could be starved and strangled spiritually in a relatively short time when they were deprived of all means of communication with the faithful beyond the church building."[100]

Chuck Donovan, whose father served in the OSS, writes about what happened in Nazi Germany:

> At first Nazi leadership feigned a desire for peace with Christian churches through the Concordat of 1933 with the Catholic Church and pledging to honor the freedom of Protestant churches, so long as the churches gave up their

involvement in political issues. Then the Nazis began tightening the screws. "Under the pretext that the Churches themselves were interfering in political and state matters, the [Nazis] would deprive the Churches step by step, of all opportunity to affect German public life. Breaking the back of Christianity in Germany was aimed at cutting off the education and formation of the rising generation from its heritage of faith [eerily similar to what is happening in government schools today]. As extreme as these goals seemed then, capturing youth and pressuring the Church to abandon its witness in the public square are almost universal phenomena now.[101]

The assault on religious freedom also extends beyond the church walls to individual believers in the workplace and religious organizations that do not accept and embrace homosexual behavior. If intimidation does not work, homosexual activists are willing to unleash the power of federal, state, and local governments to cow the church and believers into silence, just as Kirk and Madsen advocated back in the late 1980s.

And once the church is silenced on the sexual behavior issue, it will not take long before it is silenced on many other issues. Already in Canada, churches and other religious organizations cannot speak out on homosexual behavior for fear of finding themselves in violation of hate-crime laws. If speaking out against homosexual behavior is considered "hate," then what about other sexual behavior now called sin, such as adultery? Without moral authority, the church in the United States will become like so many are now in Europe, museum pieces from an era long, long ago. The result will be tragic for the millions of individuals who will be unable to hear and respond to the gospel—the good news of Jesus Christ—because the church may no longer be allowed to proclaim it.

Let's conclude again with the story of Lot.

The two angels arrived at Sodom in the evening, and Lot was sitting in the gateway of the city. When he saw them, he got up to meet them and bowed down with his face to the ground. "My lords," he said, "please turn aside to your servant's house. You can wash your feet and spend the night and then go on your way early in the morning." "No," they answered, "we will spend the night in the square." But he insisted so strongly that they did go with him and entered his house. He prepared a meal for them, baking bread without yeast, and they ate. Before they had gone to bed, all of the men from every part of the city of Sodom—both young and old—surrounded the house. They called to Lot, "Where are the men who came to you tonight? Bring them out to us so that we can have sex with them." Lot went outside to meet them and shut the door behind him and said, "No, my friends. *Don't do this wicked thing."* [emphasis ours]

—Genesis 19:1–7

From being forbidden by God to enter the city, to sitting in a place of authority there, to calling sexual activists his friends, Lot's behavior was not unlike all too many people of faith today.

CHAPTER SEVEN

The Seduction of Corporate America

In many regards, the workplace is the leading edge of change for the GLBT [Gay, Lesbian, Bisexual, and Transgender] community. Company CEOs and executives can often wield more power than state and local officials in creating significant changes that affect their employees' lives. They can enact new policies with the approval of a few board members rather than thousands or even millions of voters . . . . Through the enactment of DP (domestic partner) benefits, employers send the message that all employees, including GLBT workers, are valued and accepted as equal, which paves the way for more employees to come out.
—National Gay and Lesbian Task Force Organizing Manual

Betty Sabatino was an employee for a San Antonio bank. One day, she was ordered to attend a session on "fair employment practices." During a question-and-answer portion of the program, billed as being a "safe zone" and open to all questions, she inquired as to why the company would provide special considerations for employees based on their sexual behavior. After the session was over, her boss approached her and expressed "concern" about her question. A few weeks later, she was fired because of "management's loss of confidence" in her.[1]

In Hollywood, California, two homosexual employees stopped near the desk of an Orthodox Jewish employee and proceeded to have a graphic discussion of the homosexual pornographic films one of them had seen. The Orthodox Jew asked the two men to stop and they refused. When he voiced his concern to the company's human relations department, he was told it was his problem that he disapproved of the men's sexual orientation and he should "lighten up."[2]

These are just two examples of what has happened to individuals who object to the promotion of homosexual behavior in the workplace. Yet, they are a microcosm of how some in corporate America have embraced the homosexual agenda, and allowed radical homosexual activists to silence, and in some cases, fire, those who do not bow at the altar of so-called tolerance.

Radical homosexual activists have adapted numerous strategies to push their agenda through corporations and marginalize and intimidate those who would object.

Did you know that 213 companies out of the Fortune 500[3] now offer domestic-partner benefits, including 82 percent of the Fortune 50?[4] And yet, despite these numbers, many corporate leaders have no idea what the enactment of these policies of financial subsidy really mean for their companies and for society as a whole. In addition, many of these corporate leaders are also not doing this on their own initiative; they are being forced to—by local laws and unrelenting pressure from radical homosexual activists. Others are doing so because they see a potential gold mine waiting to be tapped—the homosexual community, a community mostly without children and with large disposable incomes.[5]

By pressuring corporations to accept their agenda and adopt domestic-partner benefits, homosexual legal activists hope to succeed in their goal to redefine marriage and the family. Nowhere is this better explained than in this statement from the organizing manual of the National Gay and Lesbian Task Force: "[An ideal policy would cover] a wide range of family types. If possible, an employer should offer benefits to same-and-opposite sex couples, both romantic and non-romantic, as well as the partner's children. By crafting an inclusive policy such as this, *the employer allows the employee to define his or her own family* and responds to the family's needs. Moreover, an inclusive policy is more flexible and *can adapt to employee family structures as they continue to change.*" [emphasis ours][6]

The key phrase in this statement is "the employer allows the employee to define his or her own family." That line shows the ultimate objective of radical homosexual activists: to use corporate America to advance their agenda of rejecting God's definition of the family and replacing it with one of their own, whether it be with three mommies, two daddies, or whatever arrangement they can devise. If this were not enough, domestic-partner policies open up the door to fraud and deceit. *New York Magazine* reported that a number of "straight" individuals without health insurance are now claiming to be domestic partners with friends who work for companies that offer these benefits. In the words of one executive assistant, "All we had to do was swear we were in a committed relationship. They didn't ask for any proof or anything." One human relations employee stated that a man tried to register his *cat* as a domestic partner. The paperwork had already been submitted to the insurance company by the employer before the ruse was realized.[7]

To achieve these aims, the activists have adopted a strategy that pressures corporations from various directions. Whether it is through local government ordinances,[8] shareholder resolutions, collective bargaining, or one-on-one meetings with management, homosexual activists are attacking on all fronts to achieve their goals. Again, they will keep coming back time and time again to wear down corporate decision makers. This strategy can be best summed up in an advertisement placed by IBM in support of a gay, lesbian, bisexual, transgendered leadership conference in Seattle, Washington, in 2000. Quoting Samuel Jackson, the ad states: "Great works are performed not by strength but by perseverance."

The effort to get corporations on board with the homosexual agenda is a multipronged strategy. According to the National Gay and Lesbian Task Force organizing manual, the first step is the establishment of a GLBT employee group: "Before starting to work on specific issues in the workplace, it is important to form an employee organization to identify needs, operate with [a] common cause, and link employees who are interested in working for change. Even if it is not possible to form an official group of GLBT employees, it is valuable [to] create an informal unofficial group from which the organizing efforts can be launched."[9]

The Foot in the Door

The second step in the homosexual activist strategy is for corporations to adopt a sexual-orientation policy. Although often presented as an urgently needed policy to stop egregious discrimination, the NGLTF manual readily admits that getting corporations to change their anti-discrimination policies and to provide domestic partners benefits is just the beginning of their campaign for their eventual goal of same-sex marriage and beyond. Yet at public shareholder meetings, activists publically and deceitfully claim that all they want is a limited anti-bias policy. At the annual meeting of Emerson Electric, for instance, homosexual activists stated that having a sexual-orientation policy does "not require the company to offer equal benefits to partners of gay employees."[10] However, this statement contradicts the strategy as outlined in the NGLTF training manual, which reads as follows: "Before attempting to get domestic partner benefits from your employer, it is imperative that the company's non-discrimination policy include sexual orientation. . . . Inclusion in a company's employment equal opportunity (EEO) policies also implies inclusion in any of its diversity programs, which provide many opportunities for educational work and involvement in policy making decisions . . . . A common rationale for establishing domestic partner benefits is that the failure to do so is contradictory to a non-discrimination clause."[11]

After reading this statement it is fairly obvious that the addition of sexual orientation to company anti-discrimination policies is the Trojan horse that leads to domestic-partner benefits, contrary to assertions made relating to the Emerson Electric shareholders meeting.

> *Many mainstream corporations actively seek this [homosexual] audience in their marketing and advertising for products from beer to liquor to life insurance, and depict openly gay and lesbian relationships. Further, an increasing number of major corporations are openly depicting non-traditional sexual activities in traditional advertisements and including elements of fetish attire and dominance and submission role-playing between adults.*
>
> —Judy Guerin, executive director, National Coalition for Sexual Freedom

This leads to the third step: domestic partner benefits. And, if corporations don't voluntarily offer domestic-partner benefits, they are increasingly forced by cities and municipalities with large homosexual communities to do so. In 1996, the San Francisco Board of Supervisors passed an ordinance that required all companies that do business with the city and county to offer domestic-partner benefits to their employees. Because of this ordinance, thousands of corporations have chosen to offer domestic-partner benefits rather than risk closing their businesses in one of the top five population markets in the United States. Corporations caved into homosexual activist demands not because of social concerns, but because of economic ones. Without the influence of this ordinance, the overall growth in domestic-partner benefits would be much less. According to the Human Rights Campaign, of the 4,285 companies that adopted domestic-partner benefit policies, 3,087 had done so because of the San Francisco ordinance.[12]

(A brief side note: A homosexual newspaper disclosed on March 7, 2003, that nearly three years ago (in 2001), the National Gay and Lesbian Task Force, a champion of domestic partner policies, actually tried to cut domestic partner benefits for its own employees! NGLTF said that the policies were "prohibitively expensive" but compromised by paying 50 percent after negotiations with the staff.[13] Yet, on its own Web site, NGLTF denies that these benefits will cost employers too much money. The site reads: "The most common reason cited by companies who do not implement domestic partner benefits is the perception that to do so would be cost prohibitive . . . these concerns are baseless . . . . If a company cares about its employees and about the values of fairness and non-discrimination, it should treat all employees equitably, no matter the price tag."[14])

Radical homosexual activists are now claiming that since corporate America has embraced domestic-partner policies (involuntarily in most cases), even though their statistics only show 4,285 out of 5 million corporations have adopted such policies, it is time for local, state, and federal governments to do so as well. This is despite the fact that it was compliance with a local ordinance that caused the dramatic growth in corporate domestic-partner policies to begin with!

The Alliance Defense Fund supported a case to challenge the San Francisco ordinance.[15] It involves S. D. Myers, a small Christian company that operates out of Ohio and has sold electrical transformers as low bidder to San Francisco for years. With ADF's help, Myers challenged the ordinance on state and federal constitutional grounds in the United States District Court in Oakland, California. Unfortunately, the court ruled against Myers, and it appealed to the Ninth Circuit Court of Appeals, where it lost again. The court ruled that the city and county ordinance did not place an "undue burden" on interstate commerce in violation of the federal constitution's commerce and due process clauses. While this case has been lost at the Court of Appeals level, it is now pending before the United States Supreme Court for possible review.

"Safe Spaces" (Except for Those Who Disagree)

The fourth step for homosexual activists is to then use corporate employment policies to promote homosexual behavior and stigmatize, isolate, and silence any employees who may express opposition to such behavior. The most vivid example of this is the "Safe Spaces" programs at Lucent and Xerox. (Unfortunately, the Orthodox Jewish man mentioned earlier was not allowed to have a safe space to have his beliefs respected.)

These programs encourage employees to display a sign that designates their work areas as safe spaces where individuals can talk openly (in a positive manner) about homosexual behavior. The flyer promoting this program tells employees how they can be supportive of gay people. It reads as follows:

- "Don't assume everyone is heterosexual."
- "Don't permit homophobic jokes or comments." [Since expressing one's biblically held beliefs on homosexual behavior has been labeled homophobia by radical homosexual activists, this is effectively calling for the censorship of religious speech.]
- "Treat the subject in a positive way."
- "Use inclusive language (partner or significant other)" and "Respect the privacy of the individual." [Only speech that affirms homosexual behavior is approved, and thus the gospel is silenced. Sadly, people like Betty Sabatino find themselves out of a job if they object to the promotion of homosexual behavior.]

The sign goes on to say, "Remember, most gay people remain completely or partially closeted within the work environment for various reasons including fear of rejection and lack of acceptance. Even though you may be supportive of your lesbian and gay coworkers, making them comfortable with you is more important than asking if they are gay. Displaying the 'Safe Space' emblem is a great way to start!"[16]

The sign consists of a bright pink triangle, the symbol that has been adopted by the homosexual activist movement to symbolize its cause.* Of course, this program also can be used to identify and

---

*According to homosexual activists, the pink triangle was used by Nazi Germany to identify homosexuals who were rounded up and sent to concentration camps. Their history ignores the role of homosexuals in top positions in Hitler's regime.

stigmatize those who do not agree with homosexual behavior, since individuals who do not display the sign can be easily targeted.

In the final steps the manual discusses how to enlist corporations in the public relations effort by homosexual activists to link homosexual behavior with civil rights: "Companies should clearly express to employees, consumers, and the community that domestic partner benefits are not special rights; they are equal rights. . . . The company is recognizing diversity and acknowledging the needs of all of its employees within that framework; all of its employees are equal and therefore all relationships are also equal."[17] And "[Domestic partner] benefits are not the final step in the GLBT [Gay, Lesbian, Bisexual, Transgender] quest for equality, but they are integral to its achievement."[18]

"Diversity" Training

Another way that religious freedom is threatened in the workplace is through "diversity training" sessions for employees in which biblical beliefs on homosexual behavior and marriage are openly ridiculed. Brian McNaught, who is considered the diversity guru and conducts workshops for AT&T, has written, "There are people who believe that homosexual behavior is forbidden by the Bible. This too is a personal belief."[19] With regard to marriage, he has said, "Heterosexist language can be changed. We can say, for instance, partner or significant other rather than spouse. We can say, 'Are you in a relationship?' rather than 'Are you married?'"[20] This ties into the statement from the National Gay and Lesbian Task Force organizing manual that all relationships must be perceived on equal footing with marriage, therefore devaluing marriage and exalting alternative lifestyles.

Diversity training is also used to spread misleading or untruthful statistics with regard to homosexual behavior. At one such "diversity" training session at American Express, employees were told that 11 percent of the population is homosexual, despite the fact that no credible study has shown the percentage of homosexuals to be above 2 to 4 percent of the population.[21]

Homosexual Dollars Equal Corporate Support

The fourth step is to get corporate America to financially support radical homosexual activism. The activists have achieved this with surprising ease.

Why has corporate America been such an easy target for homosexual activists to push their agenda? One of the main reasons is that the homosexual community has a much higher level of disposable income than most families,* and therefore in order to tap that market, many corporations have gone overboard in their willingness to bow to the demands of radical homosexual activists. In addition, homosexual activists, with the aid of the media, have become so adept at demonizing any corporation that does not give in to their agenda that most companies quietly cower at their feet rather than face the public relations wrath of the activists.

One example of this is the number of corporations that support radical homosexual training conferences. One such conference is the "Out and Equal Leadership Summit," held on an annual basis to develop strategies to push the homosexual agenda on corporations. The following were listed among the 2004 conference sponsors:

- American Airlines
- NCR
- IBM
- Eastman Kodak
- Chubb Insurance Group
- JP Morgan Chase & Co.
- Motorola
- Ford Motor Company
- SC Johnson
- Shell Oil
- Walt Disney World
- Aetna
- Agilent Technologies
- American Express
- Bank One

- Best Buy
- California State Automobile Assoc.
- Cargill Inc.
- Charles Schwab & Co.
- Chevron/Texaco
- Daimler Chrysler
- Cingular Wireless
- Coors Brewing Co.
- Dell Computers
- E-Trade
- Fleet
- General Mills
- General Motors
- Hewlett-Packard
- IBM

- Intel Corp.
- Kaiser Permamente
- Lucent Technologies
- Microsoft
- Proctor and Gamble
- Prudential Financial
- Qwest
- Raytheon
- Sun Microsystems
- Target
- Boeing
- United Airlines
- Verizon
- Wells Fargo ank
- Whirlpool
- Xerox

The Ford Foundation has provided grants to the Gill Foundation[22] (which promotes homosexual causes in Colorado), the National Gay and Lesbian Task Force,[23] International Gay and

---

*A study released by Simmons Research in 2000 found the average income of gay and lesbian households to be $85,000, more than twice the national average. According to a Syracuse University/Opus Comm Group/G Society study released in October 2001, the *median* household income of homosexual households is $65,000—nearly 60 percent higher than the national average of $40,800. More than a fifth of the respondents in the Syracuse study reported a household income of $100,000 or above, while nearly 60 percent of homosexual male households and 46 percent of lesbian households reported income in excess of $60,000. According to Simmons Research, 59 percent of gay and lesbian consumers buy "whatever they want." The homosexual market is estimated to be in the range of $250–$350 billion. Finally, 62 percent of homosexual men and 59 percent of lesbians are college graduates, and 47 percent of homosexual men and 40 percent of lesbians hold professional or managerial jobs—more than twice the figure for the general population. What is interesting is that homosexuals deny these demographics when they are mentioned in the context of anti-discrimination, but then trumpet them when they are convincing corporations to cater to them.

Lesbian Human Rights Commission,[24] National Gay and Lesbian Task Force Policy Institute,[25] and the Lambda Legal Defense and Education Fund,[26] which is the largest legal advocate for same-sex marriage in the United States.

The Human Rights Campaign, which bills itself as the "largest lobbying group for gay and lesbian rights in the United States," lists American Airlines, Volvo,* IBM, Washington Mutual, Cingular Wireless, Nike, John Hancock, Coors, and Capital One among the corporate sponsors on the HRC Web site.[27]

Catering to the Homosexual Market

Corporations have also been lining up to advertise in homosexual publications and to publish and air advertisements sympathetic to the homosexual agenda. This ties into a strategy of using corporate America to soften up Americans for acceptance of homosexual behavior.

Joe Landry, publisher of *Out* and *The Advocate,* says "Lots of companies are adding diversity marketing to their budgets, which used to mean money for advertising mainly to blacks and Hispanics, but now it's meant largely, and sometimes mainly, for gay and lesbian customers."[28]

In fact, from 1997 to 1999, advertising in gay publications went up *20.2 percent,* to $120.4 million. This does not include homosexual-themed advertisements in other media.[29]

And corporations eager for homosexual dollars have been able to pursue a marketing strategy aimed at those who practice homosexual behavior without much backlash. Bob Witeck of Witeck-Combs Communications says, "I think we're near a tipping point. Backlash against such [homosexual] advertising has dropped and there's a higher comfort level. I see more evidence of that all the time."[30]

Homosexual activists demand more than just advertising directed toward them, *they demand total support for their agenda.* A Human Rights Campaign survey found that "seventy-two percent of gay, lesbian, bisexual, and transgender consumers said it was important for 'companies who advertise to the GLBT community to demonstrate effective corporate citizenship by supporting their causes.'"[31]

During the 2000 Summer Olympics, the John Hancock Financial Services deliberately marketed itself to the homosexual

---

*Volvo ran an ad in homosexual publications that depicted a homosexual couple with a baby and a pregnant lesbian. The ad had the tagline "Whether you're starting a family or creating one as you go . . . Volvo. For life."

community and it appeared they did just as the radical activists demanded: The advertisement showed total support for their agenda. One commercial featured two women holding a newborn Chinese baby and telling each other what wonderful mothers they will both make. The ad ended with the tag line "We are family." Obviously, the viewer could assume the women were open lesbians. It was only after adoption groups expressed concern that the Chinese government would forbid future adoptions of children since one of the conditions of such adoptions was that they be to two-parent, heterosexual homes, did John Hancock alter the commercial. How did John Hancock alter it? By changing the nationality of the baby from Chinese to Cambodian![32]

Subaru has also been a major marketer to the homosexual community and proudly states that it is the number-one choice of lesbian households.[33] In addition, Subaru has used a homosexual ad agency to promote its product.[34] To ensure the continued support from the lesbian community, Subaru's national advertising campaign features lesbian tennis star Martina Navratilova and includes the slogan "It's not a choice. It's the way we're built."[35] The implication is fairly obvious.

The airline industry, particularly American Airlines and United Airlines, has been a big supporter of the homosexual agenda. For American, the lure of homosexual travel dollars is too enticing to pass up. American spokesman Tim Kinkaid says, "We're doing this for a great business reason. It's been very rewarding to us. We've made millions of dollars over the years simply by reaching out to this community and acknowledging that they are important to us. . . . There was a negative reaction from conservative religious organizations, but every other airline is doing it now. . . ."[36]

For United Airlines, the issue has been damage control with homosexual activists. After the 1996 San Francisco ordinance was passed, United initially balked at providing domestic-partner benefits and became the target of blistering attacks from radical homosexual activists and their friends in the media.[37] San Francisco International Airport is the airline's West Coast hub, and United controls a large number of gates there. After it became evident that the city might be willing to boot the largest leaser of gates from its airport rather than relent on the ordinance, United not only caved in, but in order to prove itself to the homosexual community, became a full-fledged supporter of homosexual organizations.

For example, the summer 2000 update from the Lambda Legal Defense and Education Fund reported on the corporate largesse of

United: "Lambda has forged a new three-year partnership with United Airlines. . . . Valued at over $300,000, it is the largest corporate sponsorship in Lambda's history to date. The benefits of this new strategic alliance *includes underwriting of all staff air travel for Lambda for the next three years,* round trip tickets to be used as prizes at Lambda events, discount coupons for event attendees, and special travel to Liberty and Partner Circle donors and new Lambda members."[38]

Can you imagine the uproar in the media and from radical homosexual activists if, for example, Delta Airlines gave three years of free flights, discounts, and so forth to Focus on the Family or to the First Baptist Church to oppose Lambda's agenda? Delta would probably be picketed and skewered on CNN, MSNBC, and the *New York Times* editorial page for providing support to an "extremist" agenda. Yet no one blinks an eye when United Airlines provides free travel to radical homosexual activists, especially in light of the government bailout of the airline industry after the events of September 11, 2001.* As Tim Kinkaid of American Airlines said, the opinion of religious conservatives does not frighten airlines at all. However, if a radical homosexual group raises one little objection, they quake in fear and give in to every one of its demands.[39]†

The WNBA—Targeting the Lesbian Market

Professional sports have also made efforts to tap into the homosexual financial gold mine. The Women's National Basketball Association (WNBA) has deliberately marketed itself to lesbians. In fact, it has been estimated that 30 percent of the WNBA's fan base is lesbian.[40] WNBA president Val Ackerman said, "We welcome any fan who wants to come out and support our sport. We have a broad range of fans. . . . To the extent that members of the lesbian community are indicating their support, I think that's terrific."[41]

The WNBA has a working relationship with the Human Rights Campaign. After the Washington Mystics home opener a few years ago, HRC hosted a post-game party attended by more than seven hundred lesbians and supporters, including the Mystics general manager and other league officials. At the party, the head of the

---

*The total amount set aside by the federal government to bail out the airlines was $15 billion. According to the airline industry, they lost $7.7 billion in 2001. Meanwhile, they are providing free travel to homosexual activists. United Airlines' application for a federal loan in 2002 was rejected, and the company has declared Chapter 11 bankruptcy.

†For more information on how corporations can stand up to the demands of homosexual activists and promote pro-family policies, see www.communityresourcecouncil.org.

Seattle Storm and the director of development for the WNBA publicly came out.[42]

The Mystics are also regularly frequented by the Lesbian Avengers (whose logo is an exploding bomb), a group that stages kiss-ins and demonstrations at which participants remove their tops in public. They include protests in front of the Family Research Council (which is across the street from the MCI Center where the Mystics play) before going to the game.[43]

Other WNBA teams besides the Mystics deliberately market themselves to lesbians. Karen Bryant, vice president of operations for the Seattle Storm, says, "Lesbians have been a strong core group of our fans in this town."[44] Kat Fox, spokeswoman for the "Davis Dykes" (the name of a lesbian organization in Davis, California) and a season-ticket holder for the Sacramento Monarchs, said, "Lesbians have been the WNBA fan base since 1997. We're saying our money is the same as the traditional family money . . . . [The WNBA] needs the money, and their marketing efforts are brilliant if they target the lesbians."[45]

What would be the reaction if a sports league specifically targeted people who go to church? It would probably result in a lawsuit. In fact, such a scenario took place a few years ago when an atheist, with the help of the ACLU, sued a minor-league baseball team that provided discount tickets for a Sunday afternoon ball game if they were presented with a church bulletin.[46] ADF was involved in the defense of the team's right to hold such a promotion, and a compromise was reached that allowed the team to continue the promotion as long as programs from civic or non-profit groups were included as well.

The WNBA's Los Angeles Sparks held events at the popular Los Angeles lesbian "Girl Bar" to help spur season ticket sales and game attendance. Sparks players provided autographs, and the fans bought Sparks pennants, notebooks, basketballs, and season-ticket packages. The Miami Sol had already appeared at lesbian bars and events more than two years earlier, and the Phoenix Mercury proudly acknowledged its marketing efforts to the lesbian community.[47]

The Phoenix Suns basketball team, which owns the Mercury, dropped the pro-family Center for Arizona Policy as sponsor of its "Church Night" promotion after homosexual activists complained about the Center's opposition to same-sex "marriage" and other pro-homosexual initiatives supporting homosexual behavior. Tom Ambrose, a team vice president, said that the Center's sponsorship was "problematic" because the Mercury had cultivated a large lesbian fan base. According to media reports, homosexual activists joined with pro-homosexual churches to get the Center booted from the church night promotion.[48]*

So, the next time your daughter asks you to take her to a WNBA game, you might want to consider the influences she might be exposed to there.

Welcome to the Gay Riviera

The travel industry has also cast a covetous eye toward the income demographics of the homosexual community. The homosexual travel market is estimated at $54 million a year.[49] Miami-Dade County has prepared a twenty-page brochure that features maps and information about hotels, shopping, and special events of interest to homosexual tourists. The pamphlet proudly proclaims, "Our 'gay' friendly environment extends beyond our local businesses to our government officials and policies. Come and see why Greater Miami is truly the gay Riviera."[50] Fodor's has produced the "gay guide" to America as well. Nicki Grossman of the Great Fort Lauderdale Visitors Bureau said, "You can't ignore the kind of spending that gay and lesbian travelers do."[51]

The city of Atlanta created an entire advertising campaign catered to homosexual tourists. Caroline Wilbert wrote in the *Atlanta Journal-Constitution*, "The thinking goes: Gay people, many of whom don't have children, have disposable income. So let's get them to spend it here."[52] The Web site promoting the campaign—gayatlanta.com—features the slogan, "We're out to show you a good time." The city spent $55,000 on the campaign.[53]

In November 2003, the city of Philadelphia announced its new $300,000 "gay travel" promotion—which included images of Ben Franklin (who is shown flying a rainbow kite), Betsy Ross, and George Washington. The campaign mixes the historical figures with rainbow banners and features the tagline "Get your history straight and your nightlife gay."[54] The campaign calls Philadelphia the "city of brotherly love and sisterly attraction."

That's just the beginning. It gets worse. The first Philadelphia spot to air featured a man in Colonial dress waiting by Independence Hall, holding a bouquet of flowers. He has just finished writing a letter to his "dearest beloved." An attractive young female walks by and makes a flirtatious overture toward him. The man quickly rejects her and hands the flowers to his male lover instead.[55]

---

*At the time of this incident, the Suns general managing partner was a prominent evangelical Christian in the Phoenix community.

Washington, D.C., also launched a homosexual ad campaign with the slogan "Where More Than Just the Cherry Blossoms Come Out."[56] Community Marketing, a San Francisco firm that helps the travel industry reach homosexual consumers, sums up the motivation of corporations and tourist destinations to market to "oppressed" homosexual travelers in the following demographic information:

- Took vacation in the last 12 months: all travelers: 64 percent; gay travelers: 85 percent.
- Took an international vacation in the last 12 months: all travelers: 9 percent; gay travelers: 45 percent.
- Hold a valid passport: all travelers: 29 percent; gay travelers: 78 percent.
- Belong to a frequent flyer program: all travelers: 25 percent; gay travelers: 64 percent
- Seventy-five percent of gay and lesbian households have incomes over the $40,000 national average.[57]

Thomas Roth, the president of Community Marketing said, "It boils down to two things: dual income and no kids. People with money and no responsibility for kids have two spending priorities— shopping and travel. When you start adding up the comparisons, you see why tourist offices and CVBs (convention visitors bureaus) are interested in reaching out to the gay market."[58]

The homosexual dollar is so powerful that corporations and destinations that were once the epitome of family values have now openly marketed themselves to the homosexual community.

If you ever plan a trip to Disney World in Orlando, Florida, here is one word of advice: don't go the first weekend in June. Why? That weekend is the annual Gay Days in the land of Mickey, Donald, and Goofy. While Disney states it does not sponsor gay days, it has done little to deter them and much to encourage them.

Gay days started in 1990 when Doug Swallow, a practicing homosexual, and his buddies from a homosexual computer bulletin board decided to get together and meet at the Magic Kingdom. Since then, their numbers have swelled to more than 125,000 attendees, all who wear red shirts to identify themselves as homosexuals.[59]

At first, Disney tried to distance itself from the event. However, as time went by and the homosexual dollars started to roll in, the event became as unofficially official as you could get, as Mike Schneider wrote in this 2000 Associated Press piece: "Walt Disney World used to keep Gay Days in the closet, fearing the wrath of religious groups. One year, Disney posted signs at the entrance warning guests that there was a gathering of homosexuals in the Magic Kingdom. In other years, passes to other Disney parks were offered to guests who might be offended by large numbers of gays. As the celebration enters its 10th year this weekend, it's now as much as part of Disney as Mickey Mouse. . . . 'During the first couple of years, their greatest fear was what other guests would think,' said Tom Dyer, editor and publisher of *Watermark,* a gay newspaper in Orlando. 'Their view has shifted to caring about how their gay and lesbian guests are treated.'"60

It is not just religious conservatives who are uncomfortable at gay days. Columnist Steve Otto, who states that he is not part of the religious right, wrote this about his family's experience at Disney World on Gay Days weekend: "Gay Days is no celebration of diversity to sit back and enjoy. Gay Days is a political statement. It's thousands of men and women wearing red shirts with labels such as 'Gay Days and Magic Nights,' groping and grabbing their way from one fantasy land to the next. . . . You couldn't help but listen as you stood in line. You could only stare into space for so long if you were trapped with them in a monorail car or a bus. Too many in the red-shirted crowd were obscene. . . . They were vulgar and they were determined to make a statement. That statement had nothing to do with acceptance or equality or even the right to stand in long lines for two-minute rides. What they were saying was that if you didn't like their vulgarity, then you were somehow a smaller person. They were saying that it's all right to be as crude in a crowd as you would be anywhere."61

What Steve Otto and his family experienced at Disney World vividly illustrates that the radical homosexual agenda is not about tolerance; it is about acceptance and an in-your-face desire to flaunt homosexuals' sexuality and related behavior at the expense of others. And, as long as their money rolls into the corporate coffers, many corporations seemingly have little or no trouble going along with them.

Yet, much of this is very sad. It is unfortunate that those caught up in homosexual behavior are now trying so hard to seek the joy that they missed in their own childhoods, by immersing themselves in the fantasy environment of Disney World.

The Bottom Line

So, what is the bottom line for radical homosexual activists and corporate America? Their strategy can be best summed up as follows:

1.   To force corporate America to accept sexual orientation as a protected class.

2. To force corporate America to provide domestic-partner benefits (which is a neutral name for sex-partner subsidies).
3. To use corporate America to force government at all levels to adopt sexual-orientation laws.
4. To use corporate America to force government at all levels to provide domestic-partner benefits.
5. To then persuade government to force all Americans to treat sexual behavior other than marriage as the equivalent of marriage.
6. To produce more "equality" for all genders, as defined by homosexual activists.

The government in states such as California has already moved to step 5 of their agenda. In San Francisco, homosexual activists have reached Step 6. Openly homosexual Congressman Barney Frank, a Democrat from Massachusetts, has adopted the line that "what is good for corporate America is good for the country" in pushing for federal domestic-partner legislation.[62] The strategy of the homosexual activists with regard to corporate America is coming dangerously close to completion.

Henry Blackaby, author of *Experiencing God,* says he believes that if revival is going to happen in America, it may very well happen through corporate America.[63] Why? Because corporations play a vital role in shaping the culture, whether it is through advertising, philanthropy, or human resources policy. A number of believers are chief executives of major corporations, but they are going to need the support of God's people to withstand the onslaught of demands by radical homosexual activists.

While corporate America can be a tool for revival in America, it can also be the tool used by radical homosexual activists to transform our country into the image they desire, an image of unlimited sexual license and a silent church. That is why radical homosexual activists have targeted corporations. They know that executives and boards of directors make most corporate decisions, and therefore it is easier to implement their agenda via this route rather than through a vote of the people.

It is going to take a concerted effort by serious people of faith to educate corporate America on the real agenda of the radical homosexual activists and why they should not adopt it. It is an agenda that not only undermines the family and promotes irresponsible sexual behavior; it is also detrimental to the best interests of both corporations and the country.

Most of all, it is going to take the persistence, prayers, and the sacrifice of God's people to help turn the tide. The gains—destructive to biblical values, the gospel, and the traditional family—made by the radical homosexual activists can be reversed and other demands halted. It will happen only if God's people are willing to take a stand, whether it be in shareholder meetings, providing economic support to companies that have stood up to radical homosexual activists, or economic punishment for those corporations that aggressively push the homosexual agenda. Corporations are run with the bottom line in mind, hence the active courting of the disposable income of practicing homosexuals. Few companies now look beyond the next quarter or fiscal year in their pursuit of a favorable balance sheet and almost none consider the next generation. Therefore, their policies are targeted to the quickest gain possible, and the affluent members of the homosexual community are an attractive market to tap. If they can be convinced that the promotion of the homosexual agenda is hurtful of that bottom line in the long run, they will change their tune.

CHAPTER EIGHT

The End of Tolerance (for Those Who Disagree)

*If I were the United Way, and all the agencies that depend on it,
I'd build a big pile of wood with a pole stuck in the middle of it.
Then I'd tie the leaders of the Boy Scouts of America to the pole, using
only the most secure half-hitches and square knots. Then I'd rub the
two sticks together and work on that campfire merit badge.*

—Mike Thomas, columnist, *Orlando Sentinel*, in response to the United Way's
financial support of the Boy Scouts of America

In the last chapter we discussed a couple of instances in which employees who objected to homosexual behavior either faced disciplinary action or were terminated because of their beliefs. In this chapter we are going to look at how this is just an extension of what can be called "The End of Tolerance" for those who disagree with the homosexual agenda.

Albert Buonanno was an employee for AT&T Broadband. When he was told that he would have to sign an employee handbook that demanded that he "value" a person's sexual orientation, he respectfully declined, citing his religious beliefs. He told his supervisors: "As a Christian, I am supposed to love my neighbor, regardless of what their sexual orientation is, but I'm not supposed to value the lifestyle of any person that contradicts the Word of God." He was fired almost immediately.[1]

A prime candidate for the football coaching job at Stanford University was disqualified because he held biblically based views on homosexual behavior. Ron Brown, an assistant coach at the University of Nebraska, had called homosexual behavior a sin while talking on a Christian radio show in 1999. Alan Glenn, the assistant athletic director of human resources at Stanford, said: "[Brown's religion] was definitely something that had to be considered."[2]

Courtney Wooten, the social director of Stanford's Queer Straight Social and Political Alliance made it clear that Brown's beliefs were a problem: "We're a very diverse community with diverse alumni. Wow, it would have been really hard for him here. He would be poorly received by the student body in general."[3]

Brown noted the different standard held for Christians who don't toe the line on homosexual behavior. He stated, "If I had been discriminated against for being black, they would've never told me that. They had no problem telling me it was because of my Christian beliefs. That's amazing to me."[4] He added:

> There was talk at a particular school [Stanford] of concern over my beliefs in Christ and how that would play out on that particular campus. It's how people live out their faith in a bold and public way that bothers people. The reason why I have not pressed forward with specifics [about what he was told by Stanford] on that is because I did not want people to lose track of the major intention, [which] is to remind Christians that we live in a world that claims to be tolerant. But they're not really tolerant of Christians [or] the Christian world view. . . . Any university or group . . . that claims the tolerance message cannot include truth in that tolerance message. The two just do not go hand in hand. If you are saying you're tolerant, and there's a Biblical mandate to stay away from a certain type of sin, then you're not going to be tolerant of that sin. You cannot possibly be tolerant over every lifestyle and every message that's given. Obviously you don't condemn other people, and you don't harm anyone else. But there's got to be some opportunity of expression of what one believes is the truth.[5]

Chris Kempling, an instructor at the British Columbia College of Teachers, was facing the suspension of his teaching license because he expressed his biblically-held view that homosexual behavior was immoral and that it should not be presented to British Columbia students as a normal and alternative lifestyle. Kempling faces a $25,000 fine as well. Jinny Sims, the head of the teachers union that should be defending Kempling said: "I really believe that as teachers we cannot let our personal religious beliefs dominate the way we communicate to our students and what we say."[6]

The bottom line is that the right of people of faith to hold sincere beliefs, along with the right to work in one's field, is under attack unless they are willing to muzzle any expression of their faith.

In Alexandria, Virginia, a Christian print shop owner refused the business of a lesbian customer who wanted him to print materials promoting a homosexual activist organization. The owner had previously printed flyers promoting the client's cleaning service, but his company's written policy clearly reserved the right to "refuse to reproduce anything that the owner deems morally questionable" and that the owner felt violated his religious beliefs. The list of objectionable material included pornography, hate literature, and pro-abortion items, as well as materials promoting homosexual behavior.

The lesbian client filed a complaint against the printer with the Alexandria Human Rights Commission. The print shop owner successfully stood up to the commission, and as a result, the city finally agreed not to bring charges against him. But the mere fact that he was brought before the commission for abiding by his deeply held religious beliefs is frightening to those who believe in religious freedom.

Larry Phillips, a Missouri state social worker, had always had exemplary performance reviews until he raised an objection to the state's licensing of practicing homosexuals as foster parents. His supervisor told him that "his religious beliefs were affecting his ability to do his job effectively"[7] and that he was "too moral."[8] He was subsequently fired on a charge that other employees just received a written reprimand on.

During oral arguments before the Eighth U.S. Circuit Court of Appeals, the deputy attorney general of Missouri argued that an employee's religious beliefs with regard to homosexual behavior could be taken into consideration when making employment decisions. *This is an absolutely chilling statement for the religious freedom of all believers.*

After the court issued a 3-0 decision in favor of Phillips, David Smith of the Human Rights Campaign put his organization's view of religious freedom this way: "Diversity of religious beliefs should be respected, as long as they don't influence public policy that should treat all people fairly."[9] Translated, that means that a person of faith has to check his religious convictions at the door and remain silent if his convictions are at odds with the homosexual agenda. Tolerance trumps religious freedom.

In Louisville, Kentucky, Dr. J. Barret Hyman, a Christian physician, challenged a city ordinance that required him to hire openly homosexual individuals in violation of his religious beliefs. The U.S. Justice Department, in an unprecedented action (under former President Clinton) became involved in the case, filing a brief in support of the local homosexual ordinance. A federal judge dismissed his lawsuit and ruled in favor of the homosexual ordinance.

Jeff Vessels, the Kentucky state director for the ACLU, stated that this decision made it clear that personal religious beliefs do not exempt someone from civil rights laws. Hyman said about the decision: "It is a sad day for Christians and most people who believe in the Bible."[10]

In the case of *Peterson v. Hewlett-Packard Co.,* a Christian was fired for putting Bible verses about homosexual behavior on the overhead bins of his work station. He did this in response to a poster of two homosexual men that the company had placed near his cubicle. When he refused to remove the verses until the company took down the poster, he was told: "You have to accept our values or be fired." He was terminated shortly afterward.

These are just a few examples of how individual Christians and religious liberty have been affected by the homosexual agenda.

Another way that religious freedom is limited is through the enactment of so-called anti-bias policies. For an example of how these policies can effectively silence those who object to homosexual behavior, consider this letter from an official in the Hennepin County, Minnesota, prison system to the volunteer chaplains who ministered there:

> A disturbing matter has come to my attention from several residents and staff of the women's facility. Without going into detail, as I understand it, an incident occurred in which volunteers told residents that homosexuality is a sin. While I will be talking personally to the Coordinator and volunteers involved, I want to make it clear to all of you that Hennepin County's overall policy is: Respect Diversity. Whether differences are based on religion, national origin, race, sexual orientation, disability . . . Hennepin County is committed to providing an environment which is respectful

of differences and free of comments or actions which may be offensive. It is crucial that all volunteers, as well as paid staff, understand this requirement. . . . I need to make it clear that in performing [volunteer service] you are required to abide by the County's diversity policy. . . . Those who, for reasons of conscience or otherwise, who don't agree to this will be requested not to be involved in the volunteer program. . . .[11]

So, if you teach what the Bible says about homosexual behavior, your volunteer service is not tolerated. Such a gag order meant that a chaplain couldn't tell an inmate whether his or her sexual behavior was a sin that Christ could forgive. If an inmate asked a chaplain, "Do you think homosexual behavior is a sin?" the chaplain would have to remain silent or have to say, "I'm sorry, government policy prevents me from answering that question." While this policy was overturned as a result of an ADF-backed legal action, it demonstrates the lengths to which homosexual activists and their allies will go to censor religious speech when it comes to homosexual behavior.

Yet another method often used by homosexual activists and their allies to deny religious freedom is their special form of diversity training. This is nothing more than indoctrination to accept homosexual behavior and ridicule anyone who holds biblical beliefs on the issue.

In another Minnesota case, three members of the Department of Corrections were forced to attend a mandatory diversity training workshop titled "Gays and Lesbians in the Workplace." When one of the employees e-mailed the warden and expressed his faith-based belief that homosexual behavior was a sin and therefore attendance should not be mandatory, the warden fired back a memo to all staff demanding participation. The three employees in the case, all Christians, attended the session, as mandated and quietly read their Bibles in the back of the room. (It should be noted that other employees were reading magazines, newspapers, sleeping, or talking with other employees during the training session.)

A month and a half after the session, the three Christian employees were singled out and given written reprimands for "inappropriate and unprofessional conduct" displayed during the training session. The reprimands specifically noted that reading their Bibles was "disrespectful and not acceptable." The three believers were the only attendees to receive the reprimands, and two of them were taken out of consideration for any future promotions. In a particularly chilling statement, one of the diversity trainers said that the mere presence of a Bible in their room created a "hostile work environment."*

With the help of an ADF funded attorney, the plaintiffs filed a federal action stating that the department's reprimand violated their rights to free speech, free exercise of religion, freedom of conscience, and Title VII† of the Civil Rights Act. The district court ruled in favor of the employees on their freedom of religion and freedom of conscience claims but denied the free speech claim.

Both sides appealed to the U.S. Appeals Court for the Eighth Circuit, which flipped the earlier decision on its head. The court ruled in favor of the plaintiff's free speech, equal protection, and Title VII rights, while *denying their freedom of religion and conscience claims* [emphasis ours]. The case awaits further court action.

In addition, the court included a disturbing note in its opinion that stated, "The only burden placed on the Appellants [the plaintiffs] was a requirement they attend a seventy-five minute training program on which they were exposed to *widely accepted views* that they oppose on faith-based principles."

Think about that statement for a moment. It essentially says that the acceptance of homosexual behavior is the "widely accepted view" and that biblical beliefs on the issue are marginal at best.

In early August 2002, the prison guards finally received justice. A nine-person jury unanimously agreed that the Minnesota Department of Corrections had violated the free speech and equal protection rights of the employees and concluded that they had been discriminated against because of their religious beliefs. The three prison guards were awarded punitive damages.

It is quite obvious from all these examples that radical homosexual activists have no qualms about forcing people of faith to violate their own religious beliefs about homosexual behavior or face the consequences. Now they are going after the very right of private organizations (including religious non-profits, organizations such as the Salvation Army, Christian businesses, and churches) to hold to their biblical beliefs when it comes to employment decisions.

The Attack on the Boy Scouts of America

There is no more visible illustration of this than the onslaught of attacks on the Boy Scouts of America by homosexual activists and their

---

*This reminds Alan of a trial while he was a federal prosecutor. During the trial, which took place in federal court, the defense lawyer tried a motion to bar Bibles and silent prayer by the spectators from the courtroom as they created an "atmosphere not conducive" for defense of obscenity charges.
†Title VII prohibits employment discrimination based on race, color, religion, sex, and national origin.

allies. There is no more vivid example of how far our country has fallen away from the principles instilled in young men by the Boy Scouts.

Yet it is ironic that while the media, homosexual activists, and their allies in government blast bishops of the Catholic Church for letting those who prey on teenage boys in, they criticize the Boy Scouts for its efforts to keep potential sexual predators out.

When we were growing up, the Boy Scouts of America were admired worldwide for teaching young men to be honest, trustworthy, good citizens, and perhaps most importantly, to have good morals and to be reverent toward God. Craig was a Life Scout (the highest rank one can obtain except Eagle) and an assistant scoutmaster for several years; Alan was involved in Cub Scouts.

James Dale was an Eagle Scout and assistant scoutmaster who publicly acknowledged his practice of homosexual behavior in a gay magazine. No one had gone on a "witch hunt" to "out" him. Because homosexual behavior is incompatible with the scouting oath and its admonition to be morally straight, he was asked to resign his leadership position. Dale instead sued the Scouts, stating that they were in violation of the state of New Jersey's anti-discrimination law, which included sexual orientation.[12]

This case had serious ramifications for the rights of all private organizations, not just the Boy Scouts of America. If the case had been lost, further legal challenges by homosexual activists (and we will discuss some of these legal challenges later) could have forced churches and private organizations to lose their right to determine their own criteria for leadership and related hiring practices.

Why? Because churches and religious organizations could also be subjected to public accommodation laws like New Jersey's because they invite others from the general public to attend and join, just like the Boy Scouts. The only possible way for churches to avoid this would be to just let the members in and lock the door and leave those who need to hear the gospel out in the street.

After a defeat at the New Jersey Supreme Court, which ruled that the Scouts were governed by public accommodation laws and would have to admit homosexual scoutmasters, the Boy Scouts appealed the decision to the U.S. Supreme Court.

The Supreme Court ruled in a close 5-4 decision that the Scouts were not subject to New Jersey's law. The court stated that the Scouts were a private group and were free to bar individuals from leadership whose behavior was incompatible with the group's beliefs.*

*Key precedent for this victory was established in one of the very first cases the Alliance Defense Fund supported before the U.S. Supreme Court: *Hurley v. The Irish-American Gay, Lesbian, Bisexual Group of*

This decision set up a tsunami of protest from radical homosexual activists and their allies in the media and government. Sympathetic city and county governments threatened to (and in some cases *did*) throw the Boy Scouts out of their public, tax-funded meeting places. The Boy Scouts were booed by delegates at the 2000 Democratic National Convention while presenting the colors there.[13] Numerous corporations* and thirty-nine chapters of the United Way (under pressure from homosexual activists) withheld funding from the Scouts in the form of financial blackmail to try to force them to change their policy.[14]

Rep. Lynn Woolsey, a California Democrat who represents the North San Francisco Bay Area, introduced legislation, which was defeated, to revoke the Scouts' federal charter.[15] Members of the Clinton administration also tried to enforce an executive order that would have evicted Scouts from using federal lands but backed down after public backlash.[16]

Also in San Francisco, the local bar association issued a policy prohibiting its members (including judges) "from activities that may give the appearance of bias based on sexual orientation." The policy states that judges "should not participate as members in a chapter or branch of any organization [such as the Boy Scouts] that invidiously discriminates on the ground of sexual orientation by excluding members on the ground of their sexual orientation, unless the judge's chapter or branch has disavowed that invidiously discriminatory policy." Angela Bradstreet, the president of the bar association said: "The bar association was very concerned about some of the language included in the lawyers' briefs in *Boy Scouts v. Dale,* as well as in subsequent cases, referring to homosexuals as not morally straight and unclean . . . . We are absolutely delighted that the San Francisco Superior Court bench has joined with the Bar Association of San Francisco in taking the lead on this issue of fairness . . . . We are now approaching other metropolitan bar associations and local courts to ask them to follow the Superior Court's lead in ensuring that there is both perception and actuality of equality and impartiality in our

---

Boston (GLIB). In that case, the United States Supreme Court upheld the right of the organizers of a private Boston Veterans Parade to bar advocates of homosexual behavior from participating. The homosexual activists had sued to be included in the event. The case had been lost several times by the veterans group as it worked its way through the judicial system. ADF became involved in the case when the attorney for the veterans asked for funding to appeal the case to the high court. With funding and additional training, the attorney was successful. In a stunning and rare 9-0 opinion, the Court overruled the previous decisions in this case, stating that the veterans had the right to bar the homosexual group from marching in its privately sponsored parade.

*Among the corporations that have pulled support from the Boy Scouts are Wells Fargo Bank, Levi Strauss, Chase Manhattan Bank, and Bank of America.

court system for everyone."[17] The California Supreme Court is now considering extending this ban to 1,600 judges statewide.[18]

Columnist Dave Thomas of the *Orlando Sentinel* viciously attacked the Scouts and basically called for the death of their leaders. He wrote: "If I were the United Way, and all the agencies that depend on it, I'd build a big pile of wood with a pole stuck in the middle of it. Then I'd tie the leaders of the Boy Scouts of America to the pole, using only the most secure half-hitches and square knots. Then I'd rub two sticks together and work on that campfire merit badge."[19]

If someone substituted the leaders of the Lambda Legal Defense and Education Fund or the Human Rights Campaign in the text instead of the Boy Scouts of America, homosexual activists and the media would scream "hate speech" and demand prosecution.

In Gloucester, Massachusetts, the mayor cancelled a city-sponsored fund-raiser for the United Way because of the organization's financial support of the Scouts. "You don't take a first step on the slippery slope of discrimination," Mayor Bruce Tobey said. "The Boy Scouts do a lot of good service for a lot of people, but the good cannot be coupled when there is public involvement with discrimination."[20]

In Santa Barbara, California, the county board of supervisors voted 3-2 to condemn the Scouts, finding them "incompatible" with the county's anti-discrimination policy, and therefore "unsupportable" by the county of Santa Barbara. Who would have ever thought that honesty, good citizenship, and upright morals would be unsupportable by a local government? Only after a group of citizens expressed outrage and prepared an initiative, with the assistance of an ADF-trained volunteer attorney, for the local ballot to protect the Scouts, did the board back down. Otherwise, Santa Barbara could have denied the Scouts access to public facilities.

In San Diego, California, the ACLU filed a lawsuit to evict the Boy Scouts from using public property they had leased from the city. The suit was filed almost immediately after the Scouts' victory at the U.S. Supreme Court. Dale Kelly Bankhead, an ACLU spokeswoman, said the lease "[made] the city a partner in the Boy Scouts' discrimination against gays and religious non-believers. While the Boy Scouts may not be for everybody, city parks are."[21] After a federal court ruled that the Boy Scouts were a "religious" organization because of their moral beliefs and should have their lease terminated, the city of San Diego caved in—and left the Scouts to fend for themselves against the ACLU. The city agreed to pay $950,000 in attorneys fees to the ACLU—money that can be used to continue the legal war by the ACLU and homosexual activists on the Boy Scouts.[22]

Other challenges to the Boy Scouts' right to use public facilities have occurred in Fort Lauderdale,[23]* New York City, Los Angeles, and Minneapolis, among other cities.[24]

In Berkeley, California, the mayor cancelled a meeting with a group of Japanese scouts from their sister city after receiving pressure from an openly homosexual city councilman. The mayor finally agreed to meet the Scouts but moved the meeting from city hall to a private home.[25]

A federal judge in Connecticut ruled that the state did not violate the rights of the Boy Scouts when it dropped them from a list of charities that state employees could contribute to via payroll deductions. A state human relations commission had previously accused the Scouts of violating the state's anti-discrimination laws.[26]

And, the American Medical Association went as far as to propose a resolution that stated that the Scouts' ban on homosexual leaders had "negative health consequences" because it would cause "psychological distress" for adolescents.[27]

Syndicated columnist David Limbaugh wrote:

> It's not enough that even the liberal United States Supreme Court ruled in *Boy Scouts of America v. Dale* that the Constitution guarantees the BSA's right to exclude homosexuals from leadership positions in its organization. Homosexual activists will not take no for an answer. Their brand of tolerance insists that no tolerance be accorded the Scouts. Forget the BSA's constitutional right to freely associate with whomever they please. No one dares to withhold approval of the homosexual lifestyle lest they invite the unquenchable wrath of homosexual activists who, ironically, insist their aim is to prevent hatred.[28]

One of the saddest parts of the attack on the Boy Scouts is that it is one of the few organizations that have been able to make a significant positive impact on troubled boys in poor urban neighborhoods.[29] When local governments evict the Scouts, these boys lose the moral guidance and life skills they so desperately need. However, in the view of homosexual activists and their allies it is more important, in some cases, to move the homosexual agenda forward than to save troubled boys.

Why do some homosexual activists want so desperately to become scoutmasters? In many cases so they can have key roles in

---

*The Scouts successfully sued the Broward County, Florida, school district (where Fort Lauderdale is located) to win equal access to the school buildings.

the formative years of boys and young men. As we outlined in chapter 3 on education, the activists know the earlier they can influence young people the more effective they are in advancing their agenda. One need only consider the priest sex scandal to identify a plausible theory along with their efforts in other countries to lower the age of consent for sex. In some countries, such as Spain, that age has been lowered to twelve! Homosexual activists in those countries have led this effort.[30]

Therefore, it is not too difficult to link homosexual behavior and predatory behaviors toward accessible teenage boys by those in positions of authority. The Scouts have genuine concern for those who are entrusted with the young men in their charge. As David Kupelian wrote, "The Scouting folks know what everyone with half a brain understands: that adults interested in sexual contact with young people gravitate toward careers and volunteer positions allowing proximity to their prey, positions such as coaches, teachers, scoutmasters—and priests."[31]

Columnist Ann Coulter added these thoughts to the debate:

> Despite the growing media consensus that Catholicism causes sodomy, an alternative view—adopted by the Boy Scouts—is that sodomites cause sodomy. . . . No spate of sex scandals is engulfing the Boy Scouts of America. Inasmuch as the Boy Scouts were not taking risk-assessment advice from Norman Mineta, they decided to eliminate a whole category of potential problems by refusing to allow gay men to be scout leaders. Perhaps gay scout leaders just really liked camping. But it was also possible that gay men who wanted to lead troops of adolescent boys into the woods were up to no good.
>
> For their politically incorrect risk-assessment technique, the Boy Scouts were denounced as troglodyte bigots in all outlets of appropriate liberal opinion. Cities and states across the country dropped their support for the scouts. The United Way, Chase Manhattan Bank, and Textron withdrew millions of dollars in contributions.
>
> And hell hath no fury like a New York Times editor spurned. The Times denounced the Supreme Court decision merely permitting the Boy Scouts to refuse gay scoutmasters as one of the court's "lowest moments." The Times "ethicist" advised readers that pulling their sons out of the Boy Scouts was the "ethical thing to do."[32]

And what can happen when a sexually predatory homosexual male does become a scoutmaster? In New York City, the leader of a Boy Scout troop pleaded guilty to four counts of third-degree sodomy after admitting that he had sexually abused a boy in his home.[33] Between 1971 and 1991, more than eighteen hundred—1,800!—Scout volunteers had to be dismissed because of sexual activity.[34*] And, the pedophilia advocacy group, NAMBLA (the North American Man-Boy Love Association)† has written a letter to the Scouts' national office asking the Boy Scouts of America "to cease its discrimination against openly gay and lesbian persons in the appointment of its scoutmasters and scouters and in membership. This will permit scouts to be exposed to a variety of lifestyles and will permit more of those individuals who genuinely wish to serve boys to do so."[35]

Unfortunately, some Boy Scout chapters in liberal areas of the country are cracking under the attacks from homosexual activist groups and their allies in the media. The Boston Minuteman Council has introduced a new diversity merit badge, adopted a so-called anti-discrimination clause that included sexual orientation, and had an openly homosexual Boston radio personality host its annual fundraiser.[36] The radio personality, David Brudnoy, said: "There are a lot of straight guys out there who could do this [emcee]." He added that the council wanted to send a signal, through his hiring, that it would not discriminate because of sexual orientation.[37]

It is not just the Boy Scouts that are under attack however. Religious-based businesses, non-profit organizations, and churches are finding themselves increasingly painted into a corner by homosexual activists.

Employers' Rights in Jeopardy

Kentucky Baptist Homes for Children (KBHC) is a religious non-profit organization that contracts with the state of Kentucky to provide a range of services for at-risk youth. It is the state's largest provider of child-care services and has a statewide network of shelters and care centers.

---

*This issue particularly hits home for Craig. Several years after he had been a Boy Scout, one of his former scoutmasters was arrested and later confessed to and was convicted of sexually molesting teenage boys in a home for troubled youth where he was providing counseling. Fortunately, Craig was not a victim of such abuse at the hands of this individual. While no system is foolproof and these actions happened after this individual was no longer a scoutmaster, it illustrates the potential danger of letting anyone openly displaying or even boasting of a proclivity for homosexual behavior (and in some cases pedophilia) be a leader of teenage boys.

†NAMBLA's literature states that one of its goals is "cooperating with the lesbian, gay, and other movements for sexual liberation." See NAMBLA: Introducing the Man-Boy Love Association, 1980.

Alicia Pedreira worked as a therapist at KBHC. When she was hired for the position, she agreed to the terms of employment that stated that KBHC had biblical objections to homosexual behavior and that any employee who engaged in such behavior would be immediately asked to resign or would be terminated. When Pedreira identified herself as an advocate of lesbian behavior, KBHC asked for her resignation. She refused, and KBHC had no other choice but to discharge her.

> *If I had been discriminated against for being black, they would've never told me that. They had no problem telling me it was because of my Christian beliefs. That's amazing to me.*
>
> —Ron Brown, who was denied the head football coaching job at Stanford University because he said homosexual behavior was a sin

Pedreira, with the help of the ACLU and Americans United for the Separation of Church and State, then filed a lawsuit in U.S. District Court that directly challenged the right of private religious organizations to determine their employment policies. She claimed that she had suffered "religious discrimination"* under Title VII† of the Civil Rights Act and that use of government funds by KBHC violated the establishment clause of the U.S. Constitution.[38] ADF supported allied attorneys assisting KBHC's defense.

The *New York Times* on April 1, 2001, hailed this case as "the most important gay rights case since *Boy Scouts of America v. Dale.*"[39] It is obvious that radical homosexual activists know that this case could open a Pandora's box full of trouble for religious organizations because a victory for Pedreira could conceivably force religious organizations that receive any form of funding from the state to employ persons who engage in homosexual behavior.

For an example, if a seminary accepts a student who has received a student loan through the federal government, the seminary could become subject to anti-discrimination laws that include sexual orientation. Why? Because the seminary is the indirect beneficiary of government funds, since those monies are going to the school to pay for a student's tuition. Or, for instance, a church runs a soup kitchen and accepts a few cases of government-excess foods to help feed the needy. The church, too, could then be made subject to the same law.

On July 23, 2001, the U.S. District Court ruled that KBHC did not violate Title VII of the Civil Rights Act when it terminated

---

*Note the argument that acting on one's religious beliefs is illegal "religious discrimination," a far-fetched but ominous legal argument.
†See footnote on page 170.

Pedreira's employment. The court correctly stated, "The civil rights statutes protect religious freedom, not personal lifestyle choices."[40] However, the judge did leave open related questions of whether the acceptance of government funds by religious organizations violates the establishment clause of the U.S. Constitution. As this case will continue to wind its way through our judicial system, the rights of faith-based organizations that receive any form of government funding will continue to remain in doubt. This case is still pending.

Bill Smithwick, the president of KBHC, stated the threat to religious freedom succinctly, "The final ruling on this issue will affect thousands of non-profits and faith-based organizations across the country."[41]

To its credit, KBHC has said that it will forgo the state funds rather than compromise its principles. Smithwick says if the court rules against KBHC, "We may have to break ranks with public funding."[42] In fact, it is already taken steps in that direction. It has announced that it will try to rely solely on donations from supporters instead.[43]

This case also bears watching because of President Bush's faith-based initiative programs. Pro-homosexual lawmakers, both Democrats and Republicans, and the media have seized upon this sincere effort by the president to allow religious groups to play a larger role in dealing with social issues, to push the homosexual agenda and force religious organizations to violate their beliefs.

On July 11, 2001, the *Washington Post* ran a scathing report on how the Bush administration had cut a "secret deal" with the Salvation Army to make sure that it was exempt from anti-discrimination laws (many of which include sexual orientation) if it accepted funds from the president's faith-based program.[44] A media and homosexual activist firestorm erupted, which led the Bush administration to back down.

Homosexual activists are relentless in trying to force religiously affiliated organizations to bow to their agenda. For example, the Greater Louisville YMCA found itself attacked by a homosexual rights group called The Fairness Campaign because it denied family memberships to same-sex couples. The group said that the YMCA's policy of offering the memberships only to heterosexual families violated the spirit of the Louisville and Jefferson County fairness ordinances, both of which include sexual orientation as a class that cannot be discriminated against in housing, employment, and accommodations. Sadly, the YMCA formed a committee "to reexamine the policy," rather than take a stance in defense of its policy.[45] The result: the YMCA gave in to the demands of those who practice homosexual behavior.* When one Christian organization caves in, it makes it tougher for those trying to stand up against the assault of homosexual activists.

The Big Brothers/Big Sisters of America announced in July 2002 that it would require its local affiliates to allow practicing homosexuals to mentor children of their gender. At least a dozen of its local affiliates have formally protested the change in policy and are in the process of severing their relationship with the national office. One executive director noted that donations were down 10 percent since the change in policy. She said that the change had "zapped our energy and our focus. It's taken countless man-hours and time and energy away from what we all want to be doing and that's serving kids." Another local director reported 100 percent opposition from parents and others to the change.[46]

The Big Brothers/Big Sisters made this change despite problems with homosexual counselors in some of its affiliates. In one example, a thirty-four-year-old mentor sexually molested a ten-year-old boy. Another homosexual Internet child pornography sting operation resulted in the arrest of two Big Brothers. Finally, another thirty-four-year-old mentor was indicted by a Kentucky grand jury on seventy-three child-sex related changes involving young boys.[47]

Salvation Army chapters across the nation are beginning to pay the price for refusing to provide health care benefits to domestic partners. In Portland, Maine, the Army lost $60,000 in annual local government funding because it refused to offer such benefits and therefore violated the city's ordinance that all groups that receive funding from the city must provide such benefits.[48] The Portland City Council rejected an amendment that would have allowed a religious exemption for faith-based organizations with sincere religious objections to homosexual behavior.[49]

Freedom of Speech?

One other method used by homosexual activists to silence believers are so-called speech codes. These codes are pernicious, since they so blatantly violate the First Amendment of the U.S. Constitution.

---

*The Young Women's Christian Association (YWCA) proclaimed in November 2002 that it had been a "very, very long time" since the organization had focused on Christian values. "Now the focus is empowering women and families," said spokesperson Crystal McNeal. That "empowerment" consists of dispensing contraceptives and condoms to girls and women, as well as support for legalized abortion. See Michael L. Betsch, "Christianity No Longer Focus of Christian Group," CNSNews. com, November 12, 2002.

The State College (Pennsylvania) Area School District instituted a speech-code policy in order to stop students from expressing negative views about homosexual behavior, among other things. When David Saxe, a professor at Penn State University, heard about this speech code, he realized the possible ramifications for his two children who were students in the school district. Saxe felt that Christians have the right and duty to share their beliefs with other students, including beliefs regarding sexual behavior.

If his children shared the gospel or called homosexual behavior disordered or something similar, they could have been subjected to a range of disciplinary actions, from a warning to expulsion, under the district policy.

Saxe, with the help of ADF-allied attorneys, challenged the constitutionality of the speech code. The United States Court of Appeals for the Third Circuit ruled in his favor, stating that such speech codes "[strike at the very] heart of moral and political discourse—the lifeblood of constitutional self-government [and democratic education] and the core concern of the First Amendment."[50]

While the result was favorable for the free speech rights of people of faith, we cannot count on the courts to continue to rule in this direction. We only need to look at what is happening internationally (for example, Bill C-250 in Canada that added "sexual orientation" to the nation's "hate speech" law) to see how far the silencing and punishment of those who do not comply with the homosexual agenda can go. Here are just a few examples:

- In Canada, serious limits have been placed on Christian broadcasters who take a biblical stand against homosexual behavior. Focus on the Family, for instance, cannot air programs that might portray homosexual behavior in a negative light, or it will face sanctions from the Canadian Communications Commission.

- In the Canadian Province of Saskatchewan, the Human Rights Commission ruled that a newspaper ad with biblical references against homosexual activity exposed homosexual men to "hatred." The advertisement featured an icon of two stick figures holding hands. The figures were covered with a circle and a slash and were accompanied by four references from the Bible, without ever quoting the words. The commission said: "the slashed figures alone were not enough to communicate the hatred . . . but the addition of Biblical references are more dangerous." The newspaper that carried the item and the man who placed the advertisement were forced to pay $1,500 to three complainants. Attorney Valerie Watson, who represented the homosexual activists, said, "It is obvious that certain of the Biblical quotations suggest more dire consequences and there can be no question that the advertisement can be objectively seen as exposing homosexuals to hatred or ridicule."[51] This ruling has now been upheld by the Court of Queen's Branch in Saskatchewan.[52]

- Students at Trinity Western University, a Christian teachers college in British Columbia, were refused accreditation to teach in public schools because they might be "unsympathetic to homosexual students" since the Christian university's policy forbids homosexual sexual relations. Students who wanted to be accredited would have to finish their training at a secular school that promoted the acceptance of homosexual behavior. John Fisher, the head of a Canadian homosexual activist group, said the Trinity students would not be able to counsel homosexual students "in a sensitive and non-judgmental way." While the Canadian Supreme Court eventually ruled 8-1 in favor of the school and said that its students did not have to go elsewhere to receive a teaching degree, the one dissenting justice, Claire L'Heureux Dube wrote that "a lack of expertise among school staff creates missed opportunities to help lesbian, bisexual, and gay youth before a crisis develops."[53]

- In British Columbia, a high school teacher was suspended for a month because he wrote letters to the local newspaper stating that homosexual behavior is not a "fixed orientation" but a condition that should be treated.[54]

- Also in British Columbia, the Human Rights Tribunal was told that the provincial ministry of education discriminates against homosexual and bisexual students if it does not provide "positive" messages of sexual orientation and gender identity in the classroom.[55]

- In New Zealand, two Christian videos that dealt with the link between AIDS and homosexual activity, questioned "safe sex," and investigated the homosexual agenda were subject to being outlawed by the New Zealand parliament as promoting "hate speech."[56]

- One more British Columbia example: All marriage commissioners in the province who were not willing to perform same-sex "marriage" ceremonies were told they had to resign unless they relented and did so. Vancouver city councillor Tim Stevenson said, "You either do it or you look for another job."[57]

• In Sweden, the parliament approved an amendment that bans all speech and materials opposing homosexual behavior and other alternative lifestyles. Violators could spend up to four years in jail. According to Annalie Enochson, a Christian member of parliament, Christians could be arrested for speaking about homosexual behavior in churches. "That means people coming from [the homosexual] lobby group could sit in our churches having on the tape recorder and listen to somebody and say, 'What you're saying now is against our constitution.'"[58] In June 2004, a Swedish court sentenced a Pentecostal pastor to a month in prison, under this law, for "offending" homosexuals in a sermon.[59]

• Also in Sweden, a company was forced to pay a former employee approximately $6,800 in damages after the employee accused her boss of homophobia for expressing his displeasure over a public lesbian kiss she shared with her girlfriend. The lesbian said that she felt "ostracized" at work and felt that she had to quit.[60]

• The French government approved a bill outlawing "homophobia." The bill made "incitement to discrimination, hatred, or violence against a person on the basis of gender or sexual orientation" punishable by a year in prison or a 45,000 euro ($54,000 American) fine. Of course, like C-250, religious speech that disapproves of homosexual behavior could be construed to cause "incitement," just as innocent Christian leaders were accused of in the days after the Matthew Shepard case here in America.[61]

• In Great Britain, homosexual activists tried to challenge the charitable status of a Christian organization that had spoken out against the liberalization of age of consent laws (again the link between homosexual behavior and the sexual pursuit of teenage boys). While the charitable status of the organization was upheld, it was silenced when it agreed to "no longer influence public policy."[62]

• In England, Prime Minister Tony Blair's government has sought to repeal a law that barred the use of public funds to promote homosexual behavior because the law served "no public purpose" and would "offend 'gays.'"[63]

- In the Netherlands, Dutch authorities pondered whether or not to prosecute Pope John Paul II on discrimination charges after he said that a homosexual advocacy march in Rome was "an offense to Christian values."[64] While they eventually recognized that the pope had "global immunity" because of his position as the head of the Vatican, the very thought of possible prosecution of a worldwide religious leader for his stance on homosexual behavior in another country demonstrates where the concept of speech codes and hate crimes legislation can eventually lead.

Many Christians still say to themselves, "But that is happening over in Europe and in Canada; it's not happening in America." Well, we have some bad news for such wishful thinkers. It is beginning to occur here as well.

Matt Foreman, the executive director of the National Gay and Lesbian Task Force, said in *Between the Lines,* a Detroit homosexual news magazine, that he will "punish," "terrify," and "torture" anyone who opposes the homosexual agenda. He went on to say that such actions would bring him "endless satisfaction." He said, "I'm interested . . . in going after, politically, local legislators and leaders that have launched these anti-gay initiatives (to protect traditional marriage). We beat you; now we're gonna go back and we're going to affirmatively punish you."[65]

After a pro-marriage rally staged by the Center for Arizona Policy, E. J. Montini, a columnist for the *Arizona Republic,* wrote mockingly, "We are at war with extremists whose hatred is based on moral superiority and religious fanaticism."[66]

A California state appeals court has found that two Christian doctors in San Diego County were wrong when they refused to artificially inseminate a lesbian. The lesbian's attorney, Jennifer Pizer, said her clients were "traumatized" by the "discrimination."[67] The attorney said on "Hannity and Colmes," "When the doctor is in her church, she can do religion, but not in the medical office."[68] David Limbaugh added, "Gay rights groups . . . are always the first to demand tolerance, but apparently their idea of tolerance is a one-way street. To demonstrate their commitment to tolerance, they should respect the doctors' religious convictions. Until they do, they will be signaling that it is not tolerance they seek, but conformity to their worldview they demand."[69]

In Pennsylvania, a recent amendment to the state's "hate crimes" law added "sexual orientation" and "gender identity" as "motives that trigger heavier penalties for individuals found guilty of 'harassment.'" In addition, the definition of *harassment* was expanded to include "harassment by communication." Kevin Hasson, president of the Becket Fund for Religious Liberty, said, "Although legislators expressly disavowed the motive at the time, one might be forgiven the impression that one purpose of this legislation was to generate a fear of prosecution among those who would preach and teach in favor of the traditional prohibition on homosexual behavior . . . . It is a measure of our times that religious leaders have lately considered taking out liability insurance to cover remarks made from the pulpit."[70]

Where do radical homosexual activists want to take us with regard to religious freedom and public acknowledgment of God? One needs to look no further than the United Kingdom, where a British homosexual group has demanded that all references to God be stricken out of the preamble to a new European Union constitution. Gay and Lesbian Humanist Association spokesman Terry Sanderson said, "Religion is dying throughout Europe and we have to realize that." The group added, "To include references to God or our 'Christian heritage' would start turning back on our 500-year journey from the Enlightenment. Instead, we should be proud of our progress and growing humanity."[71]

Or we can take another look to Canada. At a February 12, 2003, University of Toronto symposium on "Religion vs. Sexual Orientation: A Clash of Human Rights?", Dr. Robert Wintemute of the School of Law at King's College at the University of London said, "The religious majority may seek to have their beliefs reflected in secular laws, but they must do so through reasoned secular arguments. Religious text or doctrines must be excluded from legislative and judicial debates because unlike secular law, they rely on [an] inaccessible, extra democratic source of authority, which cannot be challenged or overturned by reasoned arguments. . . . Religious doctrines must be deemed absolutely irrelevant in determining the content of secular laws."[72]

Canadian lawyer Barbara Finley, an open lesbian, said, "The legal struggle for queer rights will one day be a struggle between religious freedom versus sexual orientation."[73]

Finally, we can look to the United Nations. At a meeting sponsored by the UN Gay, Lesbian, Bisexual Employees, or UNGLOBE, a multipronged strategy for a "showdown with religion" on homosexual "rights" was launched. At this meeting, attended briefly by UN Secretary General Kofi Annan, Roman Catholics and evangelical Christians were targeted as the "chief opponents" of the homosexual agenda. Princeton University professor Anthony Appial pondered whether religion should be "limited" because it poses a "challenge" to homosexual activists. Svend Robinson, the author of C-250, openly mocked born-again Christians, saying, "Do they have to come back as themselves?"[74]

In the radical homosexual activist manifesto *After the Ball,* Marshall Kirk and Hunter Madsen wrote, "[In regards to those] who feel compelled to adhere rigidly to an authoritarian belief structure (i.e., an orthodox religion), that condemns homosexuality . . . our primary objective regarding die-hard homohaters of this sort is to cow and silence them."[75] As we have seen in this chapter, their strategy is being played out on a daily basis against people of faith and religious organizations. We have a choice: We can either stand up and fight for our religious freedoms or allow the radical homosexual activists to cow and silence us. The choice is ours to make, and sad to say, to this point, many believers have chosen the latter option.

CHAPTER NINE

The Full Weight
of the Government

*Their goal is to get sexual orientation included [into "hate crimes"
legislation]. Once they do that, this is laying the foundation for law
enforcement to take care of those people that they consider to be
members of the hate group. Churches, pastors, the whole nine yards.
I don't think there will be any group left untouched
when their agenda is finally completed.*

—Kevin McCoy, West Virginia Family Foundation

On June 25, 2001, Judy Guerin of the National Coalition for Sexual
Freedom gave a speech at the fifteenth annual World Congress of
Sexology in Paris. Her speech discussed her organization's plan to
reform sexual laws in the United States. Her talk outlined the agenda
of radical homosexual activists and their allies to push their agenda
through federal, state, and local legislatures and bring the full weight
of government pressure and laws down on those who hold biblical
standards of sexual behavior.

In her speech, Guerin discussed at length the changing "sexual
ethos" of Americans, much of it driven by the gains made by the radical homosexual activists in the past decade. She stated: "The public
discussion of sex appears to have increased tolerance for a broader
range of sexual expression. As a result, the time seems right to press
for the abolition of laws that prohibit consensual sexual activities

such as sodomy, adultery, pornography, sadomasochism, and what constitutes public sex."[1]

In June 2004, the National Gay and Lesbian Task Force (NGLTF) stated that it was time to repeal America's "archaic and unjust" sex laws. NGLTF launched a project to "identify" which laws need to be done away with. The task force press release said that the point of the project was "to educate Americans about the prevalence and abuse of antiquated and unjust sex laws in the nation, and to give grassroots activists policy and organizing tools to work to change these laws." Targeted laws included those against public lewdness that, in the words of NGLTF, "are routinely misused to persecute and prosecute people who participate in non-traditional forms of sexual expression." NGLTF also said that it looked at age-of-consent laws as well.[2]

As we have discussed earlier, the increasing exposure to and "tolerance" of homosexual behavior leads to the normalization and acceptance of other disordered sexual behaviors. As former law professor and federal circuit court judge Robert Bork put it so succinctly, we, as Americans, are indeed "slouching towards Gomorrah" (referring to the city that God destroyed in the Book of Genesis because of the rampant sexual sin there).* The result is that sexual disorders and extreme behavior are exalted, and the traditional family and religious freedoms are attacked.

What is alarming though, is that the radical homosexual activists and their allies want to write into law their special manifestations of a so-called right to privacy (a right that appears nowhere in the Constitution and was created in its present form by a majority of the Supreme Court in the infamous *Roe v. Wade* decision). This will allow them to openly practice and celebrate any variety of sexual behavior and to punish those who hold to biblical standards of sexual behavior. Guerin said, "The right to privacy must be extended to include one's choice of an adult sexual partner, or partners, *in or outside of marriage* [which used to be called adultery] and the full range of consensual sexual behaviors in which people engage, so, too, must the definition of 'privacy' be broadened to include public spaces such as sex clubs and live entertainment."[3] [emphasis added]

In fact, in December 2002, the radical homosexual activists had one of their long-term wishes fulfilled when the United States Supreme Court accepted a legal challenge (*Lawrence v. Texas*) to its 1986 decision in *Bowers v. Hardwick* that held that states could proscribe

---

*See Genesis 19.

same-sex sodomy.* Oral arguments were held on March 26, 2003, and a decision was issued on June 25, 2003.

In this case, two homosexual men living in Texas were engaging in same-sex sodomy when police and other emergency personnel entered their property, responding to an emergency call to investigate a report that a man was "going crazy" with a gun.[4] Since same-sex sodomy is illegal in Texas, the two men were fined.

Overturning the *Bowers* decision has been the top item on the wish list for homosexual activists since 1986. If they got rid of *Bowers,* their sexual behavior (which carries tremendous public health risks, including the rapid spread of HIV/AIDS and other sexually transmitted diseases) can no longer be proscribed by the state. These behaviors that have cost Americans billions of dollars, millions of broken, wounded souls, and the very lives of thousands will be recognized as a protected activity!† With this they believe all of the other legal "dominoes" that stand in the way of their agenda will begin to fall, such as prohibitions on same-sex "marriage," the lifting of the "don't ask, don't tell" policy on homosexuals in the military, nationwide adoption of children by same-sex couples, and most of all, the restricting of free speech rights for all who have biblical or faith-based objections to endorsing, funding, or supporting the sexual behavior.

In fact, in their petition to the Supreme Court to hear the case, the radical homosexual organization Lambda Legal Defense and Education Fund wrote that laws that prohibit or restrict sodomy are used to "justify discrimination against 'gay' men and lesbians, in parenting, employment, access to civil rights laws, and many other aspects of everyday life."[5] The homosexual activists have made it clear where they want to go if they win *Lawrence.*

---

*The Lambda Legal Defense and Education Fund is basing their case in part on the so-called "right to privacy" that was the linchpin in the infamous *Roe v. Wade* decision. This "right to privacy" was fabricated from a moon shadow by former Justice William O. Douglas in the case of *Griswold v. Connecticut.* Douglas claimed that he "discovered" this "right to privacy" in the "emanations" from the "penumbra" mystically hidden in the 3rd and 4th Amendments to the Constitution and between the 9th and 10th Amendments. What is a "penumbra"? It is a cloudy shadow around the moon. This ended up being the basis for the Roe decision.

†In February 2003, *Rolling Stone* magazine, hardly a conservative publication, ran a story on "bug chasing, the behavior of homosexual men who deliberately engage in activities that could cause them to contract HIV/AIDS as a "badge of honor." The writer cited sources estimating that 25 percent of all newly-positive HIV positive men had contracted the disease this way. Radical homosexual activists immediately went into spin control and tried to discredit the study in *Newsweek* magazine and other sources. Whether or not the 25 percent figure is accurate, "bug chasing" and the abandonment of so-called "safe-sex" has been well-documented over the years in several mainstream media sources, including the *New York Times* and *San Francisco Chronicle.* See Gregory A. Freeman, "Bug Chasers: The Men Who Long to Be HIV+," *Rolling Stone,* February 2003. Also see Seth Mnookin, "Is Rolling Stone's HIV Story Wildly Exaggerated?" *Newsweek,* January 24, 2003.

Annise Parker, an openly lesbian member of the Houston City Council said about *Lawrence:* "It's one more battle, one more step. I think there will be a huge celebration if we win it."[6] Ruth Harlow, a Lambda attorney arguing the case, said: "It's the most important gay rights case in a generation."[7]

Christians had reason to be concerned when the Supreme Court granted review of this case, which challenged Texas's law designed to protect marriage and the public health by barring same-sex sodomy (thirteen states still had such a bar as of 2003). The court rarely grants review to a case that challenges a previous High Court opinion if the voting justices do not believe they have the votes to overturn it.

Remember, just seventeen years ago, then Chief Justice Warren Burger said this about sodomy in his 1986 concurring majority opinion in *Bowers:* "Decisions of individuals relating to homosexual conduct have been subject to state intervention throughout the history of Western civilization. Condemnation of those practices is firmly rooted in Judeo-Christian moral and ethical standards . . . . [Sir William] Blackstone described 'the infamous crime against nature' as an offense of 'deeper malignity' than rape, a heinous act 'the very mention of which is a disgrace to human nature' and 'a crime not fit to be named.' To hold that the act of homosexual sodomy is somehow protected as a fundamental right would be to cast aside millennia of moral teaching."[8]

In a 6-3 decision, the U.S. Supreme Court provided exactly what the radical homosexual activists wanted: the extension of the so-called "right to privacy" to include homosexual sodomy. In his majority opinion, Justice Anthony Kennedy did not look to the U.S. Constitution for guidance but instead to "trends" in state laws and, even more alarmingly, to "international law" as the basis for the decision! Quickly afterward, radical homosexual activists started to use the Lawrence decision to press for the total completion of their agenda, including same-sex marriage, adoption, and the elimination of the "don't ask, don't tell" policy of the U.S. military.

Still some people may be saying, "So what? Who cares what homosexuals do in their bedroom?" But as former Chief Justice Warren Burger wrote, good governments have always regulated sexual behavior. Once one state law protecting marriage and regulating sex is found to be unconstitutional, all others are fair game, such as laws against pedophilia, sex between close relatives, polygamy, bestiality, and all other distortions and violations of God's plan. In addition, to the impact on human and marital relations, the state has a great interest in the public health costs and the moral impact on the culture.

The efforts to reverse the experience of Western civilization all ties into the overall strategy of desensitization toward deviant and now often unlawful sexual behavior, as outlined by Kirk and Madsen. Once homosexual behavior is seen as something to be tolerated or even affirmed then other sexual activists can come back and say, "Then what about our sexual preferences and behaviors?"

Another issue is the definition of consent by sexual liberation activists. Efforts to lower ages for consent would apply it to all kinds of deviant sexual behavior. Guerin stated that she felt that the homosexual movement had forced Americans to "confront" and "begin to overcome" traditional gender roles. She was encouraged the most by the "non-judgmental" attitude that Americans had adopted to deviant sexual behavior.[9]

She continued: "The new societal attitudes of openness and tolerance as to sexuality are evidencing themselves in a variety of ways. A major indication is the inclusion of an ever-broader range of sexually-defined groups in the U.S. anti-discrimination laws at the Federal and State levels: women, gays and lesbians, transgender people (the latter only in a few recent instances), with the types of protection (jobs, housing, parental rights, etc.) also expanding."[10]

Guerin concluded that the time is ripe for the United States to legislate acceptance of more and more forms of sexual behavior. She called for the elimination of all statutes and government regulations regarding the choice by so-called sexual minorities of a marriage partner (including those who are "gender variant" or engage in wife-swapping); extending the principles of freedom of speech to all forms of pornography; and changing the attitudes of law enforcement and the medical professionals toward all forms of sexual behavior.[11]

California: The Brave New World

Much of the brave new world of sexual liberation that Guerin described is already occurring in the state of California. A cadre of homosexual lawmakers, working with political allies and with a sympathetic governor, have begun turning the state into what they describe as "the friendliest place in America for homosexuals."[12] And, not coincidentally, it has become one of the increasingly hostile areas in the country for religious liberty.

What is happening in California may eventually occur at the federal level if people of faith continue to turn a blind eye to what is happening in local and state governments. The result will be increasingly dramatic losses of religious freedom and mandatory (under penalty of law) violation of conscience.

As so-called "anti-discrimination" laws are expanded to include more and more sexual minorities and an ever-expanding list of what constitutes discrimination, serious Christians will find themselves more and more isolated and discriminated against in a society that has turned its back on God's plan for human sexual behavior.

For example, in 2001, former Governor. Gray Davis signed AB1475. This bill removed the "religious exemption" that had protected religious health care providers, such as Catholic or Baptist hospitals, from being subjected to anti-discrimination laws that include sexual orientation. The bill stated that it would "make the provisions of the act prohibiting harassment [which is defined in the bill as refusing to hire or employ a practicing homosexual or to fire someone because of his or her sexual orientation] applicable" if the hospital accepts patients who are non-adherents of the religion of the hospital.[13] Thus, if a Catholic or Baptist hospital accepts a non-Catholic or non-Baptist patient as part of its ministry, the hospital is immediately subject to anti-discrimination laws that include sexual orientation.

Another bill the governor signed into law was SB225. This bill required that private (which in many cases means religious) schools with interscholastic sports teams adopt non-discrimination policies supporting sexual orientation and "perceived gender" or face the prospect of being banned from the California Interscholastic Federation (CIF) or other interscholastic sports programs.[14] In a nutshell, schools, both public and private, must have a non-discrimination policy that includes sexual orientation in place or otherwise they can no longer compete in interscholastic sports. As the law is written, a religious-based school that refuses to abandon its convictions and challenges this law may have to explain its "religious tenets" to a judge who will ultimately decide the case.*

In May 2002, the California Senate approved a tax break for unmarried couples that gives them the same property tax exemptions as traditional married couples. Unmarried couples that have lived together for at least five years will not be subject to property tax assessments when one of them dies. Jackie Speier, the sponsor of the bill, said: "We can no longer define the family in the traditional way,

---

*In chapter 5 we discussed former Governor. Gray Davis's signing a domestic partners bill (passed on September 12, 2001, the day after the attacks on the Pentagon and World Trade Center) that gave domestic partners a dozen of the same rights as married couples. This was in despite of a 2–1 popular vote in March 2000 that reaffirmed marriage in California as being between one man and one woman. See Jim Wasserman, "California Governor Signs Gay Rights Bill," Associated Press, October 15, 2001.

and the state should not be judging individuals' living arrangements."[15] But of course, the state is making a judgment by granting this special exception to advance fornication, sodomy, and other behaviors leading to non-normal living arrangements.

In early August 2003, then-Governor Davis signed into law AB196, authored by openly homosexual assemblyman Mark Leno of San Francisco. This bill prohibits housing and workplace discrimination based on "gender characteristics" (i.e., "transgenderism"). The bill was coauthored by four members of the state's "Legislative Lesbian, Gay, Bisexual and Transgender Caucus."[16] Leno tried to take advantage of the war in Iraq by stating, "Particularly at this time when we are at war supposedly defending democracy, everyone without exception should have an opportunity to pursue their dreams and become all that they are God-given."[17] The bill contains no exemption for religious business owners, owners of Bible bookstores, or for non-profit organizations such as the Boy Scouts if they refused to hire someone because they are a transsexual. Those found in violation of the proposed law would be fined $150,000.[18]

The Pretense of Tolerance Is Over Part 2

While many would tend to dismiss what is happening in California because of its liberal reputation, it still illustrates the growing national threat to people of faith. This is because it is the largest state in the nation, and if it were an independent nation it would be the sixth largest economy in the world. Homosexual activists have had virtual carte blanche in the state legislature in efforts to advance their agenda and restrict the freedoms of those who hold and practice sincere religious beliefs opposing homosexual behavior. California is not the only place that has begun to open its doors wide to homosexual activism. It is happening at the federal, state, and local levels nationwide. Here are just a few examples, including some more from the Golden State:

- In Philadelphia, Mayor John Street signed an ordinance that added gender identity to the city's anti-discrimination ordinance. It was adopted on April 30, 2002. New York, San Francisco, Denver, and Minneapolis also have similar laws.[19]
- When San Francisco's law was passed back in 1994, former Supervisor Terence Hallinan said: "Very seldom do we have the opportunity to make history, to reach out beyond the mundane and make justice. We are doing it here. We are creating a new civil right."[20]

- In July 2001, the state of Rhode Island enacted a measure that extended civil rights protection to transsexuals and cross-dressers. The Associated Press reported, "The measure was enacted on the final day of the legislative session, barely raising a fuss—a sign perhaps of the growing trend around the country of offering anti-discrimination protections to transgendered individuals."[21] Even homosexual activists didn't expect this bill to pass. "We thought it would be very controversial, but legislators seemed to understand it was an issue of basic human rights," said Tina Wood of the Rhode Island Alliance for Lesbian and Gay Civil Rights.[22]

- A New Jersey Appeals court ruled that the state's anti-discrimination law applied to transgendered individuals. The decision read as follows: "It is incomprehensible to us that our Legislature would ban discrimination against heterosexual men and women; against homosexual men and women; against bisexual men and women; against men and women who are perceived, presumed or identified by others as not conforming to the stereotypical notions of how men and women behave, but would condone discrimination against men or women who seek to change their anatomical sex because they suffer from a gender identity disorder."[23] Such a decision opens up a whole slew of expanding rights for various sexual behaviors.*

- On May 1, 2002, the *New York Times* expressed its editorial support for a "transgendered rights" bill that was signed into law by New York City Mayor Michael Bloomberg. The *Times* wrote, "The transgendered category covers a wide array of people who do not fit into traditional gender groups, whether due to appearance, behavior or physical attributes. . . . Because the rights of the transgendered have gotten little attention, it might seem that New York broke new ground yesterday. But in fact, more than 40 towns, counties, cities, and states—including Iowa City, Louisville, Kentucky, and Rhode Island—have written transgendered people into their anti-discrimination laws. New York City's action yesterday was not path-breaking, but it should light the way for other jurisdictions to extend protection to their own transgendered citizens."[24] In regard to such laws, Paisley Currah, associate

---

*Many homosexuals acknowledge implicitly that deviating from God's norms for marriage get worse and worse. Now, many use the word *queer* because it embodies more sexual minorities than just homosexuals.

professor of political science at City University of New York, said, "It's [transgendered protection] totally exploding—in law, the amount of litigation, the laws passed, the law reviews written. Transgendered people have become more organized and [are] moving beyond merely a support system for each other to actually fighting for their rights."[25]

• In Minnesota, former governor Jesse Ventura proclaimed June 2002 Gay, Lesbian, Bisexual, Transgender Pride Celebration Month after refusing to issue a proclamation in support of the National Day of Prayer. Ventura's proclamation read: "Members of the gay, lesbian, bisexual, transgender community have made significant contributions towards the enhancement of our quality of life through active involvement in the economic and political activities of the community."[26]

• In Sacramento, an elaborate display proclaiming June as "Gay Pride Month" was featured in the rotunda of the state Capitol where a Christmas nativity display would bring lawsuits and screams of protest. It included a pink triangle (the homosexual symbol of pride) and photographs of the state's four lesbian lawmakers.[27]

• The chief justice of Quebec, Michel Robert, said that the work of the Canadian judiciary had been to re-create a new and moral social order that affirmed homosexual behavior. In an interview with the *National Post,* the chief justice said that the nature of the judiciary is to create social policy and redefine public policy without public oversight and without reference to "traditional moral norms." He concluded: "We are defining the fundamental socio-economic values of the society and I don't think this will change." He then linked legalized abortion and same-sex "marriage": "If same-sex marriages are legal and being performed every day, it's because of three courts' decisions—BC, Ontario, and Quebec. The courts defined what is permitted and what is not permitted in terms of abortion in this country, and the same thing might happen with . . . same-sex marriage."[28]

• Attorney General John Ashcroft, who himself has often taken a strong stance against homosexual behavior, allowed his deputy attorney general, Larry Thompson, to speak at a "Gay Pride" celebration in the United States Department of Justice's great hall.[29] Betty DeGeneres, the mother of Ellen DeGeneres, also spoke at the Office of Personnel

Management's Gay Pride celebration.[30] The Bush adminis-
tration also appointed an actively practicing homosexual
man to the post of Ambassador to Romania, and Secretary of
State Colin Powell pointedly introduced the man's partner,
who will reside in government-funded housing, at the State
Department swearing-in ceremony.[31] Robert Steers, of the
GOP homosexual group, the Log Cabin Republicans, said,
"We have never had this much access to a Republican White
House before."[32] Finally, the Bush administration let stand
Clinton White House policies that extended workplace dis-
crimination claims to include sexual orientation.[33]

• It was reported on March 24, 2004, that in 2003 the number
of individuals discharged from the armed forces for violations of military standards relating to homosexual behavior
had fallen to 787, the lowest level since 1995.[34] (For the
prior five years, the armed services discharged more than
1,000 members annually, and a total of more than 8,500
members since implementation of former President Bill
Clinton's "Don't Ask, Don't Tell" policy).

Under this policy, men and women who engage in
homosexual behavior were allowed to remain in the military as long as they kept their "sexual orientation" private
and refrained from homosexual behavior. In fact, under the
present military policy, a service member's commander—
who may *not* ask a member to reveal their sexual "orientation"—is able to initiate an inquiry or process for discharge
only if the member (1) makes a statement that he or she is
lesbian, gay, or bisexual; (2) engaged in physical contact
with someone of the same sex for purposes of sexual grati-
fication; or (3) married or attempted to marry someone of
the same sex.

Even these very limited rules were too restrictive for the
homosexual advocates who sued the military repeatedly to
challenge its rules. The Alliance Defense Fund provided
funding for allied attorneys in their efforts to help defend the
law in three separate legal challenges to the military's pro-
scription on active, open homosexual behavior in the armed
services of the United States. These legal challenges were
heard by federal circuit courts of appeal. In each case, the
Pentagon was deeply concerned about the impact of such
open behavior on the high standards of conduct and performance essential for military readiness.

The Department of Defense has not commented on the 2002 decline in involuntary separations for homosexual conduct, nor is it clear that the decline is statistically significant. Nevertheless, homosexual activist C. Dixon Osburn, the executive director of the Servicemembers Legal Defense Network (dedicated to the removal of the "don't ask, don't tell" policy and for the open participation in homosexual behavior in the military), said: "When they need lesbian, gay, and bisexual Americans most, military leaders keep us close at hand."[35] It is unlikely, however, that most commanders knowingly retain individuals who fail to obey the "don't tell" and "don't engage in homosexual conduct" policy. In fact, recruitment is up and retention standards in general are tighter than in today's armed forces. Still, considering the limited proscriptions* of the current policy, it is astounding that so many men and women each year fail to keep their homosexual desires, activities, or behaviors private and to themselves.

- In Benton County, Oregon, county commissioner Linda Modrell announced that the county would not issue marriage licenses to heterosexual couples until the homosexual couples were allowed to marry. Modrell said, "To maintain consistency with our oath to uphold Oregon's Constitution's anti-discrimination provisions, we must temporarily cease issuing marriage licenses to any couple, regardless of gender until there is a state determination."[36]

- The Centers for Disease Control launched a campaign called "STOP AIDS: Sex in the City." Included in this campaign were workshops on "Sex Toys and Gay Masturbation Techniques" and "Exploration of 'Gay' Intimacy and Fantasy" and a live bondage/sadomasochistic show featuring toys, role-playing, and "scene negotiation." This program received $698,000 in federal funding in fiscal year 2000 under then-President Clinton.[37]

- Another Centers for Disease Control Web site featured a link to Internet pages of "pro-sex" activist organizations that provided teenagers with explicit advice on homosexual behavior, sodomy, and masturbation. The link was to the Coalition for Positive Sexuality and featured statements like: "If you think you might be queer, relax! If you think you might be

---

*This comment is from Melissa Wells-Petry, a former major in the U.S. Army.

queer, try to find a lesbian/bisexual/gay/transgender community center near you."[38]

• In Portland, Oregon, Mayor Vera Katz issued an official
proclamation commemorating "Leather Pride Week" in
honor of the National Leather Association's Bondage,
Discipline, and Sadomasochism Event in the city. A
spokesman for the mayor said that the proclamation "cited
the importance of a diverse community and praised the
motto of 'Safe, Sane, and Consensual' adopted by the leather
community." Susan Brownlow, the state director of
Concerned Women for America, said: "Where are you going
to stop? Is it going to be pedophilia next?"[39]

As you can see from each of these pieces of legislation and other
actions by federal, state, and local governments, the affirmation of
homosexual behavior is just the beginning. Once homosexual behavior is affirmed by government, promoters of other disordered sexual
behaviors (behaviors prohibited by Scripture) start to demand their
rights. After all, if you are going to tolerate one, you have to tolerate
all.

For the Christian, the issue becomes especially problematic
when the government adopts special legal privileges for those
engaging in homosexual and other extramarital sexual behavior. As
we have seen with the Catholic and other religious hospitals in
California, the passage of such legislation is just one short step away
from forcing Christians, churches, and religious organizations to
violate their sincere beliefs with regard to homosexual behavior or
cease to function.

The Supreme Court has already upheld the exclusive power of the
Internal Revenue Service to determine when the "public interest"
trumps religious liberty for tax exemption purposes. In 1983, the
Court, in an 8–1 decision, upheld the revocation of the tax-exempt,
non-profit status of Bob Jones University* because school officials
genuinely believed "that the Bible forbids interracial dating and
marriage." (See appendix 1 for a more detailed discussion of this decision.) Therefore, if homosexual behavior is legally equated with race
as the radical activists demand, and is granted heretofore unimagined
constitutional protection, then the next logical step, based on the decision in *Bob Jones University v. United States of America*, could be for tra-

---

*In 1970, a federal court decision prohibited the IRS from allowing tax-exempt status for certain pri-
vate schools whose admission policies discriminated on the basis of race. See *Green v. Kennedy*, 309 F.
Supp. 1127, appeal dism'd sub nom. *Cannon v. Green*, 398 U.S. 956 (1970).

ditional Bible-based religious organizations and churches to have their tax-exempt status revoked because they engage in "discriminatory" behavior. The U.S. Supreme Court wrote: "History buttresses logic to make it clear that, to warrant exemption under 501c3, an institution must . . . *be in harmony with the public interest. The institution's purpose must not be so at odds with the common community conscience as to undermine any public interest that might otherwise be conferred.*"[40]

> *Very seldom do we have the opportunity to make history, to reach out beyond the mundane and make justice. We are doing it here. We are creating a civil right.*
> —Former San Francisco Supervisor Terence Hallinan on the city's passage of a transgender anti-discrimination law

We are beginning to see the first stages of radical homosexual activists playing this trump card. As reported in chapter 6, the Canyon Ferry Baptist Church in Montana found itself under investigation after it hosted a closed-circuit television feed of pro-marriage speakers in Colorado Springs. During the rally, a petition was circulated in support of an amendment to the Montana Constitution that would define marriage to be between one man and one woman. These actions are perfectly legal under IRS guidelines (see Gary McCaleb's letter in appendix 2). ADF counsel Gary McCaleb—with local lawyers Timothy C. Fox and Alan Jocelyn—filed a lawsuit in Helena, Montana, seeking declaratory relief from the state's efforts to apply state election law to churches that merely teach and preach in support of traditional marriage and make petitions available on church premises to qualify the constitutional amendment for the Montana ballot.[41]

In addition, as also reported in chapter 6, churches that do not perform same-sex "marriages" could also face legal challenges to their tax-exempt status if they are found to engage in "discrimination." (See appendix 1.)[42]

Therefore, if homosexual behavior is found by the IRS and the courts to be in "harmony" with the public interest, and if biblical teachings and practices of churches and religious organizations are "at odds" with the common community conscience that affirms homosexual behavior, their financial status will be seriously compromised.

The ENDA of Religious Freedom

This is where the danger of the federal Employment Non-Discrimination Act, better known as ENDA, comes in. This legislation, which was barely defeated in the U.S. Senate in 1996 (and would have been readily signed by then-President Bill Clinton) by a margin of 50-49,[43] would have added the category of sexual orientation to the 1964 federal Civil Rights Act. It continues to be brought up year after year until it is passed.

When one looks at the demographics of the homosexual community, it becomes quite obvious that those who identify themselves as homosexual or engaging in homosexual behavior are not nearly the oppressed class portrayed. In fact, the marketing strategies of entire industries, such as airlines, cruise lines, and alcoholic beverages, are based on their knowledge of the ready cash available to the active homosexual and the homosexual media's knowledge of that cash to sell advertising.

In a 2000 study released by Simmons Research, the average income of homosexual and lesbian households was found to be $85,000, or more than *twice* the national average[44] (see chap. 7). Another study by Syracuse University in 2001 found that the *median* income for homosexual couples in the United States was $65,000, *nearly 60 percent higher than the national median of $40,800.* More than a fifth of those who responded to the Syracuse study reported an income of $100,000 or more.[45] It is interesting to note that homosexual advocates, conference leaders, and activists promote these figures when trying to convince corporations, like United Airlines, to market to them or grant special privileges but then deny the existence of the very same statistics when they are trying to make the argument that they are an "oppressed" class.[46]

In fact, Rich Tafel, head of the GOP homosexual organization, the Log Cabin Republicans, questioned the need for ENDA. He said, "I can tell you anecdotally that as I travel all over the country, I almost never hear from anyone who was fired because they were gay."[47] After a firestorm of protest from homosexual activists, observers predict Tafel will either quietly reverse his position or no longer head the Log Cabin Republicans.

It becomes quite obvious that the single greatest reason for ENDA to exist is to limit, stop, and punish individuals and organizations that believe that homosexual behavior is sinful or disordered and that so-called personal sexual and related behavior can in fact have a public or employment related impact.

ENDA's supporters claim that religious organizations, including schools and institutions of higher learning owned and operated by a religious organization would have been exempt from the bill,[48] However, Roger Clegg, general counsel for the Center for Equal Opportunity, writing in the *National Review,* shows how the bill, even with a so-called religious "exemption" (which has been shown in

California to be worth practically nothing as homosexual activists incrementally strip it away) would violate the religious freedom of millions of Americans. He wrote: "Something should be said at the outset about the distinction between homosexuality and homosexual behavior. . . . Millions of Americans believe that homosexual behavior violates sincerely and deeply held religious beliefs. It is, in other words, a sin. What is the relevance of this fact for law and government? Well, sometimes sins are made illegal—murder and theft, for instance. Sometimes they are not; no one is jailed for failing to honor his father and mother. And sometimes they are made illegal but seldom prosecuted. Much fornication, including homosexual behavior, falls into this category. The idea is to stigmatize the behavior, even if it is unrealistic to prosecute it."[49]

Clegg then continued to show how ENDA would have stigmatized those who have sincerely held religious objections to homosexual behavior:

> It might be objected that this is not an appropriate role for law and government. Instead, if some people want to stigmatize certain behavior then they should find ways to do so without dragging legislators and lawyers, let alone prosecutors, into the act. Which, of course, is exactly what the Employment Non-Discrimination Act makes it impossible to do. . . . Who wants to make a private behavior [religious objection to homosexual behavior] by an adult illegal—those supporting the bill or those opposing it? And who wants to use the government to force people to act against deeply held personal beliefs? It is, of course, the *proponents* [emphasis ours] of the bill who want to make private behavior illegal, not its opponents. The private behavior is the exercise of one's freedom of association and control of one's own property to refuse, on occasion, if one wishes, to hire homosexuals.[50]

Therefore, what would have been stigmatized is not homosexual behavior, which has serious negative ramifications for society,* but religious, public health, or other objections to such behavior. The

---

*In recent years, unprotected homosexual sex has led to a serious spike in new HIV/AIDS infections. Since 1981, more than 1 million Americans have been infected with the AIDS virus, and about 450,000 have died. In addition, syphilis and gonorrhea among homosexuals in San Francisco has doubled in recent years. (Source: Rene Sanchez, "A City Combats AIDS Complacency," *Washington Post,* May 12, 2002, p. A3). Another recent study found that a majority of young homosexual men who are infected with HIV/AIDS have no idea that they are infected. (Source: Leonard Altman, "Alarming Finding on HIV in Gay Men," *New York Times,* July 8, 2002).

religious freedom to talk about the sinfulness or disordered nature of homosexual behavior and the need for redemption would be ridiculed, while the behavior that often leads to death would be exalted. It is also important to realize that the tendency of courts interpreting such legislation is almost always to expand coverage, not to retract it. Eventually religious exemptions are whittled away in subsequent legislation until no exemption is left.

Censoring the Pulpit

Another type of law that will be used to silence or punish people with religious objections to homosexual behavior is so-called hate crimes legislation. We have already shown how such legislation in Canada, Sweden, and Holland will lead to the censoring and punishment of anyone who raises an objection to homosexual behavior, even from the pulpit.

In fact, Sen. Ted Kennedy, who is the co-sponsor of ENDA and a federal hate-crimes bill, called religious objections to homosexual behavior "an insidious aspect of American life."[51]

Stop and ponder these comments for a moment. The force that launched America, the belief system that made it great, the freedom that allowed the Kennedy family to become rich and powerful is "insidious."

As can be seen from other countries, the expansion of hate crimes will be used against any religious viewpoint that objects to homosexual behavior—because the philosophy underlying so-called hate crimes goes far beyond the commitment of an actual crime—it punishes the thought in some ways, the belief system behind the crime. These laws can be quickly expanded and separated from any form of traditional crime to include any speech that homosexual activists would claim incited someone to harm a homosexual person. Therefore, it is logical to expect that, just as Dutch authorities were urged to prosecute Pope John Paul II,[52] individuals such as Dr. James Dobson—who was bizarrely blamed indirectly and wrongfully with regard to the tragic murder of Matthew Shepard—could be charged with committing a hate crime anytime they mentioned the biblical position on homosexual behavior. This same rule could possibly extend to churches (that is on the verge of happening across the Atlantic).

In municipalities with an assortment of hate crime laws or similar speech limiting laws, religious freedom is already at peril. In 1998, the San Francisco Board of Supervisors took the unusual action of denouncing an advertising campaign sponsored by a national ministry that said homosexual behavior was sinful and that homosexuals can change. The ministry's advertisement, which appeared in the *San Francisco Chronicle*, said that Christians love those trapped in homosexual behavior but pointed out the destructiveness of homosexual behavior and the need for Jesus Christ to bring healing to the lives of those practicing homosexuality. The board passed two resolutions that said such advertising "validates oppression of gays and lesbians" and creates a climate "that may encourage violence." The ministry took the board to court over the resolutions, but the Ninth U.S. Court of Appeals in San Francisco rejected the claim, stating, "The main purpose and effect of the Supervisors' actions was to promote equality and condemn hate crimes, not to attack or inhibit religious beliefs."[53] Yet that is exactly what the resolutions did. This is just a taste of what is to come if expanded federal hate crimes legislation in its various forms comes to pass. Imagine the explosion of outrage and the court's decision if on the other hand, the board had passed resolutions *supporting* the ads?

In West Virginia, it was reported that an assistant attorney general in that state had been teaching police about hate crimes. The manual he was using was allegedly written by employees of the U.S. Justice Department under former Attorney General Janet Reno. A sentence about hate groups reads, "Some groups include apocalyptic Christianity in their ideology and believe we are in, or approaching, a period of violence and social turmoil which will precede the Second Coming of Christ." Kevin McCoy, the head of the West Virginia Family Foundation commented, "[This curricula is] laying the foundation for certain types of speech that are not politically correct and how they could be possibly perceived to be not appropriate within the law enforcement community. . . . If this curricula is continued to be taught to law enforcement in this state, it will not be long before they roll out the big guns and start cracking the whip. . . . Their goal is to get sexual orientation included. Once they do that, this is laying the foundation for law enforcement to take care of those people that they consider to be members of the hate group. Churches, pastors, the whole nine yards . . . I don't think there will be any group left untouched when their agenda is finally completed."[54]

An individual who posted a message in response to the article containing McCoy's comments, wrote, "Yes, Christianity is a hate group. . . . Not all Christians are hateful but their beliefs are hateful."[55]

Still, many Christians are unaware of the threats posed to their religious freedoms by potential laws like ENDA and hate crimes legislation. Some Christians even support various forms of such laws because it seems like the "fair thing to do." What they don't know is that when they support or are ambivalent about such legislation, they are signing a death warrant for religious liberty. Many Christians will come to realize the famous lament of the German pastor, Martin Niemoeller, is true for them as well: "First they came for the Jews, but I did nothing because I am not a Jew. Then they came for the socialists, but I did nothing because I am not a socialist. Then they came for the Catholics, but I did nothing because I am not a Catholic. Finally, they came for me, but by then there was no one left to help me."[56]

CHAPTER TEN

Where Do We Go from Here?

Those who want to win the world for Christ must have
the courage to come into conflict with it.

—Titus Brandsma, martyr, who died at Dachau as a victim of Adolf Hitler in 1942

A new missionary was walking the streets of Colombia one day, a nation ravaged by organized crime and rampant drug use, accompanied by a Christian native of the country. As he walked the streets of the country, child after child would come up to the missionary and beg him for money. Even though he had limited funds, it was his inclination to give whatever he could to these poor and destitute children. However, his Christian companion quickly admonished him that giving into the demands of the children would cause the children more harm than good.

"You see," his companion said, "these children are trapped by the mafia at an early age to go begging in the streets. The crime syndicate breaks their fingers and other horrible things are done to them. But if you give in and just hand them the money, they will just take the money to the mafia and all it will do is perpetuate the problem. You may have thought that you helped the child, but all you did was treat a symptom, the cause of the problem will go on and on, and future generations of children will fall into the same trap."*

---

*This story was told to Craig by an employee of Food for the Hungry, an international relief ministry.

This story also serves as an analogy when it comes to our response to those trapped in homosexual behavior.

As Christians, we find ourselves in a difficult position when it comes to the demands of homosexual activists. How can we be compassionate toward those trapped in homosexual behavior while not also falling into the trap of enabling it? We are called to love our neighbors. For the sincere Christian, this means many things (see Matt. 25:31–46) but especially introducing them to the love and saving grace of Jesus Christ (Matt. 28:18). And what is the greatest obstacle to faith and life in Jesus Christ? It is a person's sinful nature. If a person cannot see or be told or be allowed to hear or read that their ignorance, their behavior, their sin is blocking them from God's full plan for them, they may miss the abundant life, the eternal life that Christ died to provide for all kinds of persons, including those trapped in sexually disordered behavior. Nor can they be able to understand why Christ had to die for us and be resurrected and emerge victorious over sin.

And speaking the truth in love does not mean telling those who are violating God's standards for marriage and sexual activity that what they are doing is "OK" in God's eyes.

A vivid example of the dilemma for Christians is illustrated in the following letter that we received at ADF:

> My husband and I became Christians 8 years ago. Our previous 30 plus years gives us numerous relationships that we consider our mission field. We have many close homosexual friendships that we are continuing to maintain in a godly manner.
>
> Recently, we were invited to a "commitment ceremony." When the invitation was declined I was questioned why? These friends all know our commitment to Christ and the lifestyle changes we have made. I stated that God's word states that homosexuality is a sin and we cannot support this sinful ceremony. You can imagine the justification and denial of God's word. We decided to end the conversation because no opinions were being changed.
>
> We have maintained the relationships the past eight years in a loving and godly manner. I am so disappointed that when I stated God's Word I am told that our friendship cannot continue. I was told that if I cannot accept the homosexual lifestyle then I could not be a friend. Who is being intolerant? When I became a Christian, I never

wanted to sever my homosexual friendships. The relationships have changed but [were] never denied . . .[1]

The barrier to sharing the gospel with an individual trapped in
homosexual behavior is seemingly higher every day, whether
through limits on religious freedom or hardened hearts. As Joe
Dallas, a former homosexual, has said: "If you gave homosexual
[activists] everything they want, they still will not be satisfied until
the church is silenced."[2] Yet, as Christians, we cannot give up trying
to share Christ's love, nor the gospel's full message of repentance
leading to forgiveness and wholeness, even when faced with rejection. Neither can we allow our right to share the good news of
Christ's love with homosexuals or any other persons to be taken
away from us.

It is vital for members of the Body of Christ to understand the
homosexual agenda and how it threatens many personal and religious freedoms. If we sit back and surrender, giving those involved
in homosexual behavior everything they think they want, we are just
like the missionary in Colombia who thought he was solving a problem but instead making it worse. The dear man or woman lost in the
trap of homosexual behavior and relationships will never be able to
hear and respond to Christ's redemptive love for him or her.

Not only is our ability to share Christ's love with those trapped
in homosexual behavior threatened, but our ability to raise our own
children to know and live the uncensored Christian life and faith is
at risk as well. Parental rights are also an essential part of religious
freedom: the ability to raise and guide one's children according to
one's beliefs. *So what are we to do?*

The letter we just shared with you illustrates a good place for
Christians to start. Although rejected by her homosexual friends, the
writer still tried to be a consistent witness and friend to those caught
in extramarital sexual behavior. Remember, it was the consistent witness and love of a quiet Christian couple—not just in words but in
deeds—that led John Paulk to Christ. That persistence by the couple
and the willingness to adjust, without theological compromise, to
provide what John needed and not push him into a situation that
would have made him instantly uncomfortable had the great impact.
Despite the obstacles placed in our paths, we must continue to share
the gospel with those who so desperately need to hear it, even if it
means rejection and even persecution.

Despite the need for us to demonstrate love and to be a strong
witness to our fellow citizens, including those who engage in

homosexual behavior, we cannot compromise on the church's traditional teachings of the gospel and people's need for repentance. Unfortunately, this is where many in the church and in our culture have stumbled. In our desire to be relevant and to be seen as tolerant and loving, we have failed to speak the truth both in love and *with* love. As one internationally known Christian leader says: "We cannot allow [a false understanding] of love to trump truth." In our hope of being accepted, we have often backed away from the spiritual battle for the hearts and souls of men. Rather than confront the culture, we have often chosen to conform to it. Instead of promoting self-fulfillment in our churches, we must get back to modeling self-sacrifice. Christ made the ultimate sacrifice for us, and like him, we must be humble servants and not haughty judges. We need to point the individual trapped in homosexual behavior to the true cross, not a revised, meaningless gospel that requires no sacrifice, no repentance, and provides no real lasting deliverance from sin and its pain and sorrow.

We must be willing to be salt and light in our culture, no matter what the price. When a television show ridicules fellow Christians or biblical beliefs and exalts homosexual behavior, we should speak out. For an effective example of what speaking out can accomplish we can look at what has happened in New York City. After years of blatant anti-Catholic bigotry on the Broadway stage, no play is presently running there that ridicules Catholicism. Why? Because of the brave stand taken by one man, William Donahue of the Catholic League, who has made sure, through his protests and effective use of the media, that there is a price to be paid for bashing Catholics.

We must not remain silent, we must speak up, when Christ and his teachings are ridiculed and sexual deviancy is exalted. This includes the media, our public schools, our elected officials, and our workplace. There may be a price that we will all have to pay, but whatever that price is, we must remember it pales in comparison to the price Christ paid for us. If we stay silent, our children and grandchildren will reap the consequences of our apathy.

Our voice must be consistent: we must love homosexual men and women, and because of this love for them we must want to see them redeemed from a lifestyle of certain, ultimate despair. John Paulk, Melissa Fryrear, Mike Haley, Teresa Britton, and so many others are living testaments to the joy and healing—through faith in Jesus Christ—available to the person who escapes from homosexual behavior.

We need to support ministries that provide outreach and are trying to minister to the homosexual, such as Exodus International,

Focus on the Family's "Love Won Out" conferences, the Church of the Open Door in San Rafael, California, and the efforts of individual pastors, priests, rabbis, and churches. Organizations advocating homosexual behavior such as the Human Rights Campaign, the ACLU, GLAAD, and others, dwarf all of them in comparison when it comes to allocation of dollars and other resources. We also need to support churches, synagogues, and ministries that have had the courage to speak the truth on this issue and confront the agenda of the intolerant homosexual activists.

We need to get involved in legal and public policy matters that will determine our nation's future. The Alliance Defense Fund (1-800-TELL-ADF or www.telladf.org) was founded by thirty-five ministry leaders across many denominational lines to deal exclusively in the legal arena. Through our God-given vision of strategy, training, and funding, we have been able, through God's grace, to equip God's people to stand up for religious freedom and for the gospel in hundreds of successful cases in our nation's courts. So often we who call ourselves "brothers and sisters in Christ" have fought among ourselves, while the homosexual advocacy groups and their allies have worked together with relative harmony. If we effectively coordinate our strategy by creating alliances with other organizations, recruit and train our friends and allies in how to respond to and resist the homosexual agenda, and provide the critical funding needed to battle on an equal basis with those who wish to silence the gospel, we are confident that the threat the homosexual agenda poses to religious freedom will be greatly diminished. For many years, the church and Christians were essentially AWOL from the courthouse while dozens of legal cases were litigated, setting precedents the homosexual activists rely on today. We can no longer ignore the legal realm.

On the political front, we need to be aware of candidates and where they stand on the issues. For example, here in Arizona, homosexual advocates recently ran for public office as conservative or even profamily Republicans in an apparent attempt to deceive conservative voters. While many of these candidates went down to defeat once voters became aware of their agenda, the *Arizona Republic* (whose managing editor featured the move of his homosexual partner to Phoenix in a news article) spun the story as a victory for homosexual activists.[3] That is why we need to look much further than the party label and learn about the person who is running. Focus on the Family has state family policy councils in more than thirty-five states that can provide you with the information you need to make an informed decision. You can get in touch with the one for your state by calling 1-800-A-FAMILY.

In the public schools, we have already mentioned the need for Christian parents to be organized and to confront the school administration head-on when it comes to reviewing curriculum. In addition, whether we have any children in public schools or not, we must be informed about candidates for local school boards or be willing to make the sacrifice and go to school board meetings to voice our objections to the homosexual indoctrination of our children. It will not be easy. Anyone who goes against the homosexual agenda is bound to be ridiculed and vilified and face possible persecution. If we consider the fact that the future of our children, grandchildren, and our nation is at stake, we must ask ourselves, "Is this too high a price to pay?" We think not.

Finally and most importantly, we need to pray. We must be on our knees, for those in sexual sin, for our children and grandchildren, and for our culture. Remember the words of the Lord to Solomon in 2 Chronicles 7:14: "If my people, who are called by my name, will humble themselves and pray and seek my face and turn from their wicked ways, then will I hear from heaven and will forgive their sin and will heal their land" God's promise for those with humble and contrite hearts is the same for all generations.

If God's people get on their knees and do these other things, we are confident that the Lord will honor this faithfulness and help turn around the seemingly inevitable direction our culture is on with regard to the affirmation of homosexual behavior and the silencing of the gospel.

In 1987, President Ronald Reagan stood in West Berlin and challenged the leader of the Soviet Union, Mikhail Gorbachev, to "tear down this wall." In Berlin, even in his own administration, few shared Reagan's conviction that a seemingly, all-powerful Soviet empire was doomed. Yet a few years later not only did the wall fall, but the entire Iron Curtain came down with it. With the same determination—to stand up to the radical homosexual activist community . . . and to preserve religious freedom—we can and will win.

Let us conclude with the words of the Most Reverend Peter Jensen, the Anglican archbishop of Sydney, Australia. His words sum up beautifully the position in which the church finds itself today in response to the threat of the homosexual agenda. It is an admonishment and an encouragement to us all:

Churches must have the courage to win influence back from a secular world. The role of the Christian churches . . . today is to speak the truth in love. . . . We have accepted the secular world's verdict that we have nothing of importance to say, and we have adjusted ourselves to this reality. We have become domesticated. . . . Instead of explaining and defending the Gospel, we have sought the path of relevance. . . . The Christian Gospel is the insertion of truth into the untrustworthy discourse of the world. Some of us want to be kind, so loving that we will not speak the truth. The therapeutic model of pastoral care has been perverted into mere affirmations of human behaviour. Our love is no love, for it refuses this great test: will it speak boldly, frankly, truthfully? . . . One of the chief reasons why we have ceased to speak the truth is we are fearful of the reaction of those around us. . . . We have contributed towards the gagging of God, perhaps because we are frightened of suffering. But there is one fundamental task to which we must be committed, come whatever may: Speak the truth in love.[4]

We must *speak* the truth in love. We must *live* the truth in love. This is the true love of the gospel. We cannot shy away from this task, regardless of the price. We need to ask ourselves: Are we willing to take a stand, to keep the door open for the gospel, or are we going to allow it to be silenced? Are we willing to share Christ's love with the person trapped in homosexual behavior, or will we simply walk by them like the Levite and the priest on the road to Jericho and not offer a helping hand? (Luke 10:25–37)

The answers to those questions will determine the future of marriage, the family, culture, and the gospel in America, and of America itself. They will determine the futures of millions of hurting individuals in need of a loving Father who alone can provide them with the true affirmation, true fulfillment, and the true love they so desperately need. And the good news—even a nation's heart can turn in a single day (Jonah 3:10).

Soli Deo Gloria.

APPENDIX 1

Background Brief:
The Future of Tax Exemption and Homosexual Behavior

Question: Could the application of a new legal test, of "strict scrutiny" by the United States Supreme Court as proposed in various cases or other sex/gender case decisions relating to sodomy and sexual behavior, lead to the revocation of church and charitable organization tax exemptions by the Internal Revenue Service?

Answer: In 1983, the High Court found that an organization's tax exempt status and deductibility of gifts to that organization can be revoked for acts contrary to the "public interest" as determined by the IRS and federal courts— even when those acts are based on sincerely held religious beliefs.[1]

Discussion: Many major religious colleges, denominations, churches, ministries, and charitable organizations that are tax exempt today differentiate (or in the view of intolerant radical activists "discriminate") on the basis of sex/gender and sexual behavior in employment, position, ordination, performance of marriage and other ceremonies or sacraments, and many other matters based upon their genuinely held religious beliefs. In fact, most of those who engage in such practices believe they are acting upon and in conformity with "revealed truth" from Scripture and/or tradition. Their future tax exemption status is uncertain with the advance of the homosexual legal agenda.

If the Supreme Court, or a plethora of courts of appeal, adopts a new test—a new standard for Constitutional review—for all claims of sex/gender discrimination under the same rules and policies that racial discrimination is now viewed (i.e., "strict scrutiny"), or decides that the Constitution, public policy, or law of the United States protects or provides special privileges for sodomy and other homosexual behavior, it is only a matter of time, application of legal "logic," and litigation before it is claimed that sex/gender and sexual orientation/behavior "discrimination" is akin to racial discrimination and thus is *in all instances* contrary to public policy and therefore those who engage in such actions are not "entitled" to the public "benefit" of tax exemption.

To put it plainly, there is either a lawful basis to differentiate ("discriminate") between persons based upon sex/gender and/or their forms of sexual behavior or there is not. Present sex/gender and sexual behavior law, though dramatically changed from one hundred to two hundred years ago, uses an "intermediate level" of scrutiny for sex/gender issues, and courts still permit differentiation for many things.[2]

Bob Jones University's sponsors genuinely believed "that the Bible forbade interracial dating and marriage." As a result of those beliefs, the university engaged in various practices, finally forbidding interracial marriage or dating by enrolled students. The federal courts found Bob Jones's "policies violated the clearly defined public policy" and after years of litigation determined that it was proper for the IRS, exercising its discretion, to revoke the university's tax exempt status. The courts also rejected Bob Jones's arguments that revoking the tax exemption violated the Free Exercise of Religion and Establishment Clauses of the First Amendment.

Bob Jones was permitted to "practice its religious beliefs," though held by the government to be discriminatory, *but* it was prevented from receiving the "benefit" of tax exemption and receipt of tax deductible gifts.

Until 1970, the Internal Revenue Service recognized tax exempt status and allowed tax deductions to private schools without regard to their faith-based racial policies. In 1970, a federal court decision prohibited the IRS from allowing tax exempt status for certain private schools whose admission policies discriminated on the basis of race.[3] As a result of that, and subsequent court decisions, the IRS revised its policies to state, in part, "the statutory requirement of being 'organized and operated exclusively for religious, charitable . . . or educational purposes' was intended to express the basic common law concept [of 'charity'] . . . [and] the purpose of the trust may not be illegal or contrary to public policy."[4]

The Supreme Court, analyzing the government's grant of tax exemptions or allowance of deductions, stated: "History buttresses logic to make it clear that, *to warrant exemption under 501 (c)(3), an institution must . . . be in harmony with the public interest.* The institution's purpose must not be so at odds with the *common community conscience as to undermine any public interest that might otherwise be conferred.*"[5] [emphasis added]

In its review of the national policy consensus on race, which led the courts to conclude that Bob Jones's dating policy was offensive to that policy, the Supreme Court specifically noted various congressional acts concurred that racial discrimination violated public policy and further noted, "The Executive Branch has consistently placed its support behind the eradication of racial discrimination" and that "few social or political questions have been more vigorously debated."[6]

Radical and intolerant homosexual activists are working overtime to equate distinctions and differentiation based on sex/gender, sexual orientation, and various forms of sexual behavior with the public and thus legal public policy equivalent of racial discrimination, despite the dramatic differences. If these activists are successful, there is no reason that the IRS and federal courts could not make the same findings regarding sex/gender and sexual behavior and that such "discrimination" could require revocation of tax exempt status and prohibit tax deductible contributions. In the twenty years since this decision, the IRS has not expanded the Bob Jones ruling to other forms of "discrimination," but this is no guarantee that it will not do so in the future.

Letter to Pastors

Gary S. McCaleb
Senior Counsel

June 4, 2004

Dear Pastors:

A great battle rages within our nation; a battle to determine whether the very foundation of our society—one man and one woman, joined in marriage—will survive. Advocates of same-sex "marriage" fight fiercely for new "rights," focusing on individuals' emotions and government benefits. But marriage is more than feelings and money; its about providing a mom <u>and</u> a dad for every child; about building a strong society through time-tested, certain methods rather than radical social experiments. Indeed, the very reason that governments choose to benefit and regulate marriage is because it <u>is</u> the proven basis for western civilization. Proponents of same-sex "marriage" cannot show otherwise.

I write to assure you that the Alliance Defense Fund will spare no effort to ensure that America's Christians will not be silenced in the battle for marriage.

In the past decade, radical advocates of same-sex "marriage" have sought to establish new "rights" in Alaska, Hawaii, Vermont, Massachusetts, Arizona, and elsewhere. All but one of these battles resulted in their defeat—and pro-homosexual forces may yet be defeated in Massachusetts, where court actions and constitutional amendments to defend traditional marriage remain very much alive.

Across America, citizens are fighting to save marriage by advancing pro-marriage legislation at the state and federal level. Homosexual activists know that their arguments will fail if they are put squarely before our nation's citizens, and they do all that they can to prevent the issue from ever coming to a vote. Thus, pro-homosexual groups are threatening churches across the nation with the loss of tax-exempt status, and/or they allege that various state political campaign laws were violated, when churches simply preach about marriage or allow petitions on their property. It is a simple scare tactic, designed to silence Christians.

Such tactics are not new. They have been tried time and again, <u>and have consistently failed</u>. For example, in 1996, 1998, and 2000, pro-homosexual activists targeted churches that supported a proposition in California that defined marriage as being between one man and one woman. In one mailing, activists sent out some 80,000 threat letters. *See* Erik J. Ablin, *The Price of Not Rendering to Caesar: Restrictions on Church Participation in Political Campaigns*, 13 Notre Dame J. L. Ethics & Pub. Pol'y 541, 557 (1999). These would-be censors failed to suppress Christian speech—the California measure ultimately passed and no church had its tax-exempt status revoked. These tactics of hate and intolerance must fail again in 2004.

Churches, Marriage, and Politics: No Time for Silence
June 4, 2004
Page 2 of 4

By this letter, we assure you that churches have broad constitutional rights to express their views on marriage, as explained below. Furthermore, other activities such as allowing parishioners to sign petitions for legislative action to protect marriage are almost undoubtedly permissible under federal tax law. In the same way, the First Amendment to the United States Constitution most likely prevents states from demanding that churches register as a "political committee" or report "contributions" when the churches merely preach about marriage or allow petitions to be signed at their facilities.

If you are contacted by any government official or private activist group on such issues, please call us immediately. The Alliance Defense Fund's attorneys will promptly review your situation and make every effort to defend your church's legal rights to speak freely in support of marriage. Below we briefly discuss the relevant law.

Legal Analysis: Federal tax law

There are two broad areas of concern regarding the effect of political activity by churches that hold tax exempt status under Internal Revenue Code ("IRC") § 501(c)(3). First, the IRC prohibits churches from participating or intervening in the political campaign of a *candidate* for public office. However, the IRC is much more accommodating in regard to churches that work to influence *legislation*, allowing such activity so long as a "substantial part" of church efforts is not devoted to such activities. This "legislative" issue is what we are concerned about here.

Fortunately, the courts understand that advocating morality, both in church and in civil life, is properly at the heart of religious faith:

> Religion includes a way of life as well as beliefs upon the nature of the world and the admonitions to be "Doers of the word and not hearers only" (James 1:22) and "Go ye therefore, and teach all nations . . ." (Matthew 28:19) are as old as the Christian Church. The step from acceptance by the believer to his seeking to influence others in the same direction is a perfectly natural one, and is found in countless religious groups.

Girard Trust Co. v. Comm'r, 122 F.2d 108, 110 (3d Cir. 1941) (emphasis added; omission in original). As the Supreme Court put it, "[a]dherents of particular faiths and individual churches frequently take strong positions on public issues including . . . vigorous advocacy of legal or constitutional positions. Of course, churches as much as secular bodies, and private citizens have that [constitutional] right." *Walz v. Tax Comm'n*, 397 U.S. 664, 670 (1969).

Whether a church devotes a "substantial" part of its resources to influencing legislation is a question of facts and circumstances, *Kentucky Bar Foundation, Inc. v. Commissioner*, 78 T.C. 971 (1982), and courts have taken different approaches to the matter. For example, in *Seasongood v. Commissioner*, 227 F.2d 907 (6th Cir. 1955), the court established a five percent (5%) safe harbor rule based on total expenditures applied to legislative activities. *Id.* at 912. More recently, the decision in *World Family Corporation. v. Commissioner*, 81 T.C. 958 (1983) raised that bar when the Tax Court ruled that an exempt organization's lobbying activities which utilized between five and ten percent of the group's resources were "insubstantial."

Churches, Marriage, and Politics: No Time for Silence
June 4, 2004
Page 3 of 4

It should be noted that one court relied on a balancing test, rather than a percentage of expenditures, in determining that a tax exempt religious organization had devoted a "substantial part" of its resources to influencing legislation. *See Christian Echoes Nat'l Ministry, Inc. v. U.S.,* 470 F.2d 849 (10th Cir. 1972). This court observed that the percentage test obscured the "complexity of balancing the organization's activities in relation to its objectives and circumstances." *Id.* at 855.

The *Christian Echoes* court stated that "the political [activities of a charity] must be balanced in the context of the objectives and circumstances of the organization to determine whether a substantial part of its objectives [not just expenditures] was to influence or attempt to influence legislation." *Id.* However, the lobbying undertaken by the Christian Echoes ministry went far beyond simply preaching about a moral issue or circulating petitions for proposed legislation. Rather, the group "attempted to mold public opinion in civil rights legislation, medicare, the Postage Revision Act of 1967, the Honest Election Law of 1967, the Nuclear Test Ban Treaty, the Panama Canal Treaty, firearms control legislation, and the Outer Space Treaty." *Id.* It urged its supporters to take no less than 22 different actions to influence American and international politics, including urging congressional representatives to support or oppose specific bills, abolish the federal income tax, withdraw from the United Nations, and so on. *Id.* Under these unusual facts—including support of candidates as well as legislation—the *Christian Echoes* court found that the defendant organization had devoted a "substantial part" of its resources to lobbying and affirmed the revocation of its tax exempt status. *Id.* at 858.

Unless a church has an extensive history of lobbying efforts (as exemplified by the *Christian Echoes* case) it is extremely unlikely that simple efforts to defend marriage, such as preaching about marriage or making petitions available to be signed—would be seen as a "substantial" portion of church resources. Such activities should be entirely permissible under federal tax law. Certainly, a church that devotes less than five percent of its resources to influencing legislation should be on very safe ground in this respect.

State Political Campaign Law

State governments have an interest in informing the public about campaign financing. The theory is that such information helps voters evaluate which interests are supporting particular legislation. *See, e.g., Buckley v. Valeo,* 424 U.S. 1 (1976) (upholding federal campaign disclosure requirements). Yet however strong that interest may be, it does not justify imposing campaign law willy-nilly on churches that incidentally support legislation.

It is not possible to consider the political campaign laws of each state in this brief letter. Nonetheless, any requirement that a church register as a "political action committee" or report "expenditures" supporting legislation, simply because the church preached about marriage or allowed parishioners to sign petitions, raises serious questions under the Free Speech Clause and Free Exercise Clause of the First Amendment to the United States Constitution.

Indeed, the courts have recognized that applying broadly worded campaign reporting statutes to groups that do not engage in substantial advocacy would violate the First Amendment. For example, in *New Jersey State Chamber of Commerce v. New Jersey Election Law*

Enforcement Commission, 411 A.2d 168 (N.J. 1980), various secular groups challenged a campaign reporting law as being unconstitutionally overbroad because it was triggered by virtually any communication between a private person and a legislator which sought to "influence" legislation. The court held that the law was constitutional, but only if it was narrowly construed so that it applied "only to persons whose direct, express, and intentional communication with legislators for the purpose of affecting the outcome of legislation are undertaken on a substantial basis." *Id.* at 179, *accord Bemis Pentecostal Church v. Tennessee*, 731 S.W.2d 897 (Tenn. 1987) (holding church responsible to report expenditures for purchasing media advertisements that opposed specific liquor legislation, but also held that broadcasting the church's religious services and distributing church newsletters, even if advocating a particular election result, were not subject to campaign law). In other words, campaign law is not *carte blanche* for the government to limit private church speech or religious exercise.

Other issues are implicated by unlimited application of state political campaign laws to churches. For example, demanding that churches register as "political committees" would operate as a "prior restraint" on speech, which is strongly disfavored under the U. S. Supreme Court's First Amendment jurisprudence. Similarly, it would chill the speech of other churches that would rightfully fear investigation and possible punishment by state election officials. Both situations offer solid bases to invalidate a state campaign law if that law were applied to churches in this context.

Homosexual activists' outrageous, intolerant effort to stop churches from expressing their faith will succeed only if pastors succumb to fear and stand mute when marriage is attacked. But nothing in the law supports these activists' demands, and no pastor should yield to fear. Rather, pastors can (and should) speak clearly regarding moral truth and freely participate in the political processes within the limits set forth by our laws.

This material is a brief overview of a complex area of the law and should not be construed as legal advice relevant to a particular church's situation. If you have any questions or believe your church's rights were violated, please feel free to contact us at the Alliance Defense Fund.

Sincerely

Gary S. McCaleb
Senior Counsel

Notes

Introduction

1. Testimony of John Paulk, given at Focus on the Family, October 31, 2001.
2. Ibid.
3. Robert S. Hogg and others, "Modeling the Impact of HIV Disease on Mortality in Gay and Bisexual Men," *International Journal of Epidemiology* 26 (1997), 657.
4. Eileen E. Flynn, "Former Lesbian Discusses Life-Changing Experience," *Austin American-Statesman*, February 16, 2003.
5. Robert Stacy McCain, "Kansas Pastor's Brimstone for Gays Draws Some Hellfire: Both Christians and Homosexuals Attack Brutal Tactics," *Washington Times*, July 14, 1999.
6. Marco R. della Cava, "Church Calls Acts 'Disordered,' Gays Feel Blamed," *USA Today*, June 12, 2002.

Chapter One—How Did We Get Here?

1. *The Advocate*, June 2004.
2. Alissa J. Rubin, "Public More Accepting of Gays, Poll Finds," *Los Angeles Times*, June 18, 2000.
3. Gene Edward Veith, "News They Can Use," *World*, October 12, 2002.
4. Marshall K. Kirk and Erastes Pill, "The Overhauling of Straight America," *Guide*, November 1987.
5. Ibid.
6. Rona Marech, "Nuances of Gay Identities Reflected in New Language, 'Homosexual' is Passe in a 'Boi's' Life," *San Francisco Chronicle*, February 8, 2004.
7. Ibid.
8. Ibid.
9. Kirk and Pill, "Overhauling."
10. Ibid.
11. Ibid.
12. Michael Weisskopf, "Energized by Public or Passion, the Public is Calling: 'Gospel Grapevine' Displays Strength in Controversy over Military Gay Ban," *Washington Post*, February 1, 1993.
13. Julia Duin, "NBC Flooded with Calls after Couric's Remarks: Family Groups Irked at Links to Death of Gay Man," *Washington Times*, October 16, 1998.
14. Deborah Mathis, "Many Share in the Hate-Filled Killing of Gay Student," *Orlando Sentinel*, October 15, 1998.
15. Robert B. Bluey, "Documents Reveal San Francisco Mayor's Ties to Homosexual Activists," CNSNews.com, June 21, 2004.
16. Kirk and Pill, "Overhauling."
17. Star Parker, "Gay Politics, Black Reality," Townhall.com, January 12, 2004.
18. Christopher Curtis, "Jesse Jackson: Gay Marriage Rights are Not Civil Rights," PlanetOut.com, February 17, 2004.
19. Kirk and Pill, "Overhauling."
20. "The 2000 Census and Same-Sex Households: A User's Guide," published by the National Gay and Lesbian Task Force Policy Institute.
21. Jim Hopkins, "QuarkXPress Grew out of Shy Guy's Love of Solitude, Now He's a Huge Philanthropist," *USA Today*, August 15, 2001.
22. Valerie Richardson, "Money *Can* Buy You Love: The Gill Foundation's Uphill Battle for Gay Rights," *Philanthropy*, September/October 2000, 22.
23. Jim Hopkins, "Gay Entrepreneurs Pour Tech Cash into Causes," GFN.com, June 19, 2001. See http://www.gfn.com/business/story.phtml?sid=9689.
24. Hopkins, "QuarkXPress."
25. Richardson, "Money *Can* Buy."
26. Gina Perales, "PrideFest Draws 4,000," *Colorado Springs Gazette*, August 28, 2000.
27. Ed Sealover, "Same-Sex Partners Get City Benefits," *Colorado Springs Gazette*, November 8, 2002.

28. Frank Eltman, "Bronx Attorney Named New Head of American Civil Liberties Union," Associated Press, May 1, 2001.

29. *The American Civil Liberties Union: Freedom Is Why We're Here,* ACLU position paper, Fall 1999.

30. Robyn E. Blumner, "ACLU National Director Retires for Much More Freedom," *Saint Petersburg Times,* September 3, 2000. Also see "Individual Donor Sets Record with $7 Million Donation," ACLU press release, July 18, 2001.

31. "Ford Foundation Gives $7 Million to ACLU Endowment Campaign," ACLU press release, June 28, 1999.

32. Internet News Bureau, "The ACLU on Morality: Special Web Collection on 'Public Morality' Launched," November 13, 1998.

33. See http://www.lambdalegal.org.

34. See http://www.hrc.org/corporate/index.asp.

35. Hopkins, "Gay Entrepreneurs Pour."

36. Ibid.

37. Ibid.

38. Ibid.

39. *Washington Blade,* January 30, 1991.

40. Adolf Hitler, *Mein Kampf* (Boston: Houghton Mifflin Co., 1971), 230.

41. Ibid., 232.

42. Ibid., 276.

43. Marshal Kirk and Hunter Madsen, *After the Ball* (New York, N.Y.: Plume/Doubleday, 1990), 154.

44. Ibid., 161.

45. Ibid., 163.

Chapter Two—That's Entertainment?

1. Michael Lipton and Craig Tomashoff, "Will Power: Happily Married Eric McCormack Plays a Gay Lawyer on *Will & Grace,*" *People,* October 26, 1998.

2. Correspondence between Mike Haley of Focus on the Family and Jon Kinnally.

3. "Iowa Study Suggests Tolerance of Homosexuals is Growing," Associated Press, March 23, 2001.

4. Ibid.

5. Ibid.

6. Murray Dubin, "Hollywood Living a Fantasy Where Gay Actors Concerned," *Houston Chronicle,* August 18, 1985.

7. Peter Stack, "Discovering Who's 'Out' at the Movies: Encyclopedist Tried to Respect Gay Stars' Privacy," *San Francisco Chronicle,* December 28, 1994.

8. Dubin, "Hollywood Living."

9. Dennis Drabelle, "The Box Office King of 1930," *Washington Post,* January 18, 1998.

10. Barry Paris, "Letter Bombs? Museum Will Open Garbo Correspondence to Alleged Socialite Lover," *Pittsburgh Post-Gazette,* April 13, 2000.

11. Stack, "Discovering Who's 'Out'."

12. Ibid.

13. Joanne Weintraub, "Homosexuality Was the Key to Cukor's Hollywood Success," *Capitol Times,* November 22, 2000.

14. Eleanor Ringel, "George Cukor: A Double Life," *Atlanta Journal-Constitution,* February 2, 1992.

15. Michelangelo Signorile, "Our Gay Century," *Advocate,* 2000.

16. Stephen Hunter, "Gay or Not, Cary Grant's Image is Unflickering," *Washington Post,* June 5, 1997.

17. Joe Newlin, "Drama Queens," *New Orleans Times-Picayune,* January 13, 2002.

18. Burt Styler and Norman Lear, "Judging Books by Covers," *All in the Family,* dir. John Rich, aired February 9, 1971.

19. Bob Schiller and Bob Weisskopf, "Cousin Liz," *All in the Family,* story by Barry Harmon and Harve Brosten, dir. Paul Bogart, aired October 9, 1977.

20. Bob Schiller and others, "Edith's Crisis of Faith," *All in the Family,* dir. Paul Bogart, aired December 18 and 25, 1977.

21. Jerry Reiger and Gary Moskowitz, "George," *M*A*S*H,* dir. Gene Reynolds, aired February 16, 1974.

22. Christine Sparta, "Emergence from the Closet," *USA Today,* March 11, 2002.

23. Ibid.

24. Ken Levine and David Isaacs, "The Boys in the Bar," *Cheers,* dir. James Burrows, aired January 27, 1983.

25. See the final report of the Attorney General's Commission on Pornography, 1986.

26. David Tuller, "Ellen's Coming Out No Shock to Gays, Lesbians in S.F.," *San Francisco Chronicle,* April 8, 1997.

27. Kinney Littlefield, "'Ellen' to Show a Bit of Gentle Puppy Love," *Orange County Register,* April 9, 1997.

28. Bruce Handy, "Roll Over Ward Cleaver," *Time,* April 14, 1997.

29. "Vows," *Ellen,* aired July 22, 1998.

30. Joanne Weintraub, "Ellen Finds New Place on TV," *Milwaukee Journal-Sentinel,* July 26, 2001.

31. Some of the most notable failures have included John Goodman's sitcom *Normal, Ohio; Some of My Best Friends* on CBS; and Ellen DeGeneres's second attempt, *The Ellen Show,* on CBS.

32. See http://www.glaad.org.

33. Ibid.

34. Campbell, "Gays on Prime Time."

35. Ibid.

36. Don Kaplan, "Don't Call Her a 'He,'" *New York Post,* August 21, 2001.

37. Matthew Gilbert, "Sexual Identity Getting Difficult to Keep Straight," *Boston Globe,* July 1, 2004.

38. Elizabeth Snead, "Gellar Seduced by 'Cruel' Opportunity," *USA Today,* March 8, 1999.

39. Adam Buckman, "Kiss of Death—Tonight's Girl-Girl Friends' Lip-Lock Means It's Over," *New York Post,* April 26, 2001.

40. Lisa de Moraes, "The Smooch That Drew a Crowd," *Washington Post,* November 4, 1999.

41. Tanya Richardson, "'Gilmore Girls' Goes Wild with Girl-on-Girl Kiss," *New York Post,* April 7, 2004.

42. Barbara D. Phillips, "TV: A Straight-On Look at Gay Life," *Wall Street Journal,* November 27, 2000.

43. Kim Campbell, "Gay Characters, Before and After 'Ellen,'" *Christian Science Monitor,* April 6, 2001.

44. "TV Show Depicts Gay 'Teen' Character," WorldNetDaily.com, January 23, 2004.

45. Joe Flint, "Viacom Plans a Gay Channel, but Reception Isn't Clear," *Wall Street Journal,* March 29, 2004.

46. J. Max Robins, "Gay Network Could Debut within a Year," *TV Guide,* January 7, 2002.

47. "Channels Race to Launch Gay TV," Associated Press, May 1, 2002.

48. Brent Bozell, "More Gays, More Often?" *Creators Syndicate,* January 31, 2002.

49. Ibid.

50. Ibid.

51. "MTV Networks to Launch LOGO, A New Television Network for Gay, Lesbian Viewers," *U.S. Newswire Press Releases,* May 25, 2004.

52. Some notable examples were *Sunday Bloody Sunday, The Lion in Winter* (which featured an implied homosexual relationship), and *Women in Love.*

53. Bernard Weinraub, "Play a Gay? More Actors Say 'Yes' to Portraying Gay Characters," *New York Times,* September 14, 1997.

54. Ibid.

55. David Lyman, "'Philadelphia' Goes Beyond AIDS," *Cincinnati Post,* January 14, 1994.

56. Bill Zwecker, "Hanks Pays Tribute to Gays in His Life," *Chicago Sun-Times,* March 22, 1994.

57. Richard Lorent, "Speech Brings Praise from Tom Hanks' Former Drama Teacher," Associated Press, March 23, 1994.

58. James P. Pinkerton, "Hollywood Honors a Subversive Take on Suburbia," *Newsday,* March 28, 2000.

59. "Sharon Osbourne, I Wish I Had 'Gay' Child," WorldNetDaily.com, March 31, 2004.

60. "Iowa Study Suggests Tolerance of Homosexuals Is Growing," Associated Press, March 23, 2001.

61. Hogg and others, "Modeling the Impact of HIV."

Chapter Three—*"Stupid" Parents, "Enlightened" Kids*

1. Don Feder, "Welcome to the NEA-Dominated Schoolhouse," *Creators Syndicate,* September 5, 2001.

2. Debra Saunders, "Gay-Ed for Tots," *Weekly Standard,* August 19, 1996, 21.

3. John Chase, "School's Gay-Straight Group Offers Teens a Place to Fit In," *Chicago Daily-Herald,* June 7, 1998.

4. "Teens and Adults Have Little Chance of Accepting Christ as Their Savior," Barna Research Online, November 15, 1999. See http://www.barna.org.

5. Torres, "Conference 'New Moment.'"

6. Ibid.

7. NEA 1999-2000 Resolutions, B-9, "Racism, Sexism, and Sexual Orientation Discrimination." See www.nea.org/resolutions/99/99b-9.html.

8. Matt Pyeatt, "NEA Task Force Issues Report on Sexual Orientation," CNSNews.com, February 13, 2002.

9. John Rossomondo, "NEA Mum about Homosexuality Task Force," CNSNews.com, August 15, 2001.

10. Katy Kelly, "Gay Parents Get Endorsed by Kids' Docs," *U.S. News and World Report,* February 18, 2002.

11. "Just the Facts about Sexual Orientation and Youth: A Primer for Principals, Educators, and School Personnel," authored by American Academy of Pediatrics, National Education Association and others, 3, 8, 9.

12. David Gelman, "Tune In, Come Out," *Newsweek,* November 8, 1993, 70.

13. Ibid.

14. Rona Marech, "Nuances of Gay Identities Reflected in New Language, 'Homosexual' is Passe in a 'Boi's' Life," *San Francisco Chronicle,* February 8, 2004.

15. Laura Sessions Stepp, "Partway Gay? For Some Teen Girls, Sexual Preference is a Shifting Concept," *Washington Post,* January 4, 2004.

16. Gelman, "Tune In, Come Out."

17. Rob Dreher, "Banned in Boston: Better Not Complain about the Gay Agenda for Massachusetts Schools," *Weekly Standard,* July 3–10, 2000, 16.

18. See http://www.glsen.org.

19. Saunders, "Gay-Ed for Tots."

20. Ibid.

21. Ibid.

22. Resolution B-69: Home Schooling. see http://www.nea.org/resolutions/01/01b-69.html.

23. Women's Educational Media, *It's Elementary,* dir. Debra Chasnoff.

24. Pete Winn and Kristie Rutherford, "Antifamily Agenda Becomes Law in California," Focus on the Family Citizen Link, October 16, 2001. See http://www.family.com/cforum/feature/a0018150.html.

25. "Teachers Vote to Lobby for Gay Schoolbooks," *Canadian Press,* August 15, 2001.

26. Michael Betsch, "Homosexual Activists Want to Silence Nation's Youth," CNSNews.com, April 8, 2002.

27. Melanie Hunter, "Family Group Threatens to Sue Homosexual Activists over Day of Silence," CNSNews.com, April 9, 2002.

28. Peter LaBarbera, "When Silence Would Have Been Golden," *Culture and Family Institute,* April 10, 2002.

29. Ibid.

30. Ibid.

31. Ibid.

32. "Make It Real: A Student Organizing Manual for Implementing California's School Nondiscrimination Law," ©2001, Gay-Straight Alliance Network/Tides Center and Friends of Project 10, pp. 5, 19, 44, and 50.

33. Robert B. Bluey, "Teachers Urged to Ignore GLSEN's Marriage Curriculum," CNSNews.com, May 26, 2004.

34. Dreher, "Banned in Boston."

35. Women's Educational Media, *It's Elementary.*

36. Ibid.

37. Ibid.

38. "Falling Boulder," *World,* February 14, 2004.

39. "K-12 Academy Hosts 'Queer State of the Union,'" WorldNetDaily.com, March 4, 2004.

40. "Education Priorities," *Fox News,* January 7, 2002.

41. Carol Innerst, "'Diversity' Leads to Classes in Homosexuality: Parents Seek to Control Curriculum," *Washington Times,* November 25, 1997.

42. Ibid.

43. Ibid.

44. E-mail from Alliance Defense Fund volunteer attorney, March 5, 2002.

45. John Haskins, "It's 1984 in Massachusetts—And Big Brother is Gay," *Insight on the News,* December 17, 2001.

46. Ibid.

47. Ibid.

48. Ibid.

49. Ibid.

50. Ibid.

51. Ibid.

52. Ibid.

53. Cheryl Wetzstein, "Educator Gets Laughs, Lawsuit With Her Hot Talk about Safe Sex," *Washington Times,* March 20, 1994.

54. Cheryl Wetzstein, "Sex Teacher Faces Suit for High School Performance," *Washington Times,* March 7, 1994.

55. Jerry Taylor, "In Face of Suit, Landolphi Wins Chelmsford Student Support," *Boston Globe,* September 5, 1993.

56. Joe Heaney, "Massachusetts Students Lose Suit over School Sex Program," *Boston Herald,* March 5, 1996.

57. Dreher, "Banned in Boston."

58. Ibid.

59. "'Gay' Sex Trainer Regains Job, Back Pay," WorldNetDaily.com, August 23, 2001.

60. Scott Lively, "Gay Days at Santa Rosa High School." See http://www.abidingtruth.com.

61. See http://www.centeryes.org/SIGNS/upcoming/index.html.

62. "In Groundbreaking Federal Lawsuit Settlement, School Agrees to Strongest Antigay Harassment Program in Nation," ACLU press release, August 13, 2002.

63. Christopher Michaud, "Survey: Students Hold Mostly Progay Views," Reuters, August 27,2001.

64. Ibid.

65. "Assault on Gay America" Viewers Guide. See http://www.pbs.org/wgbh/pages/frontline/teach/diversity/assault.

66. See Carroll Smith-Rosenberg, *Disorderly Conduct: Visions of Gender in Victorian America* (Oxford University Press, 1999).

67. Josh White, "In the District, Walking with Pride: 'Out in DC.' Tours Explore Events That Shaped Gay History," *Washington Post,* August 23, 1998.

68. Samara Kalk, "Lincoln Was Gay, Activist Contends," *Madison Capital Times,* February 23, 1999.

69. Ibid.

70. Jessica Kowal, "School Debate: Teach Gay Issues," *Newsday,* October 17, 1999.

71. "U.S. Teens Struggle with History," Associated Press, July 3, 2001.

72. Marilyn Elias, "Gay Teens Less Suicidal than Thought, Report Says," *USA Today,* November 26, 2001.

73. Rhonda Smith, "P-FLAG Receives Grant for $250,000: Funds Will Expand Organization's National Safe Schools Campaign," *Washington Blade,* July 16, 2001.

74. Gelman, "Tune In, Come Out."

75. Haskins, "It's 1984."

Chapter Four—The Lavender Tower

1. "Comedy and Tragedy: College Course Descriptions and What They Tell Us about Higher Education Today," *Young America's Foundation,* 2002, 14. See http://www.yaf.org.

2. Ibid., 16.

3. Ibid., 25.

4. Ibid., 32.

5. Ibid., 43.

6. Ibid., 43.

7. Ibid., 53.
8. Ibid., 60.
9. Ibid., 62.
10. Ibid., 64.
11. Ibid., 65.
12. Ibid., 65.
13. Ibid., 67.
14. Ibid., 74.
15. Ibid., 77.
16. Anne D. Neal, *Exfemina,* Independent Women's Forum, April 2001.
17. University of Colorado course catalog (www.colorado.edu).
18. Jason Pierce, "Tax Money Aids Homosexual Scholarship Fund," CNSNews.com, September 19, 2001.
19. Patrick Healy, "College Recruiters Look to Gays but Schools See Problem in Identifying Students," *Boston Globe,* May 21, 2002.
20. Ibid.
21. Ibid.
22. Gene Edward Veith, "Gay Authority," *World,* June 1, 2002, 13.
23. See www.1.law.ucla.edu/~williamsproj/about/index.html.
24. Ibid.
25. Ibid.
26. Scott Norvell, "PETA Protests Gay Dorms, Soda Jerks," Fox News, May 20, 2002.
27. William Hermann, "First Lesbian Sorority is Organized at ASU," *Arizona Republic,* February 18, 2004.
28. Gene Edward Veith, "Identity Crisis," *World,* March 27, 2004, 27.
29. Ibid.
30. Joyce Howard Price, "Transgender Restrooms Urged for Schools," *Washington Times,* February 11, 2002.
31. George Orwell, *Animal Farm* (White Plains, N.Y.: Longman Publishing Group, 1946).
32. *Chronicle of Higher Education,* August 7, 1998, B10.
33. Jeremy Beer, "Postmodern Paradise," *Countumacy,* January 2, 1998.
34. Merrell Noden, "Edmund White's Own Story," *Princeton Alumni Weekly,* March 10, 2004.
35. Ron Grossman, "At Notre Dame, A Gay Film Fest," *Chicago Tribune,* February 11, 2004.
36. Mattingly, "Campus Christian Groups."
37. Ibid.
38. Ibid.
39. John Leo, "Playing That Bias Card," *U.S. News and World Report,* January 13, 2003.
40. Laura Ingraham, "Universities Throwing Christians to the Lions," *Laura Ingraham E-Blast,* January 6, 2003.
41. Rachel Zabarkes, "Desperately Seeking Diversity," *National Review Online,* August 1, 2002.
42. "Students Protest Blood Drive Screening," Associated Press, March 17, 2004.
43. Laura Mansnerus, "Court Revives Lesbians' Suit over Housing," *New York Times,* July 3, 2001.
44. Seth Lewis, "Court Lets Homosexuals Sue for Access to Married Housing," CNSNews.com, July 2, 2001.
45. "Jefferson's Bill for Establishing Religious Freedom in the State of Virginia," 1779 Papers 2:545.
46. *Southworth v. Board of Regents University of Wisconsin System,* 221 F.3d 1339 (7ᵗʰ Cir. 2000).
47. Eugene Abel and others, "Self-Reported Sex Crimes of Nonincarcerated Pedophiliacs," *Journal of Interpersonal Violence,* Vol. 3 No. 5 (1987).
48. K. Freud and R. I. Watson, "The Proportions of Heterosexual and Homosexual Pedophiles Among Sex Offenders against Children: An Exploratory Study," *Journal of Marital Therapy,* Vol. 34, 1992, 34–43.
49. W. D. Erickson and others, "Behavior Patterns of Child Molesters," *Archives of Sexual Behavior,* Vol. 17, 1988.
50. M. Tomeo, D. Templar, S. Anderson, D. Kotler, "Comparative Data of Childhood and Adolescence Molestation in Heterosexual and Homosexual Persons," *Archives of Sexual Behavior,* Vol. 30, No. 3, 2001, 535–531.
51. "No Place for Homo-Homophobia," *San Francisco Sentinel,* March 26, 1992.
52. Edward Brongersma, "Boy-Lovers and Their Influence on Boys," *Journal of Homosexuality,* Vol. 20, No. 1/2 (1990), 162.
53. "The Real Child Abuse," *Guide,* July 1995.
54. Bruce Rind, Ph.D., Robert Bauserman, Ph.D., and Phillip Tromovitch, Ph.D., "An Examination of Assumed Properties Based on Nonclinical Samples," presented at the Paulus Kirk, Rotterdam, the Netherlands, December 18, 1998.
55. American Psychiatric Association, "Diagnostic and Statistical Manual of Mental Disorders," DSM-IV-TR, Fourth Edition, No. 302.2, p. 571.
56. "Child Sex Abuse Study Denounced," Associated Press, July 13, 1999.
57. Robert Stacy McCain, "Endorsement of Adult-Child Sex on Rise," *Washington Times,* April 19, 2002.
58. Ibid.
59. Ibid.
60. Chuck Colson, "Apples, Teachers, and Serpents: Academia's Assault on Our Children," *Breakpoint,* September 24, 2002. This quote is also posted on the Web site of the North American Man-Boy Love Association (NAMBLA).
61. John Leo, "Apologists for Pedophilia," U.S. News.com, April 22, 2002.
62. Jennifer Walsh, "Make Sex Education a Topic for the Pulpit, Black Pastors Are Urged," *Boston Globe,* July 7, 2000.

63. "Mainstream Book Advocating Adult-Child Sex Draws Howls of Protest," Fox News, April 2, 2002.
64. McCain, "Endorsement of Adult-Child."
65. Leo, "Apologists for Pedophilia."
66. Jodi Wilgoren, "Scholar's Pedophilia Essay Stirs Outrage and Revenge," New York Times, April 30, 2002.
67. Ibid.
68. "Pedophilia for Progressives," Wall Street Journal, May 6, 2002.

Chapter Five—The Family under Attack

1. Jeff Jacoby, "The End of the Gay Marriage Debate?" Boston Globe, May 17, 2004.
2. Veith, "Doing without Marriage."
3. Stanley Kurtz, "Slipping Toward Scandinavia," National Review Online, February 2, 2004.
4. U.S. Department of Health and Human Services, National Center for Health Statistics, "Births to Unmarried Mothers, 1980-92" and assorted national and monthly vital statistics reports.
5. Bureau of Labor Statistics, National Longitudinal Survey of Youth, 1996.
6. Veith, "Doing without Marriage."
7. Stanley Kurtz, "The Marriage Mentality," National Review Online, May 4, 2004.
8. "Legal Recognition of Same-Sex Marriage: A Conference on National European and International Law," King's College at the University of London, July 1–3, 1999.
9. "Netherlands OKs Gay Marriages," Associated Press, September 13, 2000.
10. "Parliamentary Vote Turns Belgium Into Second Country to Approve Gay Marriages," CBCNews, January 31, 2003.
11. "Spain's New Government to Legalize Gay Marriage," Reuters, April 15, 2004.
12. Alister Doyle, "Norwegian Finance Minister Marries Gay Partner," Reuters, January 15, 2002.
13. "Germany's First Gay Couple Wed," CNN, August 1, 2001.
14. Malcolm Thornberry, "Restricting TG Marriage Illegal, European Court Rules," 365Gay.com, January 8, 2004.
15. David Frum, "The Fall of France," National Review, November 8, 1999.
16. Chris Crain, "Gays May Ruin Traditional Marriage," New York Blade, August 3, 2001.
17. Stanley Kurtz, "Going Dutch?" The Weekly Standard, May 31, 2004.
18. Suzanne Fields, "'Queer Eye' for the Straight Courtship," Tribune Media Services, March 11, 2004.
19. Gene Edward Veith, "Wages for Sin: Marriage Benefits Are Starting to Go to Those Who Are Shacking Up," World, August 18, 2001.
20. "All Together Now," The Advocate, September 11, 2001.
21. George W. Dent Jr., "The Defense of Traditional Marriage," Journal of Law and Politics, Vol. XV, No. 4, Fall 1999, 628–637.
22. ACLU Policy Guide, 1992.
23. "Boston Globe to Cover Gay Unions," Associated Press, September 29, 2002.
24. Richard Ostling, "Same-Sex Marriages? Civil Unions? A Gay Theologian Thinks They're Only the Beginning," Associated Press, January 28, 2004.
25. "Same-sex Couple Flaunts 'Open Marriage,'" WorldNetDaily.com, May 18, 2004.
26. Elizabeth F. Emens, Monogamy's Law: Compulsory Monogamy and Polyamorous Existence, Public Law and Legal Theory Working Paper No. 58, The Law School, The University of Chicago, February 2003, www.law.uchicago.edu/academics/publiclaw/index.html.
27. Don Lattin, "Committed to Marriage for the Masses, Polyamorists Say They Relate Honestly to Multiple Partners," San Francisco Chronicle, April 20, 2004.
28. Alexandria Sage, "Attorney Challenges Utah Polygamy Ban," Associated Press, January 26, 2004.
29. Mark Thiessen, "Utah Polygamist Invokes Ruling on Gay Sex," Associated Press, December 1, 2003.
30. Camille Paglia, "I'll Take Religion over Gay Culture," Salon.com, June 1998.
31. "Uncle Sam Should Care about Who Gets Married," Insight on the News, August 27, 2001.
32. Andrew Sullivan, Virtually Normal: An Argument about Homosexuality, 1995.
33. Paul Olson, "Civil Union Study Gives Insight Into First Year Couples," Out in the Mountains, January 2003.
34. Don Feder, "Vermont Storms Citadel of Marriage," Jewish World Review May 1, 2000.
35. William N. Eskridge, "The Case for Same-Sex Marriage," 1996.
36. Michaelangelo Signorile, "Bridal Wave," OUT, December-January 1994.
37. Barbara Cox, "A (Personal) Essay on Same-Sex Marriage," National Journal of Sexual Orientation Law, Vol. 1, Issue 1, 1995.
38. Stanley Kurtz, "The End of Marriage in Scandinavia," The Weekly Standard, February 2, 2004.
39. Michael Powell, "For Some, A Sanitized Movement," Washington Post, March 31, 2004.
40. Patrick Moore, "Gays: Assimilated and Asexual?" Los Angeles Times, January 27, 2004.
41. Fredrich U. Dicker, "Wipe Out Marriage, Legislator Says," New York Post, April 8, 2004.
42. Lisa Leff, "Divorce Deemed a Benefit of Gay Marriage," Associated Press, May 22, 2004.
43. Frank Langett, "Many Evangelicals Oppose Ban on Same-Sex Marriage," Baltimore Sun, April 14, 2004.
44. See http://www.metroweekly.com/feature/?ak=1123
45. "Netherlands OKs Gay Marriages," Associated Press.
46. "Civil Liberties At Risk through Ballot Initiatives," ACLU press release, November 4, 1998.
47. "Vermont's Civil Unions," Gay-Civil-Unions.com, October 13, 2002.
48. Jeffrey Gold, "New Jersey High Court Has Record of Support for Gay Rights," Associated Press, June 27, 2002.

49. Jessica Cantelon, "Homosexuals Seek More Progress in Battle over 'Marriage Equality,'" CNSNews.com, July 8, 2002.

50. Cindy Wockner, "Transsexual Marriage Is Ruled Valid," *London Telegraph,* October 15, 2001.

51. *Goodridge v. Massachusetts Dept. of Public Health,* Docket #2001-1647A (Suffolk Co. Sup. Ct, Mass.).

52. Robert B. Bluey, "Author of Homosexual Marriage Ruling is Under Fire, Won't Budge," CNSNews.com, April 28, 2004.

53. Associated Press Raw Vote Totals, November 3, 2004.

54. Walter Shapiro, "Presidential Election May Have Hinged on One Issue: Issue 1," *USA Today,* November 5, 2004 and Lawrence Kudlow, "A Virtuous Victory," *National Review,* November 3, 2004.

55. Kentucky Registry of Election Finance.

56. Kelly Weise, "Big Campaign Spending Doesn't Translate to Victory on Moral Issues," Associated Press, August 16, 2004.

57. Carolyn Lochhead, "Gay Leaders Try to Reframe Struggle for Marriage Rights," *San Francisco Chronicle,* November 10, 2004.

58. "Gay Marriage Lawsuit Filed," Associated Press, November 9, 2004.

59. "Lords Back Appeal on Transsexual Marriage," *Scotsman,* January 22, 2002.

60. "Ontario Province Will Not Appeal Marriage Ruling," *Canadian Press,* July 17, 2002.

61. E-mail from Matt Daniels of the Alliance for Marriage to Alan E. Sears, July 13, 2002.

62. Patrick White, "Gay Civil Unions Are Legalized in Quebec," *Philadelphia Inquirer,* June 9, 2002.

63. Chris Wilson-Smith, "Lesbian Couple Seeks Divorce," *CNews,* July 21, 2004.

64. Chris Bull, "Northern Enlightenment," *The Advocate,* September 17, 2002.

65. "Lambda Legal Appeals Prudential Financial's Denial of Medical Insurance Coverage for Lesbian Retiree's

66. Winston Churchill, "Speech at the Royal Academy,"April 30, 1938.

67. "The Battle Over Same-Sex Marriage," *San Francisco Chronicle,* March 21, 2004.

68. Phillip Mattier, Andrew Ross, "Newsom Hasn't Been Ad-Libbing," *San Francisco Chronicle,* February 28, 2004.

69. Stanley Kurtz, "'Marriage' Mayhem, *National Review Online,* May 20, 2004.

70. Bruce Carroll, "A Fine Mess We're in Now," *Washington Blade,* April 23, 2004.

71. John Derbyshire, "Here to Stay," *National Review Online,* May 14, 2004.

72. Dennis Prager, "Same-Sex Marriage: Good for Gays, Bad for Children," Creators Syndicate, May 4, 2004.

73. Jenifer Warren, "Capitol Gains for Gay Pols," *Los Angeles Times,* December 10, 2001.

74. Don Feder, "Gay Marriage Undermines Institution," Creators Syndicate, August 1, 2001.

75. Matt Pyeatt, "Pennsylvania Supreme Court Extends Same-Sex Parental Rights," CNSNews.com, January 8, 2002.

76. Jane Meredith Adams, "Love vs. the Law," *Rosie,* April 2002, p. 50.

77. Ann Oldenburg, "For Rosie, Coming Out Is Merely about What's Right," *USA Today,* March 11, 2002.

78. Daniel Merkle, "More Americans Support Gay Adoption," ABCNews.com, April 2, 2002.

79. Katy Kelley, "Gay Parents Get Endorsed by Kids' Docs," Associated Press, February 18, 2002.

80. Robert Lerner, Ph.D, and Althea Nagai, Ph.D, *No Basis: What the Studies Don't Tell Us about Same-Sex Parenting* (Washington D.C.: Marriage Law Project, 2001), 13–15.

81. Ibid., 27.

82. Ibid., 28.

83. Ibid., 53.

84. Ibid., 75.

85. Maggie Gallagher, "Homosexual Parenting Findings Based on Faulty Studies," Universal Press Syndicate, February 5, 2002.

86. See Judith Wallerstein, Julia Lewis and Sandra Blakeslee, "The Unexpected Legacy of Divorce: A 25 Year Landmark Study," (New York, N.Y.: Hyperion Books, 2000).

87. Kathryn Jean Lopez, "Another Divorce?" *National Review Online,* April 12, 2002.

88. Michael Gurian, Patricia Henley, and Terry Trueman, "Boys and Girls Learn Differently! A Guide for Teachers and Parents," (San Francisco, CA: Jossey-Bass, 2001).

89. George Archibald, "U.S. to Help U.N. Redefine Families," *Washington Times,* April 22, 2002.

90. Ibid.

91. Peter LaBarbera, "Gores Give $50,000 to Promote 'Gay' Parenting," *Culture and Family Report,* March 1, 2002.

92. "Gores Court Booksellers for New Publication," Associated Press, May 1, 2002.

93. Dennis Prager, "How the Nuclear Family Became Controversial," Creators Syndicate, August 14, 2002.

94. Inga Gilchrist, "Boy in Lesbian Tug-of-War," *Auckland Herald-Sun,* January 25, 2002.

95. "Boy Officially Has 3 Parents," WorldNetDaily.com, April 18, 2004.

96. Mike Wendling, "British Study Links Single Parenthood, Social Problems," CNSNews.com, February 11, 2002.

97. James Doherty, "Anger as Lesbian Couple Wins Full Parental Rights," *Scotsman,* April 8, 2002.

98. Matt Pyeatt, "Deaf Lesbians Criticized for Efforts to Create Deaf Child," CNSNews.com, April 2, 2002.

99. Leslie Brady, "Judge's Ruling Pleases Supporters of Gay Rights," *Bergen County Record,* March 12, 2003.

100. Stanley Kurtz, "Heather Has Three Mommies," *National Review Online,* March 12, 2003.

101. Cynthia Hubert, "Birth of Change: Thanks to Medical and Legal Advances, Sadie Karpay-Brody Has Two Mothers Who Are Both Her Natural Parents," *Sacramento Bee,* November 2, 2003.

102. Tessa Mayes and Rosie Waterhouse, "Gay Couples Join Forces to Have Babies as Foursomes," *London Times,* June 17, 2001.

103. "Lesbian Couple Sentenced for Abusing Their 5 Sons," 365Gay.com, January 15, 2004.

104. Bruce Kluger, "Kids Teach Us Lessons about Gays, Inclusiveness," *USA Today,* August 27, 2001.

105. See Andrew H. Friedman, *Same-Sex Marriage and the Right to Privacy: Abandoning Scriptural, Canonical, and Natural Law Based Definitions of Marriage,* 35 Howard L.J. 173, 222–23 (1991).

106. C. S. Lewis, *The Four Loves* (Harvest Books, 1960).

107. George Dent, "The Defense of Traditional Marriage," *Journal of Law and Politics* (University of Virginia, 2001), Vol. XV, No. 4, 590–591.

108. Shaena Eagle, "College Freshmen More Politically Liberal Than in the Past, UCLA Survey Reveals." See http://www.gseis.ucla.edu/heri/heri.html.

109. Marilyn Elias, "Divorce Is Likelier for Kids of Divorce," *USA Today,* May 14, 1991.

110. David Popenoe, *Life without Father* (New York: The Free Press, 1996).

111. Ibid.

112. Elias, "Divorce Is Likelier."

113. Phillip Vassallo, "More Than Grades: How Choice Boosts Parental Involvement and Benefits Children," *Policy Analysis,* Cato Institute, October 26, 2000.

114. "Back to School 1999: National Survey of American Attitudes: Substance Abuse V: Teens and Their Parents," National Center on Addiction and Substance Abuse at Columbia University, September 1999. See http://www.casacolumbia.org.

115. Stanley Kurtz, "Deathblow to Marriage," *National Review Online,* February 5, 2004.

Chapter Six—The Silence (and Silencing) of the Church

1. Ed Magnuson, "In a Rage over Aids: A Militant Protest Group Targets the Catholic Church," *Time,* December 25, 1989.

2. Rosemary Harris, "Church Service Is Interrupted by Gay Activists Throwing Condoms," *Colorado Springs Gazette Telegraph,* November 8, 1993.

3. Steph Smith, "Gay Catholics Refused Communion at Chicago Cathedral," 365Gay.com, May 31, 2004.

4. Jonathan Peter and Jonathan Wynne-Jones, "Labour Minister Backs New 'Gay Jesus' Prayerbook," *London Guardian,* March 11, 2002.

5. Hanna Rosin, "Lesbian 'Marriage' Threatens to Split United Methodists," *Washington Post,* June 16, 1999.

6. Jason B. Johnson, "Methodist Clergy at Gay 'Wedding' Won't Be Punished," *San Francisco Chronicle,* February 12, 2000.

7. Allan Dobras, "Radical Methodist Church Ends Marriage Ceremonies in Prohomosexual Protest," *Culture and Family Report,* October 25, 2001.

8. see http://www.princetonreview.com/college/research/rankings/rankingTeaser.asp?CategoryID=3Topic ID=24.

9. Mark I. Pinsky, "Longtime Orlando Pastor Resigns," *Orlando Sentinel,* December 5, 2002.

10. Sean Salai, "Assembly OKs Transsexual," *Washington Times,* June 7, 2002.

11. Rhonda Smith, "Trans Minister Seeks Local Methodist Appointment," *Washington Blade,* June 14, 2002.

12. Sean Salai, "Transsexual Methodist Minister Resigns," *Washington Times,* July 2, 2002.

13. "Ask but Don't Tell," *World,* July/August 2002.

14. "Lesbian Pastor Acquitted of Breaking Church Law," 365Gay.com., March 21, 2004.

15. Laurie Goodstein, "Methodists Put Pastor on Trial for Declaring Herself a Lesbian," *New York Times,* March 17, 2004.

16. Marsha King, "Religions Divided over Gays in Clergy," *Seattle Times,* July 1, 2001.

17. Hanna Rosin, "Lutherans Vote to Study Gay Issues: Activists Sought More Rapid Liberalizations," *Washington Post,* August 14, 2001.

18. Jaroslav Pelikan, ed., *Luther's Words III* (St. Louis, MO: Concordia Publishing House, 1961), 255.

19. Priest Defrocked Over Church Views," Associated Press, September 6, 2002.

20. Alison Appelbe, "Homosexual Unions Pose Challenge for Canadian Church Officials," CNSNews.com, September 30,2002.

21. Gary Rohrbough, "Barry Lynn Claims Roman Centurion in Bible Had Male Sex Slave," CNSNews.com, October 3, 2002.

22. Gary D. Harwood, "North Carolina Pastor: 'Homosexuality is Not a Sin,'" *Baptist News,* October 9, 2002.

23. Michael Meade, "Catholic College Approves Gay-Straight Alliance," 365Gay.com, February 3, 2003.

24. Matt Johns, "Was Jesus Gay?" 365Gay.com, December 25, 2003.

25. Laurie Goodstein, "New Hampshire Episcopalians Choose Gay Bishop, and Conflict," *New York Times,* June 8, 2003.

26. David Gram, "Liturgy for Gay Marriages Developed in Vermont," Associated Press, June 18, 2004.

27. "Religious Left Strategizes on Homosexual 'Marriage,'" MichNews.com, June 22, 2004.

28. "A Search for God's Welcome, Two Deeply Religious Women Discover a Church that Accepts Them as They Are," *Newsweek,* March 20, 2000.

29. Ibid.

30. Ibid.

31. Martha Sawyer Allen, "New Perspective on the Divine is Attacked: 'Re-Imagine' Conference Criticized as Repudiation of Traditional Beliefs," *Minneapolis Star-Tribune,* January 23, 1994.

32. Richard N. Ostling, "No Mention of 'Man' in New Bible," Associated Press, January 29, 2002.

33. Stephen Bennett, "Was Jesus 'Gay'?" WorldNetDaily.com, July 16, 2002.

34. Carol Stenger, "On Being Christian and Gay." See http://www.hrc.org/familynet/chapter.asp?article=582.

35. Josh Friedes, "Can Anyone Show Just Cause Why These Two Should Not Be Lawfully Joined Together?" *New England Law Review,* Spring 2004.

36. Dennis Prager, "Who Supports Same-Sex Marriage?" Creators Syndicate, March 9, 2004.

37. David D. Kirkpatrick, "Gay-Marriage Fight Finds Ambivalence from Evangelicals," *New York Times,* February 28, 2004.

38. Chuck Colson, "Why Bother? Why Some Christians Aren't Fighting Same-Sex 'Marriage,'" *Breakpoint,* June 23, 2004.

39. Tony Campolo, *20 Hot Potatoes Christians Are Afraid to Touch* (Nashville, TN: Thomas Nelson, 1988), 13.

40. Ibid.

41. Ibid., 16.

42. Speech by Tony and Peggy Campolo at North Park College Chapel, February 29, 1996.

43. Ed Golder, "Campolo Shares His Convictions," *Grand Rapids Press,* February 20, 1993.

44. Ibid.

45. "Baptist Pastor Won't Respond to Challenge," *Maranatha Christian Journal,* June 7, 2002.

46. Catechism of the Catholic Church. United States Conference of Catholic Bishops, Article 6, The Sixth Commandment, 2nd edition, 2002.

47. Ibid., No. 2357.

48. Ibid., No. 2358.

49. Ibid., No. 2359.

50. George Weigel, *The Courage to be Catholic* (New York: Basic Books, 2002), 109.

51. Paul Likoudis, "New Ways Ministry Forges Ahead with Defiance," *Wanderer,* March 21, 2002, 1.

52. Michael Novak, "The Fall of the Progressive Church," *National Review Online,* May 1, 2002.

53. Lawrence Morahan, "Lay Group Calls on UN to Sanction Vatican over Sex Abuse," CNSNews.com, April 24, 2002.

54. Bill Keller, "Is the Pope Catholic?" *New York Times,* May 4, 2002.

55. Ibid.

56. Pat Buchanan, "Anti-Catholicism at the New York Times," *Creators Syndicate,* May 8, 2002.

57. Jon Meacham, "Sex and the Church: A Case for Change," *Newsweek,* April 30, 2002.

58. Ibid.

59. Ann Coulter, "Should Gay Priests Adopt?" Universal Press Syndicate, March 21, 2002.

60. John Leo, "A Gay Culture in the Church," *U.S. News and World Report,* June 3, 2002, 16.

61. Carl Ingram, "Panel Backs Child Abuse Bill," *Los Angeles Times,* May 8, 2002.

62. Lawrence Morahan, "RICO Sex Abuse Lawsuit Names Vatican as Defendant," CNSNews.com, April 19, 2002.

63. David Lazarus, "Church Problems Include Insurance: Scandal May Mean Higher Rates," *San Francisco Chronicle,* April 24, 2002.

64. Rod Dreher, "The Gay Question," *National Review,* April 22, 2002.

65. "'NAMBLA' Priest Arrested for Child Rape," Fox News, May 2, 2002.

66. Nick Madigan, "Sent to California on Sick Leave, Boston Priest Bought Racy Gay Resort," *New York Times,* April 15, 2002.

67. "'NAMBLA' Priest Arrested for Child Rape," Fox News, May 2, 2002.

68. David France, "Gays and the Seminary," *Newsweek,* May 20, 2002.

69. Ibid.

70. Joel Mowbray, "Homosexuality a Factor in Sex Abuse by Priests," copyright 2002 Joel Mowbray.

71. John Leo, "Of Rage and Revolution," *U.S. News and World Report,* April 1, 2002.

72. Joyce Howard Price, "Predator Priests," *Washington Times,* April 16, 2002.

73. "The Church, Holy and Immortal, Shall Prevail!" *Wanderer,* April 25, 2002.

74. NACDLGM 2002 National Conference.

75. Dreher, "The Gay Question."

76. Paul Bedard, "Father Gay," *U.S. News and World Report,* April 29, 2002.

77. Allyson Smith, "Homosexual Groups Go into Spin Mode on Catholic Crisis," *Culture and Family Institute,* April 25, 2002.

78. Anthony DeStefano, "Loyal Catholics Defend Church," *USA Today,* May 5, 2002.

79. "The Church, Holy and Immortal," *Wanderer.*

80. Charles A. Donovan, "A Red Hat for a Stop Sign," *Washington Times,* April 23, 2002.

81. "Letters Threaten 3 Priests," Associated Press, October 1, 2002.

82. Ken Garfield, "Lotz's Views on Gays Meets Dissent," *Charlotte Observer,* May 14, 2002.

83. "Federal Judge Upholds Firing of Madison Firefighter," Associated Press, June 23, 1999.

84. Sworn testimony of Ralph Ovadal before the U.S. District Court for the Western District of Wisconsin, No. 96-C-0292-S.

85. See http://www.skeptictank.org/firegay.html.

86. News release: official statement by Dr. David Innes. See http://www.hsbchurch.org/riot1.html.

87. della Cava, "Church Calls Acts 'Disordered.'"

88. Melanie Hunter, "Pastors Urge Apology from Senator for Remarks Regarding Marriage Amendment," CNSNews.com, March 8, 2004.

89. Kelli Samantha Hewett, "Two Men Preparing to Carry Crosses Charged with Disorderly Conduct," *The Tennessean,* May 9, 2004.

90. "Canada's Anti-Gay Violence Law Worries Some," Fox News.com, May 18, 2004.

91. Lynn Vincent, "Remaining Silent," *World,* May 8, 2004.

92. Ibid.

93. Ibid.

94. "Senator Delivers Death Wish to Christian," WorldNetDaily.com., February 18, 2004.

95. "Christian 'Properly Convicted' for 'Anti-Gay' Sign," WorldNetDaily.com, January 15, 2004.

96. Allison Ferrell, "Gay Rights Group: Church Broke Law," *Billings Gazette,* May 27, 2004.

97. Robert B. Bluey, "Marriage Changes May Shake Churches' Tax Exemption," CNSNews.com, February 23, 2004.

98. Michael P. McConnell, "Pro-Gay Group Wants Police Chaplain Removed," *The Daily Tribune,* October 16, 2002.

99. "Religious Beliefs Underpin Opposition to Homosexuality," The Pew Forum on Religion and Public Life," see http://www.pewforum.org/docs/index.php?DocID=37.

100. Office of Strategic Services Research and Analysis Branch, "The Nazi Master Plan: The Persecution of Christian Churches," July 6, 1945. See http://www-camlaw.rutgers.edu/publications/law-religion/. Also see Claire Hulme and Dr. Michael Salter, "The Nazi's Persecution of Religion as a War Crime: The OSS's Response within the Nuremberg Trials Process," *Rutgers Journal of Law and Religion,* Vol. 3 No.1, 2001-2002.

101. Chuck Donovan, "At War with God," *Focus on the Family Citizen,* August 2002, 28-29.

Chapter Seven—The Seduction of Corporate America

1. Robert Knight and Kenneth L. Ervin II, "Can I Question Homosexuality? Don't Bank on It," from *The Other Side of Tolerance: Victims of Homosexual Activism,* Family Research Council, 1997, 8.

2. Ibid.

3. The Human Rights Campaign (HRC), www.hrc.org.

4. Ibid.

5. See www.glcensus.org.

6. Sally Kohn, "The Domestic Partnership Organizing Manual for Employee Benefits," *Policy Institute of the National Gay and Lesbian Task Force,* 6. See http://www.ngltf.org/library/index.cfm.

7. Amanda May, "Odd Couples," *New York Magazine,* July 8, 2002.

8. Human Rights Campaign press release, June 15, 2001.

9. Kohn, 8.

10. A. Stamborski, "Guests Add Spice to Emerson's Annual Meeting," *St. Louis Post-Dispatch,* February 7, 2001.

11. Kohn, 8.

12. See http://www.hrc.org.

13. Lou Chibbaro Jr., "NGLTF Leaders Quit Amid Major Reorganization," *Washington Blade,* March 7, 2003.

14. The NGLTF Domestic Partnership Organizing Manual, 11.

15. *S. D. Myers, Inc. v. City and County of San Francisco,* 253 F.3d 461 (9th Cir. 2001).

16. "Safe Space" flyer, published by Galaxe Pride at Work. See http://www.galaxe.world.xerox.com.

17. Ibid., 26.

18. Ibid., 1.

19. Brian McNaught, *Gay Issues in the Workplace* (New York, N.Y.: St. Martin's Press, 1993), 10.

20. Ibid.

21. Personal conversation between American Express employee and Craig Osten.

22. Information from the Ford Foundation Web site. See http://www.fordfoundation.org under "Peace and Social Justice: Governance and Society, 2001 Grants."

23. Ibid.

24. Ibid., under "Peace and Social Justice: Human Rights and International Cooperation, 2000 Grants."

25. Ibid., under "Peace and Social Justice: Human Rights and International Cooperation, 1999."

26. Ford Foundation advertisement in the Out and Equal Leadership Summit 2000 Program.

27. See http://www.hrc.org.

28. Adam Pertman, "In Gay Market, Ads Target Big Dollars, Not Big Change," *Boston Globe,* February 4, 2001.

29. Ibid.

30. Greg Jonnson, "More Advertisers Pursue Gay and Lesbian Customers," *St. Louis Post-Dispatch,* June 22, 2001.

31. See http://www.hrc.org.

32. "Hancock Changes 'Adoption' Commercial Again," *Chicago Tribune,* September 22, 2000.

33. Pertman, "In Gay Market."

34. Catherine Donaldson-Evans, "Fortune 500 Companies See Money in Gay Families," FoxNews.com., May 26, 2004.

35. Ibid.

36. Jonnson, "More Advertisers."

37. Edward Epstein, "S.F. Warns Airlines on Partners Law: United Must Comply to Get Facility Lease," *San Francisco Chronicle,* January 15, 1997 and "Airline Fears Global Effects from Domestic Partner Law:" Associated Press, January 28, 1997.

38. Donor Profile: United Airlines, *Lambda Update,* Summer 2000.

39. Pertman, "In Gay Market."

40. Ira Berkow, "A Lesbian Group Protests Too Much," *New York Times,* August 5, 2002.

41. Tom Weir, "WNBA Sells Diversity," *USA Today,* July 24, 2001.

42. Al Dobras, "Women's Pro Teams Reach Out to Lesbians," *Culture and Family Report,* July 11, 2001.

43. Marc Fisher, "Caught in the Mystics' Net: Basketball Team's Diverse Fan Base Is in a League of Its Own," *Washington Post,* August 4, 1998.

44. Dobras, "Women's Pro Teams Reach Out."

45. Weir, "WNBA Sells."
46. Todd Richissin, "Lawsuit No Longer in the Lineup for Suns," *Baltimore Sun,* January 12, 2000.
47. Dobras, "Women's Pro Teams Reach Out."
48. Michael Clancy, "'Church Night' Drags Suns Into Gay Marriage Debate," *Arizona Republic,* January 15, 2004.
49. Maya Bell, "Miami Beckons to Gays: Visit the Gay Riviera," *Orlando Sentinel,* February 13, 2002.
50. Ibid.
51. Deborah Sharp, "Cities Come Out About Wooing Gays—and their Dollars," *USA Today,* December 7, 2003.
52. Caroline Wilbert, "Wanted: Gay Tourists, Atlanta to Follow Lead of Other Cities with Ad Campaign," *Atlanta Journal-Constitution,* May 16, 2002.
53. "Rolling Out the 'Rainbow Carpet,'" *World,* June 1, 2002, p.12.
54. Susan Jones, "Betsy Ross, Ben Franklin Part of 'Gay Friendly' Tourism Campaign," CNSNews.com., November 14, 2003 and Sharp, op.cit.
55. "Philadelphia Debuts First Commercial Aimed at Gay Travelers," Associated Press, June 2, 2004.
56. Sharp, op. cit.
57. "News, Tips, and Bargains: Just the Facts: Gay Travelers," *Los Angeles Times,* January 23, 2000.
58. Ibid.
59. Mike Schneider, "Christian Group to Show Gay Days Video at Disney Meeting," Associated Press, February 12, 2002.
60. Mike Schneider, "Gay Days Part of Disney Landscape," Associated Press, June 3, 2000.
61. Steve Otto, "A Weekend Visit to the Gay '90s," *Tampa Tribune,* June 14, 1999.
62. Lawrence Morahan, "Domestic Partnership Bill Would Hurt Families," CNSNews.com, April 17, 2001.
63. Speech at Alliance Defense Fund Fall Briefing, September 5, 2001.

Chapter Eight—The End of Tolerance (for Those Who Disagree)

1. Steve Jordahl, "Employee Says Beliefs Prompted Firing," *Family News in Focus,* May 9, 2002.
2. "School Rejects Coach over Christian Beliefs," *Lincoln Daily Nebraskan.*
3. Ibid.
4. Ibid.
5. Christine Hall, "Coach Says Christian Beliefs Doomed His Chances for New Job," CNSNews.com, June 13, 2002.
6. Claude Adams, "Teacher Battles Union Over Published Views," *National Post,* November 25, 2002.
7. *Phillips v. Missouri,* Text of Complaint.
8. "The Other Side of Tolerance," *Family Research Council,* 1997, p. 14.
9. Joyce Howard Price, "State Erred in Firing Worker Opposing Gay Foster Parents," *Washington Times,* July 22, 2001.
10. "Federal Judge Dismisses Suit vs. 'Fairness' Ordinance," Associated Press, March 21, 2001.
11. Letter from Marilyn Schoonover, Specialist/Volunteer Department to Chaplaincy Coordinators and Volunteer Members, April 7, 1995.
12. *Boy Scouts of America v. Dale,* 530 US 640 (2000).
13. Charley Reese, "An Incredible Attack on the Boy Scouts," *Grand Rapids Press,* September 4, 2000.
14. Joyce Howard Price, "Scouts Lose United Way Funds over Gay Ban," *Washington Times,* March 15, 2002.
15. "House Rejects Effort to End Boy Scouts' U.S. Charter," Associated Press, September 14, 2000.
16. Michael J. Sniffen, "Attorney General Will Keep Federal Lands Open to Scouts," Associated Press, September 3, 2000.
17. Press release issued by Bar Association of San Francisco, July 23, 2002.
18. Adam Liptak, "California Might Bar Judges From Scouts," *New York Times,* December 21, 2002.
19. Mike Thomas, "United Way Makes Giving Not Easy," *Orlando Sentinel,* July 23, 2001.
20. Seth Lewis, "Massachusetts Mayor Boycotts Boy Scouts," CNSNews.com, July 31, 2001.
21. Ken Ellingwood, "Scouts' Use of San Diego Park at Issue," *Los Angeles Times,* December 4, 2001.
22. "Boy Scouts Statement in Response to City Settlement," Desert Pacific Council of the Boy Scouts of America Press Release, January 8, 2004.
23. Bill Hirschman, "Boy Scouts Sue to Stay in Schools," *Orlando Sentinel,* December 6, 2000.
24. Laura Parker, "Debate Simmers Over Scouts' Ban," *USA Today,* June 15, 2001.
25. Olga R. Rodriguez, "Japanese Scout Troops Left in Lurch by Berkeley Councilman," Associated Press, August 7, 2001.
26. "Connecticut Can Bar Scouts as Charity," Associated Press, July 30, 2002.
27. Robyn Suriano, "Doctors Say Scout Rules Damage Health of Gays," *Orlando Sentinel,* June 20, 2001.
28. David Limbaugh, "Boy Scouts Still Under Heavy Fire," Creators Syndicate, June 4, 2001.
29. Annette Scalise, "On the Recruiting Trail, The Boy Scouts Extend Their Efforts in Ethnic Communities," *Newsday,* May 24, 2002.
30. See http://www.ageofconsent.com.
31. David Kupelian, "Pedophile Priests and Boy Scouts," WorldNetDaily.com, May 8, 2002.
32. Coulter, "Should Gay Priests Adopt?"
33. "Scout Leader Pleads Guilty to Sodomy," Associated Press, May 8, 2002.
34. Brief of Amici Curiae Public Advocate and others. *Dale v. Boy Scouts of America,* 734 A.2nd 1196 (N.J. 1999) (No. 99–699). Also see Steve Geissinger, "Scouts Remove 1800 Scoutmasters for Suspected Abuse Over Two Decades," Associated Press, October 14, 1993.

35. Letter from Leland Stevenson, co-recording secretary, NAMBLA, to Ben Love, Chief Scout Executive, Boy Scouts of America (Nov. 1992). See http://www.abidingtruth.com/pfrc/archives/livelybites/3-21-2001.html.

36. Ken McGuire, "Local Boy Scout Council Takes Another Stand for Diversity," Associated Press, June 10, 2002.

37. Ibid.

38. *Pedreira v. Kentucky Baptist Homes for Children, Inc.*, 186 F. Supp. 2d 757 (W.D. Ky. 2001).

39. Eyal Press, "Faith Based Furor," *New York Times Magazine*, April 1, 2001, p. 62.

40. Mary Leonard, "Judge Sees No Bias in Firing of Lesbian," *Boston Globe*, July 25, 2001.

41. Chris Poynter, "Baptists' Homes' Firing of Lesbian Is Upheld," *Louisville Courier-Journal*, July 25, 2001.

42. Ibid.

43. Peter Smith, "Baptist Homes Prepares to Do without State Money," *Louisville Courier-Journal*, November 15, 2001.

44. "Salvation Army Memo Cites Deal with Bush," *Washington Post*, July 11, 2001.

45. Chris Kenning, "Gay Rights Group Questions YMCA Member Rules," *Louisville Courier-Journal*, June 7, 2002.

46. Lynn Vincent, "Brothers Up in Arms," *World*, October 26, 2002.

47. Ibid.

48. "Salvation Army Gives Up City Money," Associated Press, July 2, 2002.

49. Oubai Shabandar, "Salvation Army to Lose Funding over Domestic Partner Flap," CNSNews.com, June 20, 2002.

50. "U.S. Court of Appeals Strikes Down Public School's Hate Speech Code," AFA press release, February 15, 2001.

51. Joanne Laucius, "Bible Had Role in Exposing Gays to Hatred," *Ottawa Citizen*, June 20, 2001.

52. *Owens v. Saskatchewan* (Human Rights Commission).

53. Debra Fieguth, "Justices Affirm Ban on Homosexual Conduct at Christian University," *Christianity Today*, July 9, 2001.

54. John Leo, "Stomping on Free Speech," Universal Press Syndicate, April 12, 2004.

55. Rich Peters, "Schools Which Do Not Teach GLBT Sexuality Discriminate," 365Gay.com, January 7, 2003.

56. Patrick Goodenough, "Videos on Homosexuality: Free Speech or Hate Speech?" CNSNews.com, March 12, 2003.

57. Elaine O'Connor, "Edict on Gay Weddings: Do Them or Split," see www. canada.com.

58. Bob Kellogg, "Sweden Moves to Criminalize Opposition to Homosexuality," *Family News in Focus*, June 10, 2002.

59. "Swedish Pastor Sentenced to One Month's Jail for Offending Homosexuals," ENI News, June 2004.

60. "Lesbian Kiss Comment Costs Firm," News.com.au, July 3, 2002.

61. "France to Outlaw Homophobia," News.com.au, June 23, 2004.

62. Patrick Goodenough, "UK Christian Group Challenged by Homosexuals Keeps Charity Status," CNSNews.com, August 23, 2001.

63. "UKGovernment Supports Repealing Gay Law," Associated Press, January 7, 2003.

64. "Dutch Will Not Prosecute Pope for Antigay Remarks," Reuters, July 18, 2000.

65. "Homosexual Leader Vows to 'Torture' Opponents," WorldNetDaily.com, April 30, 2004.

66. E. J. Montini, "Rally Crowd Takes a Vow to Love, Honor, Abhor," *The Arizona Republic*, May 18, 2004.

67. "Can Doctors Refuse to Artificially Inseminate Lesbians Because of Religious Beliefs?" *Hannity and Colmes*, February 18, 2003.

68. David Limbaugh, "Tolerance is a Two-Way Street," *Creators Syndicate*, February 22, 2003.

69. See http://www.samesexmarriage.ca/equality/bertha_wilson.htm.

70. "Becket Fund Warns Clergy of Amendment to State's Hate Crimes Law for Preaching About Sexual Orientation and Gender Identity," see ww.becketfund.org.

71. Kirk and Madsen, *After the Ball*, 176.

72. Mike Wendling, "Group Wants God Left Out of European Constitution," CNSNews.com, February 4, 2003.

73. *Leo*, April 12, 2004, op.cit.

74. "U.N. Group in 'Showdown with Religion,'" WorldNetDaily.com, August 8, 2003.

75. Kirk and Madsen, *After the Ball*, 176.

Chapter Nine—The Full Weight of the Government

1. Guerin, "The Politics of Sexuality."

2. Susan Jones, "Sexual Freedom Activists Target 'Archaic, Unjust' Sex Laws," CNSNews.com., June 1, 2004.

3. Guerin, "The Politics of Sexuality."

4. Gina Holland, "Supreme Court Hears Arguments in Major Gay Rights Case," Associated Press, March 27, 2003.

5. To access Lambda's brief on-line go to:http://www.lambdalegal.org/binarydata/LAMBDA_PDF/pdf/177 .pdf.

6. Kristin Hays, "Case of Two Texas Men Turns Into Major Gay Rights Battle Before the Supreme Court," Associated Press, March 23, 2003.

7. Carolyn Lochhead, "Top Court to Rule on 'Most Important Gay Rights Case,' Texas Law Forbids Sodomy Only by Same-Sex Couples," *San Francisco Chronicle*, March 26, 2003.

8. *Bowers v. Hardwick*, 1986, Burger C.J. concurring opinion.